The African American Press

The African American Press

A History of News Coverage During National Crises, with Special Reference to Four Black Newspapers, 1827–1965

CHARLES A. SIMMONS

McFarland & Company, Inc., Publishers
Jefferson, North Carolina, and London

LIBRARY OF CONGRESS CATALOGUING-IN-PUBLICATION DATA

Simmons, Charles A., 1933–
   The African American press : a history of news coverage during
national crises, with special reference to four black newspapers,
1827–1965 / Charles A. Simmons.
      p.   cm.
   Includes bibliographical references and index.

   ISBN 0-7864-2607-1 (softcover : 50# alkaline paper) ∞

   1. Afro-American press—History.   2. Afro-American newspapers—
History.   3. United States—Race relations—History.   4. Press and
politics—United States.   I. Title
PN4882.5.S57   2006
071'.3'08996073—dc21   97-40233

British Library cataloguing data are available

Cover photograph ©2005 Photodisc

Manufactured in the United States of America

McFarland & Company, Inc., Publishers
   Box 611, Jefferson, North Carolina 28640
      www.mcfarlandpub.com

CONTENTS

Preface   1
Introduction   5

1 The Beginning of the Black Press   9

2 The *Chicago Defender* and the Move Northward,
       1915–1928   25

3 *Pittsburgh Courier*   43

4 *Black Dispatch*   51

5 *Jackson Advocate*   63

6 World War II, 1939–1945   69

7 The Civil Rights Movement, 1960–1965   91

Conclusions   159
Notes   167
A Selected Bibliography   187
Index   193

PREFACE

In researching this book, I found that the history of black newspapers in the United States could be thought of in terms of nine distinct historical eras. In the first era, the antebellum, antislavery movement era, 1827 to 1861, newspapers fought for the freedom of slaves more than anything else.

In the second period, the Civil War and Reconstruction era, 1861 to 1877, newspapers shifted to educating Negroes and, according to Martin E. Dann's *The Black Press, 1827–1890: The Quest for National Identity*, attempted to gain recognition for black national identity.

During the third era, the era of reaction and adjustment, 1877 to 1915, black people encountered more lynching and other violence than during any other period in the history of the United States. That era began with the ending of Reconstruction and ended with the death of Booker T. Washington. The black press fought for an end to lynching and violence against blacks.

The fourth era, encompassing the Great Migration and World War I and extending from 1915 to 1928, runs to the beginning of the depression and covers a period in history when many blacks migrated from the South. During that period the black press fought for equal treatment of black soldiers, provided assistance through housing and job notices, offered guidance on where to obtain transportation and how to travel safely, and printed notices on how family members and friends were doing, whether they had gone north or were still in the South. While doing all of this, the black press also continued to fight for an end to violence against all blacks.

The fifth period, the Great Depression era, 1929 to 1939, began with the depression and ended with the beginning of World War II. The black press fought to end violence against blacks and the unfair treatment of blacks with regard to employment.

During the World War II era, 1939 to 1945, an end to violence

1

and the equal treatment of military personnel were high on black editors' lists.

The cold war era, 1946 to 1959, covered the period from after the war until the beginning of the civil rights movement. An end to violence and segregation was still on black editors' lists of things for which to fight. Although the Montgomery bus boycott did occur during that period, it did not spread across the country, and it ended before the decade was over. Some business sit-ins also sprang up during that time, but they were sporadic and ended a short time after they had begun.

The civil rights movement era, 1960 to 1976, was started in 1960 at Greensboro, North Carolina. Organized civil rights activities and demonstrations were conducted throughout the decade and spread across the nation. That was a time when black editors found themselves faced with a different editorial situation. Rather than providing the guidance and leadership for obtaining equal civil rights as they had done so many times in the past, they found themselves merely reporting it.

In reviewing the numerous magazines, books, pamphlets, newspapers, clippings, and journals for this book, I have noticed the tendency of writers and historians to rely on Armistead S. Pride's tally of nearly 3,000 newspapers as the total number of black newspapers published in the United States since 1827. Pride's *A Register and History of Negro Newspapers in the United States: 1827–1950*, Irving G. Penn's book *The Afro-American Press and Its Editors*, and Warren Brown's *Check List of Negro Newspapers in the United States (1827–1946)* are essential references for a study of the history of the black press, but the dates when each of these studies ended suggest that further research is necessary. I began to research the period after those cutoff dates to see how many additional newspapers I could find. I began my study in 1981, but by 1985 the research had ballooned into a raging monster which only a computer could control. A computer database makes the possibilities for extracting information almost limitless. My research in this area continues and concerns newspapers whether religious, fraternal, business, collegiate, or for general interest, so long as the target audience was primarily black readers. As of this writing, I have discovered close to 4,000 newspapers. Information from this database is now available to any interested researcher upon request.

I would also like to express a special thanks to Dr. Alberta Mayberry and Ronald Keys in the Langston University Library, Langston, Oklahoma. I was given access to a wealth of information at that university, including a large general collection and a valuable collection of black newspapers on microfilm.

Also, special thanks to the library staff at the University of Central Oklahoma, Edmond, Oklahoma, where there is also a large and valuable collection of black newspapers on microfilm. The staff's patience and assistance with all of my requests for information were genuine and extremely helpful.

I wish to express sincere appreciation to my committee chair, Dr. Bruce Petty, for his counsel, suggestions, and advice throughout my graduate program. I would also like to thank Dr. William Segall, Dr. John Steinbrink, and Dr. Lynn Arney for serving on my graduate committee. Their suggestions, enthusiasm, encouragement, and support were helpful throughout the study.

Finally, a special thanks to Dr. Ray Tassin, professor emeritus, University of Central Oklahoma, who suggested that I become involved in minority press research. His patience, understanding, and support made this project succeed.

Also a special thanks to Dr. Clif Warren, dean of the College of Liberal Arts, and Dr. Clyde Jacob, vice president for academic affairs, University of Central Oklahoma, for their genuine support during the doctoral period.

During the time span covered by this study, the way black people and others thought of race identities within the United States has changed a number of times. The question I asked when preparing this work was which name for members of the Negro race could I use throughout the study? Acknowledging that none of the various names used at different times has ever been placed before the Negro masses within this country for a vote, I decided to use at least three different names in this book: Afro-American, Negro, and black. I use *Afro-American* because it was well respected in 1827 when the black press was founded. I have generally not used that name in any 20th century context, however. I have also considered the fact that an overall majority of Negroes at that time were, indeed, Afro-Americans. Equally important, I have personally fought battles to restore some dignity to the word *Negro*, for that is the name under which I was born and raised. I use it with pride. At the same time, I have chosen to use the word *black*, with a small "b," which originally was intended to be parallel to Caucasian use of the word "white." My understanding is that *black* is not intended to be the name of the race but merely a descriptor. Finally, the reader will note that this book is titled to reflect predominant present-day usage, incorporating the phrase *African American*. Because this phrase became widely used only after the time period covered herein, I have not used it in the text.

In the quotations I have used from various newspapers throughout the text, linguistic and typographical errors in the original versions have been reproduced accurately and largely without comment; the device "[*sic*]" has been used in a handful of cases thought to be unclear.

I should note that the founding date for the *Black Dispatch*, one of the newspapers used in this study, has come under question. Richard Keaton Nash, a former editor of the newspaper, mentioned to me that the date used most commonly by historians, November 5, 1915, is incorrect, and that the newspaper was actually founded sometime in 1914. He also provided a broadcast interview tape on which Roscoe Dunjee, the editor and publisher, stated that he founded the paper in 1914.

In reading over many copies of old *Black Dispatch* newspapers in preparation for this book, I discovered a January 2, 1920, editorial in which Roscoe Dunjee provided a founding date of November 4, 1914. However, as I continued my research of old newspapers, I also found a news story in the September 14, 1940, edition mentioning a founding date of November 8, 1915. Additional research in this area is clearly needed.

INTRODUCTION

The basic editorial philosophy of the black press has not changed much since 1827, when *Freedom's Journal* was founded. The goals of all editors were to deliver messages in unity to their readers, deliver them with passion and emotion, and let white editors and citizens know that black citizens were humans who were being treated unjustly. But the role of a black editor was more than that.

It has been shown throughout the history of the black press that black editors were effective in delivering their messages to readers. After all, these were well-respected men and women in the community, most with some education, who knew or could find out the fate of Afro-Americans within the country. With some degree of subtlety, it has also been shown that black editors after delivering their messages faced a serious problem of survival, particularly when what had been said was accusatory, was based on facts, and pointed clearly to identifiable white individuals. Many groups of white citizens who did not appreciate what a black editor had said had little difficulty in forming a mob and wrecking the office of that newspaper. If the editor had not been careful or quick when the mob arrived, he or she might have been run out of town or killed.

For many black editors, survival was a serious problem throughout the nineteenth and early twentieth centuries. In spite of the dangers facing these men and women of the press, many blacks, even those who could barely write, sought the job of editor not merely because they had something to say or because the profits were worth the aggravation but primarily for its position of respect and influence in the black community. The success of that job, however, depended on how well the editor could deliver a resounding blow to whatever was causing the problem and survive thereafter.

Editors had to be aware of the problems involved in publishing black newspapers: readership in the black community was limited because the economic base and the literacy rate was low, white readers who had high economic and literacy rates were not particularly interested in much of what blacks had written, and the advertising base was limited because blacks had little or no money to engage in businesses. It was essential that black editors show some backbone in their writing to gain black respect and what little readership was available. But showing backbone meant that editors could lose their newspapers, which were essential to the survival of the black people, or even their lives. An editor had to be bold and show a position of strength, but had to be canny enough to live through the consequences.

The need for editors to deliver their message with courage continued throughout the nineteenth century until the time of Booker T. Washington and W.E.B. DuBois, when a division over the use of accommodation rather than militancy surfaced. This division was primarily concerned with the methods that should be used when seeking ways to elevate the race literally and economically. From that point in history and even into the civil rights movement, there have been some subtle divisions, and sometimes clear and overt divisions, of thought among black editors and publishers, but the basic editorial philosophy has remained the same—deliver the message with strength and survive. Some of those divisions are said to have been injurious to the progress of black people; some are said to have been responsible, even if indirectly, for a breakdown of efforts to remove racial barriers.

To provide some insight into what black editors faced, four black newspapers from separate geographical locations have been chosen for study. They are examined in light of the survival techniques used by the editors, their effectiveness when the black press was unified, the problems incurred when an editor failed to see the importance of race unity, how some editors reacted when faced with threats or physical dangers, and how ineffective an editor became when the interests of the primary readers were ignored.

The *Chicago Defender* was chosen because, in addition to being located in the North, it was the first newspaper to depart successfully from the traditional manner of reporting black news. Heretofore, black owners, publishers, and editors of black newspapers had followed a rigid and conservative style of providing straight news and opinion about racial problems without any sensational flair. The idea was to provide the news with dignity and honor reflective of the newspaper's solid position in the black community. In the early nineteenth century, black readers perused the paper to read about injustices, but the intensity of occurrences in many instances was rarely sensed. As a result, their interest in newspapers was low. To compound the situation, in the South during the era of reaction and adjustment, the many acts of violence dampened editorial intensity because black editors had to consider their own survival. Thus a credibility gap between reader and writer was created.

Robert S. Abbott, editor of the *Chicago Defender*, did not follow that conservative tradition. Ignoring the sacred canon of black editors, he overcame the economic problem through the use of graphic and detailed accounts of violent news and large and glaring headlines in red type. He also created news. Did such a bold and unwelcome move set the black press back in its quest for national believability? Not only did this organ have the audacity to use a different style for reporting black news, but this new style proved to be so successful among black readers that circulation figures increased to heights never before obtained by a black newspaper.

Robert Abbott is also given credit (even if incorrectly) for starting the Great Northern Drive, an exodus in which thousands of blacks in the South gave up their homes at the suggestions of the editor and moved north. This tradition of militant reporting carried over to include criticism of the federal government for allowing the unfair treatment of black military personnel during World War I.

Another Northern newspaper, the *Pittsburgh Courier*, had a much less conspicuous beginning. Once the editors changed their staffs until a proper mix of personnel had been found, the *Courier*, particularly during World War II, began a militancy that propelled that newspaper to a circulation count no other black newspaper had ever before obtained. Unlike the *Defender*, which was not always careful about the accuracy of what it printed, the editors and staff of the *Pittsburgh Courier* were careful, stuck to the truth, and, when they attacked, did so with unarguable authority. This newspaper was chosen for the perseverance of its staff despite the extreme governmental pressure for it to tone down its bold voice and militancy during World War II.

The *Black Dispatch* of Oklahoma City was chosen because it was a rare, bold newspaper located in the South with an editor, Roscoe Dunjee, who was persistent in advocating militancy to obtain civil rights for blacks. And though the editor faced financial and physical pressures that would eventually run him out of business, he accepted this outcome rather than change his stance. This organ was clearly an example of a black publication in the South which survived for many years and never muted its contents because of its geographical location. Although this paper was not prominent nationally to the same degree as the *Chicago Defender* and the *Pittsburgh Courier*, it was recognized nationally and internationally for its unwavering pursuit of justice through the use of biting and accurate editorials.

Another Southern newspaper, the *Jackson Advocate*, is a study in contradiction. This Mississippi newspaper, which did not have national recognition or a national circulation as did the other three papers, was considered somewhat militant during World War II, but its editor reversed his role during the civil rights movement when the newspaper could have become an organ on which the entire nation would have focused. What was even more startling was its shift from militancy to innocuous accommodation. Rather than calling for unity among the members of the black race to fight against injustices in Mississippi, the editor, Percy Greene, sought to chastise his black readers for not progressing rapidly. Greene ignored the incalculable and successful attempts by state officials to keep Mississippi blacks "in their place" but was quick to recognize what he thought were insufficient efforts of race members to get along with members of the white race. What was a possible motive for the editorial shift from militancy to accommodation? It has been determined that the editor accepted bribes from a governmental body which "suggested" that he refrain from calling for support of equalization of the races. The state organization responsible for derailing Greene's association with his readers further suggested that the *Jackson Advocate* should show no overt approval at all to civil rights efforts.

Three of the newspapers in this research obtained credibility beyond question. One did not.

1

THE BEGINNING
OF THE BLACK PRESS

*Antebellum Period and the Antislavery Movement,
1827–1861*

Mordecai M. Noah, the editor of the *New York Enquirer*, showed strong support for the back to Africa movement being urged by the Colonization Society during this period. It would be much easier, he stated, to get rid of the free Afro-Americans roaming the streets of New York than to assimilate them into American society.[1] But he continued to emphasize that the "institution of slavery" should remain intact. Noah further insisted that since free Afro-Americans were a threat to the institution of slavery, they should be deported.[2]

Prior to Noah's campaign, much of the censure of Afro-Americans was answered only by friendly white supporters because Afro-American New Yorkers were given no journalistic voice. Many Afro-Americans believed, however, that Noah's accusations had gone too far and that a retort of some kind had to be delivered, not from their friends in the white race, but from the people who had been insulted.[3]

With this in mind, a group of representative Afro-Americans gathered in New York City to draw up plans for a newspaper and to select men capable of conveying their messages. Thus *Freedom's Journal* was begun on March 16, 1827.[4] Its initial role was to confront all charges made by the *New York Enquirer*. The *Journal*'s Prospectus read:

> We shall ever regard the constitution of the United States as our polar star. Pledged to no party, we shall endeavor to urge our brethren to use their right to the elective franchise as free citizens.... Daily slandered, we think that there ought to be some channel of communion between us and the public, through which a single voice may be heard, in defense of five hundred thousand free people of colour. For often

9

has injustices been heaped upon us, when our only defense was an appeal to the Almighty: but we believe that the time has now arrived, when the calumnies of our enemies should be refuted by forcible arguments.[5]

The Reverend Samuel E. Cornish, a noted orator and Presbyterian minister with a flair for assertive editorials, was senior editor. The junior editor and business manager was John B. Russwurm, the second Afro-American man to have graduated from a college in the United States.[6] According to I. Garland Penn, an Afro-American historian, no other newspaper in the country encountered as many attempts to shut it down as did the *Journal*. It also set the unfortunate precedent of having to survive without the benefit of adequate subscribers and sufficient advertisers.[7]

In addition to challenging published attacks on Afro-Americans, the role of *Freedom's Journal* was to pursue an editorial policy against slavery and efforts to colonize. Those roles had been convincingly embedded in the minds of Russwurm and Cornish, but it wasn't long after the paper had started that the editorial pursuits of the editors became somewhat clouded. Russwurm began to believe that hatred for the free Afro-Americans in the United States was very deeply ingrained within too many whites. So strong did his feelings grow in that regard that he began to back away from his original promise of militant reporting. Cornish, who had held steadfast to his original promise, frequently argued with Russwurm about his change of direction. But Russwurm would not reconsider his decision. Failing with his arguments and deciding that his differences with Russwurm threatened the existence of the newspaper, Cornish gave up and resigned in September, just six months after the paper was founded. Ironically, it wasn't the frequent though unsuccessful attempts by outside forces to shut down the *Journal* throughout that turbulent period that caused it to fold, although its demise may have been inevitable. Instead, the newspaper couldn't survive the serious internal difference of editorial opinion.[8]

Russwurm continued as editor after Cornish's departure, but he didn't have Cornish's flair and style for writing biting editorials. Instead, there was hesitation, compromise, and uncertainty. But readers and supporters of the paper were patient, being aware of the recent internal problems, and waited for their remaining editor to return to his former position of protest.[9]

By 1829, Russwurm's views on moving to Africa had reached a point where his writings totally favored the position of the Colonization

Society. Those readers who had faithfully supported the paper finally turned against it, charging that Russwurm had "sold out to the Colonization Society."[10] On March 28, 1829, Russwurm ceased publication.[11] What was even more distressing was that Russwurm accepted a generous gratuity from the society, closed the doors of the *Journal*, and departed for Liberia, where he established the *Liberian Herald*.[12]

With the departure of Russwurm, Cornish returned and revived the *Journal* on May 29, 1829, changing the name to *Rights of All*. But the previous enthusiasm for the paper just wasn't there anymore. Or perhaps readers had been too dismayed by what had happened previously. Unfortunately, just five months later, Cornish, was himself forced to close down the paper. But even as he issued his final edition on October 9, Cornish maintained his position of protest[13] and he is credited "in part for the black press becoming identified with the role of protest."[14]

Over the years, the idea of protest newspapers was slow to catch on. The lack of readers may have been a major factor. And though the editors of that first newspaper did survive, their newspaper did not. Some papers did eventually turn up, however, to continue in the protest vein. Among the major papers included in this group were *African Sentinel* (Albany, N.Y.), 1831; *Albany Argus* (Albany, N.Y.), 1832; *Spirit of the Times* (New York), 1836; *Weekly Advocate* (New York), 1837; *Colored American* (Philadelphia), 1837; *Colored American* (New York), 1837; *Elevator* (Albany, N.Y.), 1841; *Emancipator and Free American* (Boston), 1842; *National Watchman* (Troy, N.Y.), 1842; *Mystery* (Pittsburgh), 1843; and *Palladium of Liberty* (Columbus, Ohio), 1844.

Although the state of New York did not have the largest concentration of free Afro-Americans at the time, it continued in 1845 to be the focal point for civil rights issues. Of concern were the unfair voting qualifications outlined in the New York state constitution which stated that no person of Afro-American heritage should have the right to vote "who was not actually worth two hundred and fifty dollars of real estate, accurately rated and taxes paid thereon." This "colored clause" went even further by stating that any white man who was twenty years old or older could vote.[15] There were no other stipulations.

After a group of Afro-Americans protested, the New York legislature pondered the clause and after much debate decided to place the issue before the New York voters. The *New York Sun*, a newspaper published for white readers, endorsed the colored clause and encouraged its readers to vote no for Negro suffrage. Those Afro-Americans who desired some sort of rebuttal to the *Sun*'s position faced the same problem which had existed in 1827. They had no Afro-American newspaper in New York or anywhere else in the country in which they could air their views and essentially had no Afro-American voice.[16]

Willis A. Hodges, a disgruntled Afro-American citizen, drafted a rebuttal and delivered it to the editor of the *Sun* for publication. The rebuttal was accepted by the newspaper's staff, but Hodges had to pay the sum of fifteen dollars, a very hefty amount, to have it published. Even when the rebuttal was printed, the editor made extensive mitigating modifications to what Hodges had written. The rebuttal was also printed as an advertisement. Upon protesting the treatment of his rebuttal, Hodges was told by a staff member: "*The Sun* shines for all white men, and not for colored men." Hodges was also told that if he wanted to further the cause of Afro-Americans, he should print his own newspaper.[17]

Having to endure such treatment and personal abuse from staff members was frustrating. But even more frustrating was the total absence of an Afro-American newspaper in the country in which Hodges could air his views without alteration. He was determined to end that drought. By engaging in white-washing work around New York to earn some money, he was able to start his own newspaper, as the *Sun*'s staff member had suggested. The *Ram's Horn* began publication on January 1, 1847.[18]

Penn notes that throughout the existence of the *Ram's Horn*, Hodges was "crude in his English" but "was one of the most sagacious and practical men of his time." That became evident when he chose Thomas Van Rensselaer as coeditor and Frederick Douglass as a contributor to the paper. Both were gifted writers and capable men.[19]

The paper did reasonably well until 1848, when a disagreement between Hodges and Van Rensselaer erupted that could not be resolved. As had been the case with the editors of *Freedom's Journal*, the division was deep enough that Hodges resigned from the paper rather than work under such conditions. Rensselaer, who was not as crucial to the paper as was Hodges, was able to print just one issue before he also gave up and closed down in June.[20] The events leading to the demise of this paper are so similar to what occurred with *Freedom's Journal* that they cannot be ignored.

Before the *Ram's Horn* folded, however, a new newspaper was begun in Rochester, New York, on December 3, 1847. The *North Star*, edited by Frederick Douglass, served notice almost immediately that the paper would be a fighter:

> The object of the *North Star* will be to attack slavery in all its forms and aspects, advocate Universal Emancipation; exact the standard of public morality; promote the moral and intellectual improvement of the colored people; and to hasten the day of freedom to our three million enslaved fellow countrymen.[21]

The entrance of the *North Star* into the newspaper arena signaled the beginning of journalistic excellence for Afro-American newspapers. This paper was widely read and widely received. It read well, and because of Douglass's connections, its messages were given greater consideration by readers. Douglass published his paper during a critical time in black history, when thousands of Afro-Americans traveled with the aid of the Underground Railroad, mostly after sundown, "at night in the dark, towards freedom above the Ohio River, guided by nothing but the North Star."[22] But the *North Star*, as had been its predecessors, was soon racked with problems: persistent and sometimes violent opposition from anti–Afro-American elements, a shortage of qualified staff, and the problem that would haunt the black press throughout most of its existence—insufficient financial assistance. But the paper clearly was not lacking in leadership, journalistic style, and effective antislavery rhetoric.[23]

Before the Civil War, 42 Afro-American newspapers had been founded. This total includes secular and religious publications but does not include magazines. All of the newspapers during that period made some kind of protest against the mistreatment of Afro-Americans in the North and called for an end to slavery in the South.

The Civil War and Reconstruction, 1861–1877

When the Civil War was in progress, the power structure in the South no longer had a total crushing grip on Afro-American civil affairs because its attention was diverted primarily to the war effort. Many Afro-Americans were able to escape successfully from their plantations, but those who escaped the bondage of slavery were on their own. Many did not know where to go, and those who did had no idea what they should do once they got there. Others just roamed the streets looking for someone to provide them with food or shelter.[24]

Five days after the Emancipation Proclamation had been signed and long before the war had ended, *L'Union*, the first general circulation Afro-American newspaper in the South[25] was begun on September 27,

1862, in New Orleans, Louisiana.[26] Thus was signaled the first change in editorial philosophy—from one of freeing the slaves to one of reestablishing the racial identity of Afro-Americans and educating them so that they could survive in society.

The editor of *L'Union* tried to soften the newspaper's sudden appearance in the South by announcing in his first issue, "We inaugurate today a new era in the destiny of the South ... to further the cause of the rights of man and of humanity."[27] After all, starting a paper for the benefit of Afro-Americans at that time in the heart of the South took great courage. To start an overtly militant paper would have been foolhardy. The South's power structure may have been preoccupied with the war, but it still had plenty of bite on the home front.

The day *L'Union* was launched was a very historic day for the Afro-American press, but it was one which began in a very dubious way, dubious because *L'Union* made its debut printed in French. Afro-American Creole descendants of French settlers began that paper and used the French language as a symbol of their heritage.[28] Unfortunately, not many Afro-Americans or whites in Louisiana at that time spoke French.

The editor listed on the masthead was Frank F. Barclay, a Caucasian. Armistead S. Pride, in his Ph.D. dissertation, states that Paul Trevigne, an Afro-American, was the actual editor, but Barclay's name was used for "diplomatic" reasons.[29] The newspaper was well received outside the South. Horace Greeley said, "It is a press organized to fight for the cause of liberty and to aid the federal government in reestablishing the Union." In the South, however, harsh criticism was the usual response.[30]

Two months after its founding, Louis Dutuit took over the editorship of the paper. He increased the number of pages being printed, changed from the practice of cramming print onto the page to that of using "clearer type faces," and started a companion newspaper called the *Union*.[31]

L'Union and *Union* were different newspapers with different styles, audiences, languages (one was printed in French, the other in English), and advertisers but both had the same political convictions. Unfortunately, the tenure of both papers was very short. On Tuesday, July 19, 1864, the final editions of those historic organs appeared. No reason was given for their demise.[32]

Two days later, however, the *New Orleans Tribune* and its companion *La Tribune de la Nouvelle-Orleans* appeared.[33] The *Tribune* began as a triweekly, another first for the Afro-American press. A short time later, it was published five times a week, including Sunday. Those two papers took over the same facilities as their predecessors, including the same ads, mailing and subscription lists, and prices. The *Tribune* introduced itself by stating that "Under the above title we publish a new paper devoted to the principles heretofore defended by the *Union*."[34] Dr. L. C. Roudanez was the owner. As was customary for a newspaper during this era, the editorial philosophy centered on political equality and progress for Afro-Americans. This time, however, the moderate tone of the French version had been replaced by one of militancy.[35]

There were 115 Afro-American newspapers founded during the Civil War and Reconstruction era. The longevity of most was short, an average of eight years, but at least nine papers lasted up to or beyond the turn of the century. Of those that folded, their longevity ranged from a low of four months for the *Colored American*, Augusta, Georgia (October 1865 to February 1866), to a high of 67 years for the *Jackson Index*, Jackson, Tennessee (1870 to 1937).

During the Civil War and Reconstruction era, all Confederate states witnessed the arrival of their first newspaper published by Afro-Americans: Alabama, *Nationalist*, Mobile, 1865; Arkansas, *Arkansas Freeman*, Little Rock, 1869; Florida, *New Era*, Gainesville, 1873; Georgia, *Colored American*, 1865; Louisiana, *L'Union*, New Orleans, 1862; Mississippi, *Colored Citizen*, Vicksburg, 1867; North Carolina, *Journal of Freedom*, Raleigh, 1865; South Carolina, *Leader*, Charleston, 1865; Tennessee, *Colored Tennessean*, Nashville, 1865; Texas, *Freeman's Press*, Austin, 1868; and Virginia, *True Southerner*, Norfolk, 1865.

L'Union's appearance in the South had been made with a great deal of caution. When what the editor viewed as a trial period was over, the role of protest began. But most of the issues of protest involved locations outside the immediate geographical area and outside the South, a survival technique used when the editor wanted to overtly protest but also stay alive. Records show that those editors who elected to protest with militancy about racial problems in the South and within their immediate areas usually had an extremely short existence, physically and professionally.

Freedom from slavery and the arrival of Reconstruction brought high hopes to the thousands of Afro-Americans roaming the countryside. And though they had no ideas about their future, they were free. As Afro-American editors saw the situation, before a new life for ex-slaves could begin, major adjustments from the role of slave to the role of free man had to be made. Since no other organized effort had been established before the end of the war for race members, the Afro-American press with its role of educator and restorer of racial identity shifted to yet another new and totally different challenge. In addition to publishing survival techniques, it made greater efforts to educate the masses by arousing, informing, and mobilizing them. Yet it never relinquished its unified role of protest.

The Era of Reaction and Adjustment, 1877–1915

The era of reaction and adjustment unexpectedly came rushing in when President Rutherford B. Hayes began pulling the Union soldiers out of the South in 1877.[36] Once the federal troops were removed, that period in history became the most dangerous and brutal for Afro-Americans.[37] Even the Afro-American press, which had surfaced and fought against the odds, faced its greatest challenge. In fact, so effective was the brutality during that era that much of the Afro-American press abandoned an editorial philosophy of militancy and became virtually mute on race issues. Those editors who became mute on rare topics survived; many of those who did not suppress or tone down their views did not.

Exceptions to this muted role came primarily from newspapers outside the South such as the *Chicago Conservator*, 1878, and the *New York Age*, 1887. Within the South, the Memphis *Free Speech and Headlight* was an exception without parallel.

As in many other cities in the post–Civil War South, Afro-Americans in Memphis, Tennessee, had advanced to the point where they had the right to vote and even had placed some of their members on the police force. Other Afro-Americans also had the good fortune to serve in public offices. When the federal troops were pulled from the South, Afro-Americans in Memphis were unceremoniously jerked from respectable jobs. Many faced clashes, other violence, and denial of civil opportunities. In the midst of this turmoil, the Reverend Taylor Nightingale published the *Free Speech and Headlight*. But it wasn't until Ida B. Wells became one of its editors in 1889 that the newspaper became noted for its militant protest.[38]

Throughout her tenure as editor, Wells pursued an editorial philosophy of racial justice and of protest against unfair and brutal practices, particularly lynching. So deep was her hatred and revulsion of lynching and so convinced was she that most of those who accused Afro-Americans of crimes were lying that she began to keep records so that she could identify trends in these crimes and make evaluations. In one of her evaluations based on her compiled data, she disputed claims of Memphis officials by reporting that "Negro lynch victims were accused of rape in less than one-fourth of lynching occurrences and that some were lynched for such trivial causes as insulting whites or failing to move aside."[39]

With her militant editorials, Wells provoked strong reactions from whites in Memphis. Although she was employed as a city school teacher, a position which would seem to have called for her to be prudent and to bend to the whims of school board members, she instead openly "criticized the poor facilities within the Afro-American public schools and the morally dubious manner by which the school board selected certain women to teach within those schools."[40]

The boldness with which Wells continued her militancy eventually brought about the expected results. When her teacher's contract came up for renewal, a simple formality under normal circumstances, it was turned down by the school board. Wells was out of a job.[41]

The action of the school board, however, did not curb Wells's tongue. Now that she no longer needed to divide her attention between jobs, she could spend more time editorializing on the conditions of Afro-Americans within the city. Lynching, a problem she could not ignore, was still being carried out unchecked and with alarming regularity with no arrest made of guilty parties.

Wells noted that when one lynching was in progress in Kentucky a group of Afro-Americans fed up with such lawlessness formed its own mob and clashed with the would-be lynchers. Wells issued an editorial praising the Afro-Americans in Kentucky for their reaction. Two white Memphis newspapers, the *Weekly Avalanche* and the *Public Ledger*, took exception to her comments and openly supported lynch mobs "as a violent but necessary abrogation of civil law in cases involving rape."[42]

By now the Afro-American people in Memphis had begun to sense that they had an editor with some backbone, that Wells was a fighter for their cause. Subscriptions to the newspaper began to increase, jumping from 1,500 to 4,000 per week. Personal appearances and travel by Wells also added to the popularity of the newspaper. Outside of Tennessee, circulation was increasing to include readers from those states with very muted presses, Arkansas and Mississippi.

Even with the financial success of the newspaper, however, this "Princess of the Press" was far from being satisfied with existing conditions.[43] She had established an editorial philosophy of militancy and intended to stick with it and bring about some change or at least bring problems to the attention of her readers. And no one, not even members of her own race, was exempted from her lashing when she believed one was necessary.

For instance, one of the things that had irritated Wells was the behavior of the one Afro-American who had had the opportunity to disrupt the ease with which laws detrimental to Afro-American advancement could be enacted. Isaiah Montgomery, the founder of Mound Bayou, Mississippi, supported the "Understanding Clause" at the Mississippi Constitutional Convention of 1890. Wells attacked him because he "had cast a vote allowing the state of Mississippi to circumvent the Fifteenth Amendment and subsequently undermine Negro voting potential."[44]

In another instance, Wells attacked Booker T. Washington, who had not yet reached the lofty position of "race leader," not for his criticism of some members of the Afro-American ministry for some of the things they had done, but for using a white Northern publication to convey his message. "She thought it was counterproductive to air such sentiments in the land of one's 'enemies'; better that Washington had made the same statement 'at home' where it would have a more direct impact."[45]

But of all the issues that stirred Wells's wrath, the arbitrary practice of lynching and the overt absence of law enforcement before, during, and after the killings, brought about the sharpest editorials. Her reactions on that issue engendered both national and international attention to her as editor.

Having seen enough lynching of her race members and realizing that Southern practices towards Afro-Americans would not change, particularly after two Tennessee lynchings in 1892, Wells decided that the living conditions for Afro-Americans in Memphis were beyond hope. Rather than remain within a state where law and order for the protection of Afro-Americans did not exist, she believed it would be far better to move somewhere else. Wells began writing rousing editorials encouraging Afro-Americans to get up, mobilize, leave, and "migrate to the new Oklahoma territory, where a lynch-free world could be found." Heeding her call to seek a better location, many Afro-Americans packed up what belongings they had and began heading west. Thus began the initial period of migration for Afro-Americans.[46]

Wells's encouragement for members of her race to leave Memphis had not, however, escaped the ever-watchful eyes of some white Memphis officials. They approached her and tried to justify the use of lynching, not to bring about law and order, but to make examples of those Afro-Americans who raped white women. Wells did not suppress her anger when she responded in writing to those comments. In another biting editorial, "She inferred, with little subtlety, that white women were accountable for provoking such alleged violations."[47]

For the sake of physical survival, no Afro-American editor had ever before gone so far as to place the responsibility for rapes on white women. With such an attack, Wells had touched on sacred grounds. Two white newspapers, the *Memphis Scimitar* and the *Memphis Commercial*, reported that whites had suffered "the ultimate indignity, and ... were compelled to insure the heresy would never be repeated."[48] Such a call for lynching by white newspapers normally sparked instant and brutal results. Wells, not at all remorseful for what she had written, realized that her life was in serious jeopardy.

But strangely enough, the danger did not come as swiftly as had been expected, but came on May 27, 1892, almost three months after her article had appeared, while Wells was visiting Jersey City. In her autobiography, Wells indicates that although she had expected immediate reaction from angry white citizens, it never came while she was in Memphis. She also anticipated that the tolerance level of whites when viewing her militant editorials would be very low. Even so, she continued to write fearlessly because of her anger at the ease with which white mobs could do as they pleased with Afro-Americans and not be challenged by lawful authorities.[49]

As a defensive gesture, Wells had purchased a pistol to confront members of the mob when they arrived: "I felt that one had better die fighting against injustice than to die like a dog or a rat in a trap. I had already determined to sell my life as dearly as possible if attacked. I felt if I could take one lyncher with me, this would even up the score a little bit."[50]

It was after her arrival in Jersey City that T. Thomas Fortune, editor of the *New York Age*, greeted Wells by suggesting that she make New York her home. She was surprised at such a suggestion and remained perplexed until Fortune showed her a copy of the *New York Sun*. She read with shock an article which stated: A committee of leading citizens had gone to the office of the *Free Speech* that night, run the business manager, J. L. Fleming, out of town, destroyed the type and furnishings of the office, and left a note saying that anyone trying to publish the paper again would be punished with death."[51]

Wells also expressed puzzlement over why that group responsible for the destruction of her newspaper had waited so long after the inflammatory editorial was published before taking action.

> The reader will doubtless wonder what caused the destruction of my paper after three months of constant agitation following the lynching of my friends. They were killed on the ninth of March. The *Free Speech* was destroyed 27 May 1892, nearly three months later. I thought then it was the white southerner's chivalrous defense of his womanhood which caused the mob to destroy my paper, even though it was known that the truth had been spoken. I know now that it was an excuse to do what they had wanted to do before but had not dared because they had no good reason until the appearance of that famous editorial.[52]

Such violent reaction in the South to what militant editors printed could be expected if they did not choose their words carefully. Slavery had ended and the Civil War and Reconstruction periods were over, but many of the practices the Afro-American press had fought against were still in evidence. One of the things that made the era of reaction and adjustment so noteworthy was that editors found it more difficult to survive during that time than they had during times of slavery.

The turn of the century brought no ray of hope for Negroes. Lynching and segregation were still an unwelcome part of life. Negroes continued to be the main victims in race riots, and many continued to move from the rural South because all hope of being treated with compassion had disappeared. As a result of these mass moves, thousands were being pushed into already overcrowded neighborhoods.

Those were new and different situations the Negro press had to face—uplifting race and community consciousness, protesting against discrimination, and reporting the news of Negro life back home in the South.

From the time *Freedom's Journal* was launched in 1827 until Negroes were officially freed in 1863, approximately 42 Negro newspapers had raised banners in protest against slavery and the unfair treatment of free Negroes. One hundred and sixteen more raised their banners in protest from 1861 through 1877 in an effort to educate. From 1880 to 1890, more than 504 Negro newspapers made efforts to warn and alert society to the increasing number of Negro citizens being lynched and the lack of law enforcement when it pertained to members of that race. It was during that time in history that editors of white newspapers began to notice the Negro press and to quote extensively its news and opinions.

The number of Negro newspapers which started during the era of reaction and adjustment was by far the highest total of any era in the history of Negro Americans. More than 2,099 papers made attempts to tell what was going on. During the period from 1895, when Booker T. Washington was chosen as the "leader" of Negroes, to 1915, when he died, a total of 1,219 Negro newspapers were begun. The pinnacle year was 1902, when 101 papers were begun. An argument for this significant rise could suggest that subsistence payments from Booker T. Washington were a major contributing factor. Subsistence payments could be seen as either good or bad for the Negro press, depending on an individual's point of view. But there is a more poignant possibility for the increase in numbers.

Also overlapping the era of reaction and adjustment was what the National Association for the Advancement of Colored People (NAACP) called the "lynching era," 1889–1939.[53] Their records for the thirty-year period from 1889 to 1918 show that 3,224 persons were lynched. Of that number, 702 were white or Native American and 2,522 were Negro. And according to the records of lynching kept by Tuskegee Institute, 115 Negroes were lynched in 1900 and 130 more were lynched in 1901, a record year.[54] Throughout U.S. history, the rise in the number of Negro newspapers has been consistent with the rise in lynching.

In addition to lynching, the Negro press reported other alarming news such as the calculated destruction of property, legal and political inconsistencies between the races, overcrowded living areas, street crimes, and race riots, which were increasing with distressing regularity. Gunnar Myrdal, a noted historian from Europe who researched the plight of blacks in the United States, has indicated, "As lynching was primarily a rural weapon which was characteristic of the South, riots were an urban weapon and characteristic of the North."[55] Editors were just as alarmed about the willful destruction of property as they were about the absence of punishment for participants in lynch mobs. The situation for Negroes was out of control, yet Booker T. Washington continued to call for accommodation, a concept which other Negro "leaders" saw as woefully ineffective.

One of the last newspapers to oppose vigorously the status quo and fight for equalization of Negro rights up to this time in history was the Memphis *Free Speech*, which had been violently shut down in

1892. Since that time and with the arrival of Washington and his conciliatory policies, the Negro people had but few directions in which they could look for some sign of compassion. It has been suggested that Washington may have been responsible for the silence of the Negro press during that period. Those newspapers which were somewhat militant were few and were located in the North. In those areas where Washington could not silence or tone down a newspaper with his policies, he attempted to muzzle it by subsidizing its competition.[56]

In 1901, with the arrival of William Monroe Trotter and the Boston *Guardian*, the militancy within the Negro press editorials began to resurge. Trotter began the *Guardian* as "a weekly newspaper devoted to securing absolute equality for the Negro people."[57] He said of Washington: "What man is a worse enemy to a race than a leader who looks with equanimity on the disfranchisement of his race in a country where other races have universal suffrage by constitutions that make one rule for his race and another for the dominant race."[58]

Trotter's attacks, however, were not aimed solely at Washington. He castigated any Negro politician who "failed to speak out against Washington's 'traitorous' surrender of the rights of Negro men."[59]

W.E.B. DuBois, educator, author, and editor of The *Crisis* magazine, also did not escape Trotter's wrath. DuBois, looked upon by many Negroes as "the Negro leader," still thought that Washington's philosophy had a chance of working if it were carried out exactly as Washington had proposed. But Trotter said of DuBois, "Like all the others who are trying to get onto the bandwagon of the Tuskegeean, he is no longer to be relied upon."[60]

The *Guardian* wanted someone to oppose Washington for the leadership role of Negroes, and there was no one better than DuBois. But since DuBois steadfastly supported Washington, Trotter attacked him for not providing the opposing leadership that would pull the race from the deep quagmire into which the South seemed to have placed it.

Strangely enough, it took less than a year for DuBois to shift from his position of support for Washington. That shift caused a major rift in the ranks of the Negro people. DuBois seemed to change for no apparent reason but insisted that the change was necessary in view of Washington's growing power. More than anything else, DuBois thought press support for the lackadaisical way in which Washington treated the growing number of laws on segregation and the disfranchisement of Negroes was far greater than it should have been. Other sources closer to the situation thought that Trotter probably persuaded

DuBois to side with the opposition. How this was done so effectively and so quickly was never discovered. But Trotter drew no lines in his efforts to put some spirit back into the thinking of Negroes.

Trotter also used the *Guardian* to arouse, mobilize, and "kick" some backbone into lethargic race members who once had been very active but recently had retreated to the role of accommodation. He saw them as a beaten people who lived with no purpose whatsoever.[61]

Actually, the issue between the two giants, Washington and DuBois, concerned the methods which should be used for the advancement of Negroes. DuBois wanted to practice the equality which had been given to the race and push for those things they did not have. Those were not his initial ideas but may have come about when he saw that Washington's philosophy was not working. On the other hand, Washington saw the need for accommodation, the role of waiting, and the theme of patience.[62] Such a confrontation between those two men at such a critical time also divided the Negro press when survival of the race needed a united front.

"None struck harder blows at the wrongs and weaknesses of the race," Penn had said of Ida B. Wells.[63] But that was before the arrival of Trotter. In one editorial, for example, in which Trotter admonished Washington and other members of his race, he was far from being subtle when he wrote: "Silence is tantamount to being virtually an accomplice in the treasonable act of this Benedict Arnold of the Negro race. O, for a black Patrick Henry to save his people from this stigma of cowardice."[64]

The *Guardian* wasn't alone in its criticism of Washington. Over in Ohio, the *Cleveland Gazette*, founded in 1883, also chipped away at the philosophy of accommodation. The Chicago *Conservator*, 1878, the *Richmond Planet*, 1883, the Washington *Bee*, 1882, and the *Christian Recorder*, 1852, initially were critical of Washington but later changed their viewpoint in his favor.[65]

Washington wanted the editors of the Negro press to use a more moderate tone in their editorials. Many did as he suggested, but not out of respect for him, although it could be argued that respect was there even if it had been purchased with gratuities. He really believed that only by using an accommodating tone would Negroes be able to overcome white hatred and survive. It must be remembered that at one time in his life Washington had been a slave. He was offering his message of trying to overcome white hatred in order to survive during a time in history when record numbers of people had already been killed or were being killed and the problem was getting worse. In reality, the Negro people had already listened to Washington's message and had sent up the signal, "Water, water; we die of thirst!" but no one seemed to be there to cast down a bucket.[66]

2

THE *CHIGAGO DEFENDER* AND THE MOVE NORTHWARD, 1915–1928

"Make the world safe for democracy."[1] The slogan used within the United States during World War I had such a paradoxical twist as far as Negroes were concerned that editors of the Negro press decided it was time for a change of editorial emphasis in what they had to say.

The use of such a slogan meant that the government either did not realize what was going on with Negro Americans or was unconcerned. After all, the government had already turned over the welfare of the Negro race to Southern authorities, so it was their problem. Or, worst yet, government officials may have believed that since Negroes had been given their freedom, they, as anyone else in the country, should solve their own problems.

The editorial philosophy the Negro press assumed during that era was to point out the contradiction between the slogan "Make the world safe for democracy" and the realities as they existed within the United States. The Negro editors therefore decided to use that slogan in their publications so that the words being used by the government to preach to the world and the lack of understanding of what was actually going on would not fade from the minds of their readers.[2]

No longer was there the question of how much coverage to give lynching and other local violence. Those usual headline-grabbing events became secondary. Instead, one of the main issues involved Negro loyalty to the United States and the treatment, or mistreatment, of Negro soldiers. Should they, the editors, encourage Negroes to fight and save the country for a democracy they did not experience? In their hearts they said no, but they concluded it would be necessary for Negroes to fight for their country despite how they felt. For if they

25

did not, the Kaiser, if he were to win, clearly would not be sympathetic to their cause.[3]

Another problem for Negro editors in addition to problems concerning the war was the absence of advertising revenue. Up to that point in history, advertising had been so scarce and undependable that editors and publishers were forced to turn their attention to other ways in which revenue could be obtained. An increase in the price of the paper was seen as one probable solution. Unfortunately, several factors, which were not apparent for some time, still prevented many Negro newspapers from obtaining wide circulation and thus the funds necessary for a profitable existence.

First of all, those major Negro newspapers which faced no physical threats of violence because of their militant editorial philosophies were located in the North. The readers those newspapers needed were unfortunately located primarily in the South. That separation from potential readers made increasing circulation a challenge.

At the same time, in the South, where large numbers of potential subscribers were located, the literacy rate was significantly lower, thereby limiting the numbers of readers. Living conditions were also extremely harsh, which meant that many Negroes in the South were preoccupied with sustaining life and thus had little concern for other domestic or international affairs. Reading a newspaper was a luxury they could not afford. Yet those same people who could not afford that luxury needed the newspaper to seek guidance on survival, notices of available jobs, and ways out of their dismal conditions.

Newspapers in the North were also becoming much more militant, an editorial philosophy necessary to satisfy the demands of subscribers. The more militant the newspaper was, the more it was accepted by the reader. Some increases in circulation as a result of that militancy were apparent for some newspapers, but for most, the numbers still were understandably small. When Negro newspapers became militant in the South, as did the Memphis *Free Speech*, circulation did increase substantially and profits were satisfactory, but the tenure for such newspapers and the time in office of their editors and staff were usually very brief.

Faced with those persistent and pressing problems, some editors elected to increase prices and hoped subscribers would understand. Unfortunately, many of those subscribers who did purchase a newspaper, particularly those in the South, also faced hard times and barely had enough income to purchase a newspaper and eke out a day-to-day living. Thus when the cost of the paper was increased—usually a painful and arduous decision for editors to make—many readers dropped their subscriptions, and this often doomed the paper to failure.

With the arrival of the *Chicago Defender* in 1905, there was a major change in how editorial content and contents directed towards particular audiences were handled. This change not only brought stability and longevity to this newspaper but enabled it to forge ahead in the Negro newspaper leadership role while expanding its circulation to a national level. Such a role backed up by substantial subscribers gave notice and recognition that the Negro press no longer could be brushed aside by authorities as merely an incidental medium.

In retrospect, the Negro press, though never praised for its literary styles or tenacity in pursuit of truth, had always attempted to provide news and opinions to its readers without the use of fanfare or ridicule. Its role was to deliver the news as seen by the editor or staff as straight as possible, even if strong emotions were involved in the story. Delivering that news was generally a serious business. The editors were serious individuals, and the welfare of their readers was paramount. After all, the black editor was seen as a role model by Negro communities, someone to honor, trust and respect. The scope of the editor's influence was rarely questioned.[4]

When the *Defender* was started, its editor, Robert S. Abbott, was the first to break away from that long conservative custom. He was not a trained journalist in the traditional sense, nor did he have a flair for words as did Frederick Douglass. But like Willis Hodges with the *Ram's Horn*, he was able to find and employ those individuals who did possess the moxie for innovation.[5]

One final thought on problems facing Negro editors at the turn of the century. The demise of so many newspapers prior to 1910 could be attributed to their persistence in reaching out primarily to Negro elites and whites who were genuinely interested in how the Negro race was faring. Since the numbers within each of those groups were relatively low, mass circulation could not be generated. Abbott may or may not have consciously turned away from those Negro elites and whites interested in how the Negro was faring, but he recognized the benefits of mimicking success when he copied William Randolph Hearst's style of yellow journalism. The Negro masses may not have had the immediate clout that the elite did, but as history would eventually show, a Negro newspaper with a mass following would clearly grab the attention of advertisers (a very welcome change) and the government, all the way up to the president.

Although Abbott printed the *Defender* in Chicago, he hadn't always lived in the North. He was born on St. Simon Island, Georgia, on November 24, 1870, and attended schools in Savannah and later attended Hampton Institute, Virginia, where he learned the printing trade. In 1899 he was graduated with a bachelor of law degree from Kent College of Law in Chicago. He was later advised that such a degree would be his "white elephant" and that his skin color was "a little too dark to make any impression on the courts in Chicago." Abbott never made it to those courts because the Illinois bar did not allow his admittance. Later, after he tried and failed to be admitted to the bar in Gary, Indiana, and in Topeka, Kansas, he returned to Chicago and turned his attention to the newspaper business.[6] Abbott probably became interested in the newspaper business while listening to such speakers as Ida B. Wells and Frederick Douglass.[7]

Abbott's venture with newspapers began in rented space on State Street with just a card table in the room. He even had to borrow a chair on which to sit. And since his entire financial backing consisted of twenty-five cents, which he used to purchase paper and pencils, he had to make arrangements for the paper to be printed on credit. Salaries were not a problem because he was the only staff, but his landlady's teenage daughter provided some help occasionally. His landlady, Mrs. Harriet Plummer Lee, provided his meals, gave him money for small expenses, mended his clothes, and let him use her telephone. As for circulation, Abbott delivered each of his first 300 papers of handbill size door to door on May 5, 1905. Thus the *Chicago Defender* was born.[8]

It was fairly easy for Abbott to deliver his paper. He lived in a Chicago ghetto crammed with people, as many as 44,000 living within a few southside blocks. So compact was his circulation route that he was able to solicit advertising, scour the community for local news, and make distribution to customers without any assistance.[9]

It wasn't until 1910 when Abbott hired J. Hockley Smiley, his first full-time employee, that the *Defender* began to surge ahead in circulation. Smiley was aware of the tactics by the "yellow press" and of the success that William Randolph Hearst was having in his battle with Joseph Pulitzer. He therefore began to report and create, if necessary, stories that were certain to stir the reader's interest and increase circulation.[10]

Meanwhile, conditions were ripe in the South for what Abbott was about to do with the *Defender*—encourage Negroes to get up and move away from the South. An ongoing depression which existed in that area and the loss of cotton crops to an infestation of boll weevil found many Negroes out of what little work they had had. Negroes also still could not vote and were denied work in many areas. Those Negroes who could find work could expect low wages. Lynching remained a traumatic ordeal for the entire Negro community. The attitude that killing humans was justified in order to keep them docile had become so common that some events took on a festive air, with plenty of people, some with children, in attendance and plenty of food and games.[11] In fear and desperation, some Negroes had already given up and were in the process of migrating from their Southern homeland.[12]

The North, which also had its woes, now had World War I with which to contend. In addition to shortages of military personnel, workers—skilled or unskilled—were needed in factories. And since the immigration of Europeans had been halted because of the war, that pool of unskilled labor had been cut off. The North needed manpower to fill the gaps left by departing soldiers.[13]

Abbott, who was familiar with the gloomy conditions of Negroes in the South, was extremely good at interpreting the mood of a situation and taking advantage of it. He could not ignore the fact that many Negroes had already begun migrating northward. As he saw it, why not have more families migrate north, where the wages were higher, even for Negroes, and where the worst of conditions were better than the best of conditions in the South. Thus he and the *Defender* began to target Southern Negroes with cries of jobs in the North. It was a successful gamble. By the end of the war, the *Defender*'s sales were far greater in the South than anywhere else.[14] Providing news of jobs was not all, however, that Abbott and the *Defender* had planned for the South.

Abbott is said to have "stooped" to the use of sensationalism in his presentation of news. He did sensationalize the news. But he must be given credit for finding success in a profession where Negroes had not found such success previously. And though Negro newspapers such as the *Christian Recorder*[15] and the *Savannah Tribune*[16] were known for their longevity, they were not known for their financial stability. The *Defender* brought not only stability to a struggling profession, but stability with very large profits and editorial clout. As James Gordon

Bennett did with such success in 1835 with the *New York Herald*, Abbott "infused new life into journalism" with his *Defender*.[17]

In the past, Negro editors generally had not emphasized crime reports in news or editorials. The *Defender* not only used the yellow journalism techniques of Hearst while announcing crimes but also used sensational headlines with large letters in red type. With the exception of the editor of the *Chicago Whip*, which also made crime news prominent, the other Negro editors treated that practice with scorn and contempt. To their way of thinking that was a passing fad destined for failure and not worthy of further consideration by honorable men doing their noble jobs.[18]

If it was Abbott's goal to sensationalize the news to gain readers, he was indeed successful. Readers liked what he was doing. Not only did they like it, they savored it and began to purchase more and more copies of the newspaper. Abbott did not ignore his subscribers in the North, but he paid particular attention to events involving Negroes in the South. That was where the survival rate was at its lowest.

That Abbott targeted the South with his news and editorials should have come as no surprise. After all, the South was where he was born and raised. But that also was the region where a driving need for some sort of spark existed, where there was a thirst for some news that life somewhere else had to be better for Negroes. Hope still lingered among Southern Negroes that someone somewhere would provide the answers to their constant misery.

When Booker T. Washington was freed from slavery and made his way to Malden, West Virginia, one of the conditions with which he had to contend was the open sex and violence in his new neighborhood. Living in crowded quarters with so little privacy, visual and auditory, some inhabitants who sold their bodies to survive made no attempt to conceal their profession.[19] Abbott was faced with this same situation. But unlike Washington, Abbott had the *Defender* with which he could effect change.

When conditions in his neighborhood seemed almost out of control, Abbott resorted to the use of muckraking against prostitution, much in the same manner as Hearst.[20] When stories of prostitutes began to wane, Abbott would dig for other neighborhood problems. When those problems also fell from prominence, Smiley, as did Hearst, would sometime create "wild stories."[21] As Abbott once said, "I tell the truth if I can get it, but if I can't get the facts, I read between the lines and tell what I know to be facts even though the reports say differently."[22]

Getting Negroes to better themselves was not the only concern on Abbott's agenda. Southerners had had approximately 50 years to demonstrate in action their true feelings for Negroes. If the number of lynching incidents was an indicator, then Negroes should be advised to get out of the South. So Abbott made his decision, a bold decision, but he had already tasted success when he took a step by sensational-izing the news. If migration was an answer for the survival of Negroes, now was the time to strike.

The announcement of jobs and better conditions was a strong inducement but was not the sole reason for the migration. Lynching and frequent face-to-face confrontations with hostile white mobs was another reason some Negroes moved. Many of those who migrated were farmers living in the rural South, where lynching was most com-mon. Being innocent of wrongdoing or just being a bystander was no guarantee of safety. In many instances the innocent were swept away when hostile mobs went on a rampage to "keep the Negro in his place." Hearing about such killings was fearful enough but not nearly as dev-astating as seeing them.[23]

A second reason why Negroes began to move was coincidental. Drought, then heavy rains, and the infestation of boll weevils that flourished under wet conditions virtually wiped out crops in 1915 and 1916.[24]

The higher wages being paid to workers in the North was a third reason for migrating. The standard hourly wage in the North was between fifty cents and one dollar. Such sums were comparable to a "full day's work in the South."[25] For many, moving north was worth the trip.

Other reasons for migrating included the overall way in which Negroes were mistreated in the South. Much of the time they were brushed-off as though they were children. They were required, how-ever, to treat a white person with absolute respect, regardless of the per-son's standing in the community. That became a significant issue because the term of address Negroes were required to use was "mis-ter," "madam," "sir," or "miss," yet when Southern whites addressed a Negro doctor or preacher or school teacher, they were not expected to use these terms nor did they do so. Instead, they referred to profes-sional Negroes by title, a tactic employed to avoid using the terms of respect.[26]

More important than most other reasons for leaving the South, perhaps, was the law as it was applied to Southerners. Negroes believed without reservation that the law was designed to protect everyone. Protection was what they craved. But an accused Negro was not guaranteed safety even while under the umbrella of the law. And in the courts, justice was not always blind because it was almost a foregone conclusion that Negroes would not receive equal justice when a confrontation had occurred with a white person. Abbott saw that problem as one of the major reasons for Negroes to leave the South: "Equal protection in courts. The same laws could not be meted to white and Negro alike, they were not cruel and stringent enough for the latter."[27]

In a *Defender* editorial quoting a letter printed in the New Orleans *Times-Picayune*, one citizen wrote about the conditions for Negroes in the South:

> The unbiased observer has not long to search nor far to seek to find the real reason for the present exodus of Negroes from the South. Isolated, ostracized, humiliated, proscribed, discriminated against, practically outlawed, the patience which made him a type as a slave has become a mockery with him as a freedman. He is the negative force in every equation. His work, be he skilled, has to be accepted with the scant and sarcastic encomium that it is well done, "for a Negro." His ability in other lines is discounted on the grounds that in whatever measure it may exist, his white blood is responsible.[28]

The *Defender* has been given much of the credit for urging Negroes to migrate north. But many other organs played vital roles in that migration and should also be given credit. The *Christian Recorder*, the *New York News*, the *Dallas Express*, and the *New York Age* were a few. Other papers from Washington, D.C., and Indianapolis were also active in that regard.[29]

No editor, however, was as relentless as Abbott. He was constantly watchful for the mood of the travelers, their problems, their expectations. He even received unexpected help from friends and relatives who had already made the trip northward. They wrote home to relatives and friends in the South telling them about the "freedom and jobs in the North." The *Defender* then merely reinforced what had been written by carrying help-wanted ads in its national edition. But that was not all. To drive home the urgency for Negroes to get out of the South, each new lynching story or other incidence of violence was sensationalized and splashed across the page with large and graphic photographs and with large red headlines.[30] Abbott wanted no misunderstanding of the urgency to move from the South. Using subtlety wouldn't do it.

Reactions through increased circulation and numerous letters from Southern subscribers made Abbott aware that his efforts were succeeding. Many Negroes were actually moving north. At every opportunity, he stressed the need to seek human dignity, freedom, and economic opportunities and to shun Southern tyranny. And he never forgot the use of front-page violence.[31]

When a weakness in their workforce became quite evident, Southern officials tried to halt the migration by warning departing Negroes that they might freeze to death in the North because they were not accustomed to that kind of weather. Upon learning of that report, the *Defender* found and collected reports from white newspapers in Georgia, South Carolina, and Louisiana about Negroes freezing to death in the South. Abbott, while reprinting these clippings on the front page, explained:

> If you can freeze to death in the North and be free, why freeze to death in the south and be a slave, where your mother, sister and daughter are raped and burned at the stake, where your father, brother and son are treated with contempt and hung to a pole, riddled with bullets at the least mention that he does not like the way he has been treated?[32]

Not only did they have someone to guide them now, but Southern Negroes were quick to recognize Abbott as their guide, someone who even took on Southern officials without fear of incrimination. As a result, letters for assistance on various problems poured into Chicago from Kentucky, Tennessee, Mississippi, and Alabama. Northern merchants became aware of what the Negro newspaper was doing and the resulting reaction from Southern subscribers. Since they were sorely in need of laborers, they placed more ads, which solidified the *Defender*'s financial position even more and encouraged further the urge for Negroes to go north.[33]

Because of the significant increase in advertising, in circulation, and in the number of migrants heading north, the *Defender* became unrelenting in its push to rid the South of its Negroes:

> Every Negro man for the sake of his wife and daughters especially, should leave even at a financial sacrifice every spot in the south where his worth is not appreciated enough to give him the standing of a man and a citizen in the community. We know full well that this would almost mean a depopulation of that section and if it were possible we would glory in its accomplishment.[34]

By this time, the circulation for the *Defender* had reached numbers never before envisioned by a Negro newspaper. According to Florette

Henri, a Negro migration historian, the *Defender*'s circulation had reached 283,571 by the year 1920.[35] The number of subscribers, however, does not reflect the actual number of readers. The practice of passing a copy of the *Defender* from person to person was so prevalent that an accurate count of readers will never be obtained. And of the number of people subscribing to the *Defender*, more than two-thirds were from outside of Chicago.[36]

With the arrival of 1917, Abbott savored the results of his news formula which had brought about an increase in circulation. Even with unsurpassed financial success having been obtained, he continued his push to incite, arouse, and stir the emotions of Southerners, Negro and white, and to urge Negroes to leave the South. This time he devised a grand plan which he hoped would draw even more Negroes and increase circulation even more. His plan was to set the date of May 15, 1917, as a day for "the Great Northern Drive." And when that date arrived, he pushed for a massive northern drive. That was a day he hoped the South would always remember.[37]

So many people leaving one geographical area at one time would require planning, and, to some degree, a major focal point where request for assistance could be directed. Preparing for the trip would not pose a major problem for many Negroes because they had very little to carry, but leaving town safely eventually became dangerous. Making the northern trip was also a traumatic ordeal for many of the travelers. The *Defender* without reservation took on the role of coordinator.[38]

To assist in the preparation for the trip, the *Defender* was called on to provide the necessary information or advice on the most economical way to travel. Railroads were alerted to provide extra cars, which they did, particularly during the summer months when regular rail travel was slow. Many Northern merchants, who had become aware of the *Defender*'s preparation for the exodus, sent agents to the South to encourage travelers to sign work contracts. Arrangements were then made for travel to a specific location with the personal belongings of the contracted party held as collateral.[39]

Some travelers, in desperation for jobs, agreed to relinquish their initial wages to agents in return for promised work. Others who were wary of those agents seeking advance money or skeptical about contracts which required them to sign over two to three months' wages sought assistance from the *Defender*. Abbott responded by encouraging group travel or the formation of travel clubs for safety.[40]

For many travelers, the northern move took on an air of excursion. The railroads, reaping the bounty of the extensive number of travelers, took full advantage of the situation by providing special excursion rates. The *Defender* even made arrangements with some rail companies for special-fare travel for anyone wishing it. Letters then poured in to the newspaper seeking more information on how to obtain that more economical way of traveling.[41]

It eventually became risky in many states for so many Negroes to leave town at the same time, and some Southern whites began to make efforts to keep Negroes in the South. Many travelers arriving in the North described the many things that had happened along the way and how they had to escape:

> They had to slip away from their homes at night, walk to some railroad station where they were not known, and there board a train for the North. If they were found to have tickets, the police confiscated them. If three or four Negroes were discovered together it was assumed they were "conspiring to go North" and they would be arrested on some trumped-up charge.[42]

The migration did have a major impact on Southern economies heavily dependent on Negro laborers. The departure of so many people so hurriedly without long-range plans for future work, a place to live, or knowing how they would survive in such a strange environment must be attributed to the impact of Abbott and the *Defender*. He had the power tool and used it to address the race as a group,[43] "all you folks—the *Defender* says come!" And almost as a group, they picked themselves up and left the South.[44]

Many Negroes in extremely isolated areas were late in hearing about the move northward. When they learned of the migration, that "everyone" was leaving or had left the South, they became alarmed. They feared that if they were left behind, they would bear the brunt of Southern anger.[45]

The actual trip must have been filled with excitement, fear, and expectations for most migrants. As the *Defender* stated, they were "wearing overalls and housedresses, a few walking barefoot." In addition to using trains for transportation, they also used boats, horses, carts, and wagons.[46] Allan H. Spear had indicated in *Black Chicago— the Making of a Negro Ghetto* that making the actual trip north "took on a mythical quality that gave to the migration an almost religious significance." Many factors led to that feeling. Agents from the North related tales, made promises, and gave assistance, but perhaps the most important factor was the many letters received from relatives and friends who had already gone north. So great was the joy of one group leaving Mississippi that they asked for the train to stop once it crossed the Ohio River so they could conduct a ceremony praising their release from "the land of Egypt." Meanwhile, what little doubt that remained with some still in the South changed when conditions did not improve for those who had stayed behind, but instead got worse, and Southern efforts to keep Negroes in the region through violence continued to be routine.[47]

As the number of Negro field workers began to dwindle, Southern officials began to make serious countermoves to stop the flow of their workers. The Ku Klux Klan made visits and threatened anyone seen with a copy of the *Defender*. Two of the paper's distributors were killed, and numerous white merchants began canceling advertising in local Negro papers as a form of retaliation. If they could not hurt the *Defender* directly, they would hurt whatever was accessible. In Mississippi, a law was passed making it "a misdemeanor to print or publish or circulate printed or published appeals or presentations of arguments or suggestions favoring social equality."[48]

Eventually, many Southern towns prohibited the sale or distribution of the *Defender*. But the more Southern leaders tried to stop the circulation of the paper, the more popular it became. Having a copy in one's possession, whether the owner could read or not, became a status symbol. Distributors were killed in many areas, however, and many more were unceremoniously run out of town.[49]

In an effort to curb the distribution of the *Defender*, Arkansas enacted legislation:

> Chancellor John M. Elliott today issued an injunction restraining John D. Young, Jr., Negro, and "any other parties" from circulating the *Chicago Defender*, a Negro publication, in Pine Bluff or Jefferson County.
> The injunction was granted at the instance of Mayor Mack Hollis. It was sought following receipt here by Young of copies of the paper containing an account of the killing of George Vicks, Negro, here Thursday, February 5.
> The *Defender's* account of the affair portrayed Vicks as defending his home, his liberty and his person, and was held to be false in its entirety by the court.[50]

Even in 1915, Abbott began to realize how wide the expansion of his circulation had become in the South. Anticipating that Southern officials would eventually make some move to block the distribution of his paper if he became successful in drawing Negroes from the South, he made alternate plans to keep his distribution channels open. Abbott and Smiley took advantage of Chicago's geographical position as the rail capital of the United States and used the services of the hundreds of Negro porters and waiters employed by the railroads who traveled constantly across the nation. Such a move had almost immediate success, so much so that other traveling groups, musicians, and other entertainers easily accepted a similar role. Those groups, initially accepting that position solely for profit, eventually saw their role as "race duty." Even if Southern authorities were successful in banning the *Defender* from the mails, Abbott could still depend on his hundreds of couriers to get the *Defender* to Southern subscribers.[51]

Whether the Negro in the South would be receptive to such a militant newspaper was never an issue. In fact, Southern Negroes loved reading about members of their race and their accomplishments. But it was the way in which "their newspaper" slugged away at those who made life so miserable for them that made them swell with pride and made some finally feel good about themselves. So when "their newspaper" beckoned that they "Come north ... all you folks, both good and bad,"[52] the effect was that "many Negroes ... simply vanished" from the South,[53] as Mable Smythe, a black journalism historian, has so vividly stated.

Numerous other Negro newspapers either supported, encouraged, counseled, or otherwise became involved in some way with the migration. The *Star of Zion* (North Carolina) opposed this movement, however: "While I concede the Negro man's right to go where he likes, for he has the right of liberty and the pursuit of happiness, yet I doubt the wisdom of such wholesale exodus from the South. There are some things which the Negro needs far more than his wages, or some of the rights for which he contends. He needs conservation of his moral life."[54]

On the other hand, the *Christian Recorder* showed its support by declaring that "If a million Negroes move north and west in the next twelve-months, it will be one of the greatest things for the Negro since the Emancipation Proclamation."[55]

Reactions from the white press in the South also varied. In Athens, Georgia, a daily newspaper reported that the *Defender* was "the greatest disturbing element that has yet entered Georgia."[56] The *Macon Telegraph* reported a warning: "Everybody seems to be asleep about what is going on right under their noses. That is, everybody but those farmers who have awakened up of mornings recently to find every male Negro over 21 ... gone-to Cleveland, to Pittsburgh, to Chicago."[57]

In Columbus, Georgia, the *Enquirer Sun* also reported a warning that "The Negro laborer is the best labor the South can get, no other would work long under the same conditions."[58]

Two white newspapers in Mississippi struck out at what was suspected to be the heart of the reason for Negro migration from Mississippi. James Vardaman, who had run for governor using a typical racist platform which had been popular at that time and which had been designed to gain white voter support, became the scapegoat. His assertions about what he would do to and not do for Negroes when he was in office were believed to be the reasons many Negroes were leaving the state. The *Herald* (Biloxi) called Vardaman "The most dangerous man that ever aspired to the governorship of Mississippi." Over in Hazlehurst, the *Courier* "feared that Vardaman's words and actions would disturb these valuable laborers 'who are docile and contented.'"[59]

Even outside the South, many observers gave the *Defender* credit for the exodus. In Chicago, the *Daily News* reported that "The Defender more than any other one agency was the big cause of the 'Northern fever' and the big exodus from the South." The U.S. Department of Labor noted that in some sections the *Defender* was probably more effective in carrying off labor than all the agents put together: "It sums up the Negro's troubles and keeps them constantly before him, and it points out in terms he can understand the way of escape."[60]

When World War I began in 1914, plans for the Great Northern Drive may have been on Abbott's mind, but they were not at the forefront of his editorials. His concerns were for racial justice and equal rights and whether Negroes should fight in the war. In fact, Abbott seemed at the edge of revolution during one of Chicago's many housing incidents, when the *Defender* advised a Negro family whose home had been besieged by white mobs to arm themselves and "be prepared to fight and fight to kill." His militancy did not abate when it came to editorials concerning the war effort: "Why Fight for A Flag Whose Folds Do Not Protect? What Incentive Have Afro-Americans to Take Up Arms in Defense of the United States When the Government Will Allow Mobs to Burn and Lynch Innocent Citizens, but Will Go To Trouble and Expense When Mexican Bandits Kill an Englishman?"[61] It wasn't long thereafter that this militant style caught the eyes of the federal government, which placed the *Defender* under investigation.[62]

When the United States entered World War I in 1917, many Negro editors swung the emphasis of their militancy to oppose the ill treatment of Negro soldiers. By 1918 the government viewed many of those statements as signs of disloyalty. An uneasiness sensed by W.E.B. DuBois, editor of the *Crisis* magazine, prompted him to write an editorial directed at other members of the Negro press. With utmost candor he wrote, "Let us, while this war lasts, forget our special grievances and close ranks shoulder to shoulder with our own fellow citizens."[63] He further suggested that "Negroes had more to gain from a society in which democracy was *at least an ideal* than they would have under German autocracy."[64] Some editors thought the comments and the timing for such a proposal were extremely bad. But not wishing to appear in disunity before the government, they put aside their feelings and worked as much as they could to support the war on the home front.[65]

But not the *Defender*. As far as Abbott was concerned, the suspension of militancy to show support for the war effort was unacceptable. In that regard, he totally ignored DuBois's cry for "close ranks" support. And whether the other editors liked it or not, Abbott continued with his militancy, so much so that he was almost arrested when the *Defender*'s cartoonist, Leslie Rogers, drew a cartoon depicting "Negro troops facing Germans as they were being shot in the back by white American troops." Abbott escaped a jail sentence by purchasing liberty bonds and by encouraging his readers to do the same.[66]

The *Washington Bee*, though not as militant as the *Defender*, had William Calvin Chase, a moderate, as its editor. At one time during the war, Chase became so frustrated with the treatment of Negroes that he could not restrain his anger. And even though he agreed that moderation of editorial attacks was needed during a time when the country was at war, he couldn't resist pointing out one of the many contradictions faced by the Negro people near the turn of the century:

> But the Negro is willing today to take up arms and defend the American flag; he stands ready to uphold the hands of the President; he stands ready to defend the country and his President against this cruel and unjust oppression. His mother, sister, brother and children are being burned at the stake and yet the American flag is his emblem and which he stands ready to defend. In all the battles, the Negro soldier has proved his loyalty and today he is the only true American at whom the finger of scorn cannot be pointed.[67]

After the war was over and the Great Northern Drive had slowed to a trickle, Abbott turned his attention to other events. With such an influx of new people crowding into areas not quite ready for them, conditions had become ripe for violence to erupt at almost any point across the country. The summer of 1919 was called the "Red Summer" because of seven extremely violent riots around the nation. In Chicago a Negro youth who had been swimming in the area of Lake Michigan set aside for Negroes strayed into the portion of the lake which had been set aside for whites. When he was discovered, whites from the beach stoned him. A riot erupted when Negroes seeing and hearing about the stoning reacted in a similar manner towards those throwing the rocks. The violence spread and continued for a week, leaving at least 15 whites and 23 Negroes dead, with many more injured.[68]

The *Defender* covered the rioting. But rather than merely reporting the facts as they had occurred, Abbott ran what appeared to be a box score of the dead and injured, white statistics in one column and Negro statistics in the other. Such a display was viewed by many as race encouragement to even the score when one race fell behind in its number of dead, and it may have been the fuel that caused the riot to last as long as it did. When Abbott realized how his statistics were being interpreted, he issued an "extra" calling for peace.[69]

Later Abbott signed a Chicago Commission on Race Relations report "recommending that the Negro press exercise more care and accuracy in handling racial subjects." He was a member of that Chicago commission.[70]

Abbott, with the *Defender*, was successful in breaking away from the daily struggles of survival through routine but sensational reporting of news in the Chicago Negro community. He later extended his coverage to events that had occurred in the South, an area that craved news written by editors without fear or intimidation. There was no viable reason why Abbott should not be able to copy the success of Hearst and the *Chicago Tribune*. In that regard he was correct in following his feelings. He may have sensationalized the news and the accuracy of his description of events at times may have been questionable, but Abbott reached the people as no other Negro newspaper editor had ever done before. And the Negro readers loved what he did. If other editors had researched the history of the Negro press before they had scorned the practices of Abbott, they would have discovered how Ida B. Wells and her *Memphis Free Speech* increased its circulation. And although Wells did not sensationalize the news intentionally, she never hesitated to report the results of her investigative findings and important details about lynching, even if the results did offend her white readers and place her life in constant danger. If the short tenure of her role as editor was justification for not following her example, then Abbott must be given even more credit for starting his paper in the North rather than the South and using that geographical separation to survive in the unstable Negro newspaper business.

3

PITTSBURGH COURIER

It was at Pittsburgh, Pennsylvania, in 1907 that Edwin Nathaniel Harleston, a security guard at the H. J. Heinz food packing plant, decided to put his love for poetry to practical use. He started a newspaper. With so much idle time while on the job, rather than just sit around reading the most common and entertaining literature, he wrote poetry. His practice had been so dedicated that it wasn't long before his writing collection had grown substantially. But since there had been no avenues in which he could display his creative works, his accumulation began to gather dust. He therefore started his own publication and used it to display his works. During the early days of the paper, *A Toiler's Life*, sales were very slow. Harleston printed ten copies per edition and sold each for five cents, but rarely sold all of them. Following the same pattern as Abbott when he began the *Defender*, Harleston was the editor, reporter, treasurer, and circulation and business managers.[1]

Realizing in 1909 that his venture had not gotten off to the start he would like to have seen and doubting if things would get any better without some outside help, Harleston decided that a larger effort in the business industry was what he needed. His first move in that direction was a visit to Robert Lee Vann, a Pittsburgh attorney, for consultation. Next he consulted with Edward Penman and Hepburn Carter, also employees at the Heinz food plant, Scott Wood, Jr., and Harvey Tanner. Those men then organized a new paper and named it the *Pittsburgh Courier*. None of those men had the necessary financial backing Harleston needed, but each was willing to work on the management end of the paper. Harleston therefore continued financing the paper out of his own pocket.[2]

The first 500 issues of the new paper reached the streets of Pittsburgh on January 15, 1910. It was a four-page publication with articles slanted towards local events. Even though subscriptions to the paper began to increase and nearly all copies of each edition were sold, it wasn't long before Harleston again began to run out of money. And, once again, additional backers were found—Samuel Rosemound, William N. Page, Cumberland Posey, Sr., and William N. Hance. Those men, combined with the original backers, made for a large staff for such a financially strapped newspaper. Rather than contend with having all eight members on the management staff, Penman, Wood, Tanner, and Carter withdrew. The paper was then incorporated on May 10, 1910.[3]

Financial success, however, still eluded the *Courier*. To make matters worse, internal fighting had begun between the backers and Harleston, who thought that the owner of the paper should be given a majority of the paper's stock. Since he no longer had any money and since the new officers did have some funds, they believed that anyone should be qualified to own stock in the company, but that stock should be paid for "with cash or work." In a fit of anger, Harleston quit. Vann was then offered the job as editor, and he accepted.[4]

Vann, like Abbott, was also a Northerner by transplant. He was born on a small farm in Ahoskie, North Carolina, attended Waters Normal Institute at Winton, North Carolina, Virginia Union University in Richmond, and, ultimately, the University of Pittsburgh, where he earned a law degree in 1909.[5] Later he passed the Pennsylvania bar examination and hung out his shingle for business in Pittsburgh. While waiting for his law practice to become profitable, Vann had read and became interested in Harleston's two-page poetry newspaper. Upon noticing the interest readers had in the paper, Vann had seen the possibility of expanding that sheet into a real newspaper.[6]

Still, the beginning for that newspaper was far less than had been expected. In fact, it bordered on the mediocre at its best. But the *Courier* became a respectable organ of opinion and commentary and maintained that respect by changing personnel and using a rational editorial direction.[7] By 1914 the paper, for the first time since its founding, had a good chance of surviving.[8]

The *Courier* was not as flashy in its presentation of the news as the *Defender*. To attract its readers, Vann used a salmon-colored front and back page, rather than large red letters and graphic headlines. He also included society news and entertainment and sports pages, and he provided more than just information.[9] Vann was editor, of course, but there were also a secretary, a reporter, a proofreader, an errand boy, and a sports editor. The office was located in the heart of Pittsburgh's black belt in a second-floor spare room. Furnishings were sparse—only a desk, two chairs, and a typewriter, which was used to put out the weekly editions.[10]

It also was a struggle for the *Courier* to get advertising. In an effort to increase circulation, Vann conducted a contest by offering a new car to the person who sold the most subscriptions. When the winner arrived to claim the prize, the *Courier* did not have enough cash to purchase the car. Instead, the winner was provided with a check for half of the total subscription money collected. The check bounced, however. Vann finally paid the winner a part of the *Courier* stock and some cash from his own pocket.[11]

While the *Defender* in Chicago was racking up sales with sensational reporting of news with headlines in red ink, Vann stuck with his conservative though sometimes exciting approach. He did not see the need to venture away from his church or his social news and shunned the high-powered news the average reader sought. Even so, by 1914 the *Courier* was able to move to better offices and was able to hire a new staff member, Ira F. Lewis, a North Carolinian who excelled in selling advertising space. By 1915, Lewis had been extremely successful with the advertising sales, and the circulation of the paper had almost doubled.[12]

As thousands of Negroes poured into the larger cities in the north during the Great Migration period, many expectant migrants chose Pittsburgh's Hill District as their new home, creating massive overcrowding and pushing the few facilities that were available beyond their limits. Vann, who also lived in the Hill District, felt the pressures of overcrowding and was forced to move to another area. In fact, the crowding was so severe that in some areas there were four beds to a room, and they were never empty of occupants. After the night sleepers were up and out at work, the night workers came home to sleep in those same beds. It was during this period that Vann saw the opportunity to use the *Courier* as a means to bring about improvements for his race.[13]

Vann altered the course of the *Courier*, making it an organ of social force by calling attention to various neighborhood problems. Abbott's call of "Come North!" brought in scores of Southern Negroes. Once they were in the North, Vann tried to teach them how to better themselves. Housing and medical facilities were inadequate, and there was a need for Negro health officers "in sympathy with [our] life and methods of living." At the same time "education as a means to racial uplift" was stressed, and Negro unemployment and unfair hiring and firing practices by white employers were reported.[14] Vann also advised Negroes who had gained employment to save their money in preparation for the return of white soldiers from the war, for once they returned to this country, they would take away jobs being held by Negroes.[15]

When covering the progress of the war, Vann openly showed a love of country by calling for a regiment of Negro soldiers in the Pennsylvania National Guard. That was an opportunity in his eyes for Negroes to improve their position within the country "once they had shown themselves as fighting men as any others."[16] Vann reported that if Negro soldiers went off to war, then, "When this war shall have ceased THE NEGRO WILL HAVE ASSUMED HIS RIGHTFUL PLACE IN THE OPINIONS OF AMERICANS. He could then ASSERT HIMSELF AS A MAN—not as a black man—AS A MAN."[17]

Vann also editorialized about the many distortions about Negroes presented in the white press,[18] the many achievements garnered by Negroes, and sports, particularly prizefighting. Local news in the Negro community was also thoroughly covered. Of particular interest to readers was news of who had gone on vacation, who recently got married or had parties, general news of church events, and news concerning the Negro elite. A new section started by the newspaper, "News from Back Home," was begun to provide new immigrants from the South with information from that region. And the increased frequency of police raids in Negro neighborhoods was strongly protested by the *Courier*.[19]

Near the end of the migration period, with so many Negroes moving to the North and with housing and other facilities in short supply, it was inevitable that nerves would be on edge and tempers would erupt. Tempers did erupt in 1917 in the form of riots that spread across the country to East St. Louis; Longview, Texas; Springfield, Illinois; Washington, D.C.; Phillips County, Arkansas; Knoxville, Omaha, Memphis, Houston, Chicago, and Indianapolis. Unlike the high involvement of sensational reporting exhibited by the *Defender*, Vann decided to maintain in the *Courier* a moderate position regarding the riots.[20]

The Justice Department investigated the Negro press for its handling of each of the riots from 1917 through 1919. An official report published in November 1919 did not address the immediate causes of the riots. Instead, it asserted "that the black press must assume much of the responsibility for the summer riots and that their constant protests against disfranchisement and lynching were incendiary." At the same time, Negro newspapers, because they were so outspoken and critical of how some riots were being handled, "were accused of being dominated by Communists." Because of Vann's moderate views during the riots, the *Courier* did not fall under direct criticism by the government, but the *Chicago Defender* and two magazines, the New York *Messenger,* under A. Philip Randolph, and the *Crisis,* edited by W.E.B. DuBois, were accused of being "radical and seditious."[21]

Vann may have viewed the omission of the *Courier* from the cited names in the published report as recognition by the government of the type of behavior expected from the Negro press. He was therefore compelled to reply to the audacity of such an assumption by stating: "The only conclusion therefore is: as long as the Negro submits to lynching, burnings, and oppressions—and says nothing, he is a loyal American citizen. But when he decides that lynching and burnings shall cease even at the cost of some human bloodshed in America, then he is a Bolshevist."[22]

In 1925 the *Courier* began to make additional moves to strengthen itself even more. George Schuyler, who was already working for another Negro organ, was hired to write a column for the *Courier*'s editorial page. It was not uncommon for Negro journalists at that time to work for more than one editor because the pay among the Negro press staff was unusually low. In an attempt to build up circulation on a national level, Vann sent Schuyler on a nine-month tour of the Confederate South and to Kentucky and Oklahoma; he visited every city with more than five thousand Negroes. The results of his studies were presented "often with the satiric touch":

> For the year 1925, the great state of Florida wins the pennant in the Lynching League of America. There are eight lynching to the credit (or discredit) of the great commonwealth of real-estate boosters, while closely following it is magnificent Texas with a paltry seven. Then there are our old friend Mississippi with four; South Carolina with three; Arkansas with two; and Georgia, Kansas, New Mexico, Tennessee with one each.[23]

After such an outstanding job of covering his assignment and increasing the paper's circulation by at least 10,000 subscribers, when Schuyler returned to the *Courier* in 1926, he was given a full-time position on the editorial staff. Now he had editorial license to report what he thought was necessary in the interest of social force.[24]

Schuyler began his job in an unusual manner by attacking members of his own race, an attack he hoped would arouse them to the need to better themselves. Fraternal organizations, a source of pride for many Negroes, were also attacked "for being insensitive to the needs of the black masses" by having large office buildings at their disposal while Negroes around them were crammed into substandard housing. So confident was Schuyler because of his successes that he even attacked black leaders. One of them was Marcus Garvey.[25]

Marcus Manasseh Garvey was a self-appointed leader who was born in Jamaica in 1887. After his childhood, he went to England, where he studied at the University of London. It was by coincidence that he met many Africans there. He befriended them and often listened to the stories they told of their homelands under colonial rule.[26]

When he returned to Jamaica in 1914, Garvey organized the Universal Negro Improvement Association (UNIA), adopted Africa as the place where Negroes should live, by force if necessary,[27] and became interested in Booker T. Washington. It was Washington's school at Tuskegee that Garvey admired, not his politics.[28]

That following year Garvey came to the United States only to find that Washington had passed away. Since no one else at Tuskegee appreciated the Jamaican's philosophies or cared for his politics, he went to New York, where there were many West Indians. He found much needed support there which encouraged him to reorganize the UNIA in Harlem. As his successes began to grow, Garvey founded the *Negro World*, a newspaper he used to convey his messages to his followers or anyone else who would read it. In one of his messages, he asked: "Where is the black man's government? Where is his king and his kingdom? Where is his president, his country and his ambassador, his army, his navy, his men of big affairs? I could not find them. I declared 'I will help to make them.'"[29]

The objective of the UNIA was to create "a strong Negro nation in Africa." Garvey's dream of Negroes in the United States becoming a part of that African dream was formed when he decided that organizations such as the NAACP had been and still were ineffective. His own effectiveness continued to grow as money from his followers poured in from across the country.[30] It appeared that Garvey's back-to-Africa movement was picking up steam.

It wasn't the excessive spending which brought about Schuyler's attack on Garvey. He chastised the Jamaican for being a possible bigamist. If laws were to be obeyed, Schuyler stated, a role model should set a good example. Schuyler labeled Garvey as "America's Greatest Comedian." He further admonished Garvey for the number of unseaworthy ships which had been purchased to transport Negroes to Africa.[31]

The Negro church and other groups were next on Schuyler's list. He noted the vast number of new churches in the neighborhood, presumably built with money obtained from neighborhood church members who had difficulty just sustaining day-to-day life. As for groups outside of his race, the Communist party, for example, Schuyler attacked them for the way in which they handled—or mishandled—a rape case at Scottsboro, Alabama.[32] The nine Negro hobo boys on trial because they were accused of raping two white hobo women were not hanged as called for by the trial, but Schulyer thought the boys should have been set free because the evidence pointed so heavily in favor of their innocence. Instead, eight of them were jailed for life.[33]

The *Courier*, as had the *Defender* and Ida Wells's *Free Speech*, eventually established itself as a vital force willing to fight for the causes of the Negro community. Unlike the sensational tactics used by the *Defender* to accomplish its goals or the sharp editorials written in anger at the *Free Speech*, the *Courier* presented information with tact, diplomacy, and, most of all, unmitigated accuracy.

The *Courier* did not need to go far to find news or problems of interest for its readers. Stories were occurring all around the neighborhood in Pittsburgh. Even so, Vann saw the need for something else. To recognize and attack the cause of problems at the source was still a part of his philosophy. And even though the Negro press had been doing that relentlessly for almost a century, with little or no success, the need to continue in that regard was essential. There would, however, be one change. It was necessary to attack the victims in an effort to get them to shake loose from their passiveness and become assertive (another form of survival), assertive as a group in their pursuit of bettering themselves. Such a pursuit might not be the answer, but it would be better than doing nothing. The *Courier* had been slow to start and did not begin with stability in its staff selection, but once those issues were settled, it became a newspaper of national importance. By 1936 its circulation had reached a total of 174,000.[34]

As Eugene Gordon, a black newspaper analyst, saw it, by 1927 the Negro press had reached a high state of general excellence. The *Courier* shared in that excellence as it became the top paper with regards to its editorial page, the best-rated for its features, and the best all-around Negro newspaper.[35]

4

BLACK DISPATCH

In Oklahoma City, Roscoe Dunjee with his *Black Dispatch* took a direction with his editorial philosophy that differed from that of Abbott but was somewhat similar to that of Vann. Abbott gloried in the sensational, using explicit or shocking photographs and graphic details in his text. He saw the Southern white man as using any means, including lynching, to deter the advancement of Negroes, so he didn't hesitate to red-ink atrocities committed against the former slaves across the front pages of the *Defender*. Vann, on the other hand, centered much of his attention on city and other local race problems while attempting to get the downtrodden to help themselves. He took frequent shots at the government, however, when he believed they were warranted. Dunjee, who was unlike Vann or Abbott in his journalistic goals, did agree that a man should be given a chance to survive and better himself without a foot holding him down. He was a civil rights advocate, and the *Black Dispatch* was the mouthpiece he used to convey his messages. He was almost fearless in what he had to say and attacked racial discrimination in all of its forms. He attacked anyone from anywhere, even the governor of the state, regardless of political or commercial clout, if he determined that their treatment of Negroes or anyone else was not justified.[1]

As were his contemporaries, Abbott and Vann, Dunjee was born in the South, on June 21, 1883, at Harper's Ferry, West Virginia. He was the son of the Reverend John William and Lydia Ann Dunjee. When Roscoe was born, his father was the publisher of a local newspaper, the *Harper's Ferry Messenger*, and worked as a financial agent for a local college. At the same time, he was employed by the American Baptist Missionary Society, which sent the reverend all over the nation to organize Baptist work. His family moved to Oklahoma in 1892 and settled on a farm east of Oklahoma City.[2]

Once the family had settled, Dunjee attended the public schools, which included some study under the elementary department at the Colored Agricultural and Normal University.[3] He also gained some experience in publications while working in a print shop there. Since his father had been a publisher at Harper's Ferry, Roscoe was able to receive encouragement and the full benefit of his father's experience in the field of journalism. He also had extensive use of his father's library, 1,500 books accumulated over a lifetime.[4]

In 1902 the Reverend Dunjee passed away, leaving the family with a farm that was not in the best condition and a $1,100 mortgage. By that time, however, Dunjee was capable of tending the farm. Each day he would load his vegetables on three farm trucks and then cart them off to the city to sell. He continued this practice for the next 15 years.[5]

When he wasn't busy with his chores, Dunjee concentrated on reading and writing, and he eventually began writing for various newspapers owned by Negroes. One was the *Bookertee Searchlight*, a newspaper in Bookertee, Oklahoma. He then joined with his friend Jimmy Stewart and began to write short articles for a newspaper owned by the Abby family.[6]

With what money he could scrape together from the sale of vegetables and from what he was able to save from his job as bellhop at the Stewart Hotel in Oklahoma City, Dunjee purchased a printing plant. But going to press would not be so simple. Finding seasoned Negro journalists in Oklahoma and keeping them there would be one of his more difficult tasks. Any Negro who aspired to become a journalist in Oklahoma had to leave the state to obtain training and then return to Oklahoma to work.[7]

Abbott had been resourceful, particularly in circumventing official Southern efforts to ban his newspaper from that region. Dunjee was also very resourceful. If the community could not provide the skilled workers he needed in his print shop, he would seek them elsewhere. They came from a very unlikely place—the state prison. That was the only location in Oklahoma which did allow journalism training for Negroes.[8] As a result, on March 4, 1914, Dunjee published the first issue of the *Black Dispatch*.[9]

Prior to the start of the *Dispatch*, there had been only six other editors who had chosen to use the word *black* in their newspaper's title. The *Black Republican and Office Holder's Journal*, 1865, New York; the *Black Republican*, 1865, New Orleans; the *Kansas Blackman*, 1894, Topeka; the *Kansas Blackman*, 1894, Coffeyville; *Our Brother in Black*,

1880, Muskogee, Oklahoma Territory; and the *Black Dispatch*, 1898, Fort Worth. None of those papers had existed longer than three years. It can be assumed, then, that many Negroes may have found the use of the word *black* to represent their race a bit repugnant. Armistead Scott Pride interviewed Dunjee in 1946 and was told how the name was chosen:

> The Black Dispatch was given its name as a result of an effort to dignify a slur. Even in this day when many people seek to refer to an untruth they resort to an old expression, "That's black dispatch gossip." The influence of this statement is very damaging to the integrity and self-respect of the race. All of this has developed a psychology among Negroes that their color is a curse and that there is something evil in their peculiar pigmentation. It is my contention that Negroes should be proud to say, "I am a black man."[10]

Once work began at the *Black Dispatch*, employees had to help make up the paper, write stories, and sell advertising, the latter being their most difficult task. It took time for Dunjee to hone those journalists so they could function in the style consistent with the larger Negro papers. When their stories reflected the "fruits of their learnings," the *Kansas City Call*, the *Norfolk Journal and Guide*, the *Baltimore Afro-American*, or *Chicago Defender* would offer them larger salaries and snatch them away. Dunjee was not noted for giving generous salaries or benefits to his employees. He therefore faced the difficulty of not only getting advertisements to sustain the paper but also keeping trained workers in-house for long periods.[11]

As for his editorial philosophy, Dunjee outlined exactly what he intended to pursue and what he would avoid:

> The policy of the Black Dispatch is not to publish stories of brutality and crime in the spirit of the yellow journalist. Every week we try to rake the news field for subjects that will be inspirational to the race and promote and develop good citizenship....
>
> In keeping with this idea we feel that it is our responsible duty to let the white man know the plain truth of how we view conditions now....
>
> Suppose the editor of this paper should go to Wheeler Park in Oklahoma City, a city owned park. at the entrance we would find a sign informing us that "No Negroes Allowed" and not far from it another sign which informs him that "No Dogs Are Allowed." do you feel that the editor would feel that the taxes that Negroes have paid the general fund, that has gone to establish and maintain the splendid zoo that cost thousands of dollars and ought to be of educational service to all of the children of Oklahoma City were being handled in a democratic way.[12]

Dunjee was angry over the way his friends and neighbors were being treated because of the color of their skin. But more than anything else, he was angry over the lack of reaction by Negroes to that treatment and their deafening silence. Dunjee wanted a medium to inform, to stir, to arouse his people to fight for the right to survive and to live with common dignity.[13] Dunjee's mother agreed that injustices towards Negroes were obvious and someone should rally the people in their own interest. But not her son. She feared for his life and had urged him not to become a journalist. That feeling came as no surprise to Dunjee when he remembered his younger years. "My father was a newspaper man during the Reconstruction period. His experience during these hectic and troublous times caused my mother to doubt the wisdom of my entering the journalistic field."[14]

During the height of the Great Northern Drive, the *Black Dispatch*, more similar to the *Courier* in content than the *Defender*, showed support through its columns of advice to those making the trip. Even though more than fifty years had passed since the Emancipation Proclamation, Dunjee recognized that many Negroes who had been released from slavery had avoided any contact with authorities; therefore they had had no exposure to education or training. The offspring and relatives from that uneducated group were among those heading north for better wages and conditions. Unfortunately, they did not possess the survival skills or maturity necessary to sustain a good lifestyle in the North:

> We are compelled at this stage of race development to talk more to this Negro about his duties than his privileges. Many are not yet developed enough to appreciate their rights. Loud and coarse behavior in public places, soiled, ill-smelling work clothing worn in places of entertainment; and sometimes occupying a little more than his side of the sidewalk, is not an intelligent exercise of our rights.[15]

There were also those race members who believed that getting involved in civic affairs or becoming a part of civil rights groups was senseless and would only lead to trouble. To avoid serious trouble, in their eyes, it was necessary to bypass attempts at getting ahead, stall any moves to elevate Negro people from the lowly position they held, and thank the Lord that they were free and alive. Any attempts at political involvement were out of the question because they were seen as an invitation to certain death. These race members believed that accommodation was the answer for race survival. In the face of such beliefs, Dunjee could not restrain his pen:

The most disgusting and senseless Negro that we know is the fellow who stands around and says, "Oh I never vote; I'm not registered" and who always slurs and tells you that the Negro who is active in politics in the community is selling you out and should not be trusted.

The same Negro who thinks like that is always the first one to hide out when the mob comes. He never owned a gun in his life, for he does not know the value of it any more than he does the value of his suffrage rights. IN FACT, HE DOES NOT EVEN KNOW THAT HIS BALLOT IS A GUN, a gun with which to shoot fear into cowardly judges who, because of their spineless inaction and subserviency to the mob, make them possible.[16]

Dunjee was also akin to Vann with his attempts to "rattle some cages" and get members of the race to better themselves. He thought that such action was crucial for simple survival. He also believed it would be difficult enough for Negroes to improve with conditions as they currently were, but if outside factions continued their attempts to "keep the Negro in his place," it would be almost impossible. Dunjee therefore saw his role as twofold: strike hard to obtain civil rights for Negroes similar to those enjoyed by the mainstream and push the race members to educate themselves so that they could become aware of their own faults.

When it came to editorials, the *Black Dispatch* excelled. Dunjee was known across the nation and well known within Oklahoma for his blazing and attention-getting comments. At times they were intense or vigorous and penetrating even to those who rarely agreed with his views.[17]

Jimmy Stewart, a writer for the *Black Dispatch*, could never forget the impact of Dunjee's writing:

As we traveled throughout the country, persons remarked about Dunjee's editorials, and although all who knew him or read them knew they would be the world longest, at no place have I met a person who said they failed to read them because of their length. This, to me, is a tribute to the writer as well as to the content of his editorials.[18]

One example of Dunjee's long editorials was written in 1941 when the issue of discrimination against Negroes and their constitutional rights came under investigation. An organization known as the Oklahoma Federation for Constitutional Rights was formed "to launch a campaign against hypocrisy within democracy."[19]

The governor of the state, Leon C. Phillips, responded to the forming of that group by saying: "This organization about constitutional rights is the height of folly. No one is denied constitutional rights in Oklahoma."[20]

The governor's response triggered an editorial from Dunjee:

> Surely the governor belongs to that class spoken of in the Bible: "which have eyes, and see not; which have ears and hear not."
>
> Governor Phillips does not need to take the word of this writer; he has only to turn to the records of a trial court in Hugo January 28, where and when Judge J. R. Childers threw out of court an alleged confession cruelly beaten out of W. D. Lyons, a defenseless Negro, by an investigator employed by Governor Phillips.
>
> When Judge Childers threw out the confession, procured in the ail [sic] at Hugo, his act was an admission that attorneys for Lyons and the National Association for the Advancement of Colored People had proved to him the document was secured through force and violence. The evidence showed that not only the Governor's investigator joined in inhuman torture to secure the confession, but that two members of the state highway patrol participated. Was this unlawful act a denial of civil rights? The Oklahoma Federation for Constitutional Rights has the Lyons case on its 1941 agendum. Do the whites so consecrated have a right to fight for the civil rights of W. D. Lyons?
>
> On every train and bus in Oklahoma this writer and all Negroes in Oklahoma are denied civil rights. Can the Governor observe denial of Negroes to Pullman and chaircar accommodations on railroads, and then like Pontius Pilate, wash his hands, Saying "No one is denied constitutional rights in Oklahoma?"
>
> Down at Anadarko the Oklahoma Conference of Branches of the N.A.A.C.P. is fighting to compel a white school board to return to the separate school two new buses which the white school board appropriated without color of law from the Negro school. The method pursued was to buy the buses with separate school money and then when the buses arrived, two old buses up at the white school were moved down to the Negro school and the new Negro buses moved to the white school, where they are now.
>
> Does Governor Phillips consider this a denial of the civil rights of Negroes living in Caddo county? In many sections of the state Negroes whose property is taxed for school purposes, are not allowed to vote in school elections. The money goes to build white schools and white schools only. Is this a denial of civil rights? What about "taxation without representation"? Is not the Governor having conflict between ideal and practice?[21]

The audacity of Dunjee with his *Black Dispatch* in pointing out so incisively the unfair treatments or violations of Negro civil rights was clearly shown through his editorials directed towards other government officials, as well. On one occasion in 1917 after a train wreck had killed several Negroes in Oklahoma, Dunjee directed a front page editorial to the corporation commission:

Just a few days ago, Most Honored Gentlemen, there happened near Kelleyville, on the Frisco railroad, one of the most damnable crimes of the age. Jim Crowism flowed, gentlemen, at Kelley ville! for in the snuffing out of the lives of those twenty helpless black men and women, whose brains, arms and eyes were scattered like dung upon the soil of the land of the fair gods and there was brought to light the vile sort of "equal accommodations" furnished black men by the railroads of Oklahoma, in Democratic America.[22]

Dunjee also questioned the corporation commission about the lack of truant officers in the Negro neighborhood:

To the County Commissioners: We, the colored citizens of the Colored Oklahoma City Schools, remembering the good things you have done, would like to point out a glaring weakness in the colored system. We have no truant officer for the colored. A truant officer is more bitterly needed by us than by the white school. Negro schools are often located in neighborhoods for moral growth.[23]

When it came to the fighting soldiers, Dunjee thought their morale was very important. It wasn't easy for Negroes to enlist and fight in a war with dignity and respect in the eyes of Europeans and then return home to the same substandard conditions, violence, and uncertainty which had previously existed. Yet Negro soldiers went off to war hoping that things would be better when they returned home. In Dunjee's eyes, if they were fighting, at least officials in Oklahoma should recognize those efforts.

When Governor Robert L. Williams made an address to National Red Cross officials, he recognized the white soldiers fighting for the country but did not mention Negroes. Dunjee responded:

I was grieved to note, most honored governor, that in your report you made no reference to our approximately 2,000 brave black boys of Oklahoma who are now in the training camp at Chillicothe, Ohio, boys, who, if the state of Oklahoma had not refused them training within her borders, or if permitted to train at Camp Bowie as your report suggested, would not now be suffering in the chilly blasts of a northern state as many letters on file at my office will attest.

I would have felt that your statement that "The Oklahoma boys in training are at Camp Bowie," was an unintentional oversight, had it not been that you read from manuscript.

There is not a black man in the state of Oklahoma who is not willing to fight for a perfect democracy, but he wants to know that it is the kind and brand that begins at home and spreads abroad.[24]

On May 31 and June 1, 1921, a riot occurred in the Greenwood district of Tulsa, Oklahoma. The *Tulsa World* on June 1 issued four extras with major headlines: "NEW BATTLE NOW IN PROG-RESS; Whites Advancing into 'Little Africa;' Negro Dead List Is About 15."[25] On June 2, the *New York Times* carried a headline "85 WHITES AND NEGROES DIE IN TULSA RIOT AS 3,000 ARMED MEN BATTLE IN STREETS: 30 BLACKS BURNED: MILITARY RULE IN CITY."[26] On June 3 the *Black Dispatch* carried the headline "Police Drag Women Behind Motor Cycles—Barrett [Oklahoma's adjutant general] Says Tulsa Police Laid Down, Black Mother Gives Birth in Chaos: $2,500,000 Of Negro Property Is Destroyed."[27]

The *Black Dispatch* reported that the riot was started after a youth, Dick Rowland, was accused by a white woman, Sarah Page, of attacking her in an elevator. Rowland was arrested and taken into custody. That evening, some white men converged upon the jail and demanded the prisoner. Upon hearing that a group of white men were bent on lynching Rowland, a group of Negroes in the Greenwood district gathered and went to the jail to offer their services for protection of the prisoner. They were told to "go home and behave themselves."[28]

On the other side of the building, the sheriff was giving a similar message to the group of white men who had gathered. They, however, refused to disperse. Upon hearing that the group of white men had not dispersed from the jail, members of the Negro group, who had returned to their neighborhood, reinforced themselves with arms and returned to the courthouse. At least one of the men from the white group dashed among the Negroes and tried to disarm them. During the struggle, a gun went off. The Greenwood district then became the central battleground after members of the Negro group fled from the area and returned to their homes with the white group in pursuit.[29] En route to the Greenwood district, the white group broke into "every hardware and sporting goods store in the city" to arm themselves.[30]

According to Mary E. Jones Parrish, from the W.P.A. Writers Project of the Oklahoma Historical Society:

> As daylight approached, they (the Whites) were given a signal by a whistle, and the outrage took place... .
> More than a dozen aeroplanes went up and began to drop turpentine balls upon the Negro residences, while the 5,000 Whites, with machine guns and other deadly weapons, began firing in all directions.[31]

In addition to keeping up with the riot, the *Black Dispatch* made attempts to squelch rumors,[32] tried to keep track of Sarah Page, the accuser, and Dick Rowland, the accused,[33] and raised money for "the colored citizens of Tulsa."[34] It would be a difficult task for Dunjee, with so many uprooted Greenwood residents running from the city and others being jailed by police for being on the streets.[35] Locating the Greenwood residents, alive or dead, would be an almost impossible job.

When Dunjee investigated the cause of the riot, he learned that Rowland while entering the elevator had stumbled and stepped on the foot of Sarah Page, the elevator operator, who, thinking she was being attacked, struck him continuously with her handbag. Rowland "grabbed her hand as he stepped out of the elevator." He was later picked up by the police a few blocks from the building where the incident had occurred.[36]

After being questioned by the Tulsa police, Rowland was released with no charges filed. In fact, he was not in the police building when the white mob appeared there to lynch him, but the authorities said they "could not afford to tell where he was." So the riot started, unfortunately, not because there had been a rape or even an attempted rape but because knowledge of what had occurred between the boy and the girl had been withheld from the gathered lynch mob. On the surface, then, there was no reason for the riot or why it was carried out with such destructive intensity.[37]

But Dunjee thought there was. Unlike Robert Abbott's attitude during the riots of 1919 when it appeared important to get even with whites for stoning the Negro swimmer, Dunjee was more concerned with why so many lives were lost, why there had been so much looting, and why had there been such a total destruction of property within the Greenwood district.

It was Dunjee's belief that the Tulsa business district which desired more expansion space but which had advanced as far as it could up to the Greenwood district was geographically blocked by Negroes from further land development. Expansion into the Greenwood area could be accomplished if Negroes were not occupying that land or if they would sell a large portion of it. Although efforts had been made to purchase large tracts of that area, they had not been successful, even after large sums of money had been offered.[38]

After the riot, the *Tulsa World* reported on June 1 that "the 'black belt' was beyond the powers of all human agency to save from flames which bid fair to raze the entire section."[39] Was it a convenience or necessity when the Tulsa city commissioners came out with an extended fire limit ordinance which was interpreted to mean "THAT

THE OLD BLACK BELT HAS BEEN ABOLISHED AND THAT THE CREATION OF A NEW BLACK DISTRICT, FARTHER OUT AND REMOVED FROM THE BUSINESS DISTRICT WILL BE MANDATORY"?[40]

Since the Greenwood district which had previously blocked the Tulsa business district from expanding onto that tract of land had been burned to the ground and the Negro people legally evicted from their property and placed "farther out and removed from the business district," the land was now open for other developments, particularly business developments. Dunjee thought that was too convenient for a coincidence and said in a front-page story that "this latest FIRE LIMIT ORDINANCE SHOWS PLAINLY THAT TULSA COVETED ALSO THE VERY LAND UPON WHICH BLACK MEN DWELT."[41]

The loss of land, other property, relatives, and friends left a deep and bitter scar on Negro Tulsans. In their eyes, even if a rape had occurred, how could the destruction of an entire lifestyle be justified? How did a mob bent on a simple lynching acquire airplanes with gasoline bombs, loot the area before its destruction, and then make an effort to destroy every building in the district? And why were the Negroes rounded up and interned while the white rioters were allowed to assist the authorities? It was another race incident in which Dunjee saw his fellow race members come out on the short end.

There had been in Oklahoma many instances of direct conflict between Dunjee or others of his race and those who had opposed the civil rights of Negroes and equalization of the law for Negroes or those who had tried to circumvent the law to deprive Negroes of what was legally theirs. When Dunjee was asked by a television station in Oklahoma City about his personal feelings and whether he harbored any ill will against any Oklahomans who had confronted him, he responded:

> I think today, and at this moment, I can truthfully say, despite the many difficult struggles I've had with those who oppose my philosophy and viewpoints, there is not a man in this state white, black, or red, against whom I hold any ill-will.
> The *Black Dispatch* has had to be many times as harsh as truth and as uncompromising as justice. I assure you, however, that at no time, during such trying moments, have I tried to inspire the ire of anyone. I've never tried to make men angry. I only try to make my fellow man think.[42]

Robert Abbott had made a place in history with his introduction of yellow journalism among Negro editors. It was not liked by all, but it was at least profitable for Abbott. Robert Vann and his *Courier* had shown that delivering the news with facts but in a lively style would work, if done correctly. Dunjee went a step further by taking his facts and evaluations to the editorial page and placing another side of the issue to the reader. The other side was not always liked or appreciated by many in the white community but was savored by Negroes. Unfortunately for Dunjee, Negroes were not a strong part of the business industry, an industry he needed for advertising revenue.

5

JACKSON ADVOCATE

Mississippi's Negro press, although never reaching the editorial status of the *Defender*, the *Courier*, or the *Black Dispatch,* made up in the number of newspapers started within the state for what it lacked in substance. The state ranked fourth, with 208, in the total number of Negro newspapers begun since 1827. Alabama had the most with 276, followed by Texas with 244, and Georgia with 242. Newspapers were begun in at least 80 cities within the state. Eight years was a newspaper's average life span, but a one-year existence was the norm for many.

For thirty-seven continuous years, 1886–1923, at least one Negro newspaper was started each year somewhere in the state, which showed the tenacity, or insistence, of Mississippians to have a Negro journal. With an average circulation between 500 and 1,000,[1] it might appear that the readership for these newspapers was almost minimal, despite the large Negro population. The circulation figures do not reflect, however, the number of instances in which one copy of a newspaper may have been passed from person to person. Since 1867 when the first Negro newspaper in Mississippi was founded, only five cities have been able to publish ten or more Negro newspapers: Jackson, 39; Greenville, 23; Mound Bayou, 19; Vicksburg, 14; and Natchez, 10.

The fighting spirit which has been traditionally reflected in the names of many Negro newspapers published in other parts of the country also existed in Mississippi. Several unusual names have also graced the banners of some organs: *40 Acres and a Mule,* Jackson; *Hop-Toad Whistle,* Assbray; *People's Relief,* Jackson; *Tutwiler Whirlwind,* Clarksdale; *Benevolent Banner,* Edwards; *Pathfinder,* Greenville; *Eagle Eye,* Jackson; *Fair Play,* Meridian; *Race Pride,* Okolona; and *Golden Rule,* Quitman. Those organs may or may not have reflected the conservative attitudes of their editors. But one newspaper with a name which did not reflect the editorial philosophy of its editor, Percy Greene, was the *Jackson Advocate.*

It must be remembered that many factors determined the course of events for Negroes in Mississippi, particularly the editorial philosophy pursued by Negro editors. Abbott from Chicago and Vann from Pittsburgh, operating from relatively safer havens in the North, faced some dangers now and then but not of the immediate magnitude as those faced by Dunjee in Oklahoma or Greene in Mississippi. To sustain segregation, some white Mississippians resorted to the use of fear and intimidation through lynching to discourage any attempts at change and to remind Negroes of their place in the state's societal hierarchy. As a result, economic advancement, the right to vote, and any ability to influence the state's political environment continued to elude Negroes.[2]

One of the things which made Mississippi a leader in the effort to suppress Negro rights was the state's adoption of the Segregation Movement in 1890. The Mississippi Constitutional Convention which adopted that movement also voted to place legal "handicaps on black civil rights in Mississippi" through the use of the Mississippi Plan. What made the adoption of that plan so poignant for the Negro in Mississippi was the appearance of the one Negro at the convention, Isaiah Montgomery, founder of Mound Bayou, an all-Negro town near the Arkansas state line, who actually agreed with the intent of the established law. It was interesting, too, that some members of the Negro press in Mississippi also seemed to approve.[3] The Mississippi Plan was definitely designed to eliminate the possibility of Negro involvement in politics through the use of poll taxes and the issuance of literacy tests.[4]

Not very long after that convention, Percy Greene was born on September 7, 1898. He was raised in Jackson and attended public and private schools there, but went to Illinois in 1915 on his first leg of seeing the world. Greene later joined the army, and then went to England. After being discharged, he became involved with bookkeeping and accounting in Jackson. Soon after, he became a postal carrier. Upon graduating from Jackson State College, he became an apprentice in a law office, where for years he studied law. Unlike Abbott and Vann who did manage to obtain their law degrees, Greene was denied a passing grade on his bar examination. He then went into the newspaper business and founded the *Jackson Advocate* in 1938.[5]

Greene was a strong believer that the "solution to racial betterment is to be found in the ability of the Negro to look inward. He is not going to be worth anything as long as he awaits the contributions of foundations and the federal government."[6] He adopted that philosophy without reservation and made every attempt throughout his life to abide by its concepts.

But when he made that "look inward" statement, Greene apparently forgot or disregarded what had happened to him in 1927. At that time, he was a law apprentice under Dr. S. D. Redmond. After he took the bar examination, his name did not appear on the published list of those who had passed the examination. He therefore assumed that he had failed and asked Redmond to investigate and find out exactly where he had placed among those who had failed. Redmond consulted with Senator Walter W. Caples, who, upon doing some additional investigation, was later advised by yet another investigating source that "Yes, that 'nigger' made the highest mark on the list ... but as long as I am Secretary of State he [Greene] would never be a lawyer in Mississippi." Greene had looked inward, had proved to be the best man for the job, but was rejected. He continued nevertheless to totally support a philosophy that was not working for members of his race.[7]

While Abbott with his *Defender* was shouting boldly for Southern Negroes to "come North" to a better life, Vann with the *Courier* was trying to teach Negroes to improve themselves and their neighborhoods for a better way of life. Dunjee with the *Black Dispatch* in Oklahoma City also had taken up a cause by trying to get his race members to develop some backbone and stand up for their civil rights. But the Negro press in Mississippi near the end of the depression years called for Negroes to stay calm, resist attempts to get involved with politics, and leave the situation in the South the way it was. Without any sign of reservation or remorse, Greene also continued to push his philosophy of "looking inward" to get ahead. That was the only way, he believed, that Negro Mississippians could survive in the state.

If history can be accepted as a barometer to justify Greene's feelings, there were several reasons why much of the Negro press in the South had trod so lightly during the late nineteenth and early twentieth centuries. First, there was always the overt threat of deadly physical harm to editors who did not choose their words and their stories wisely. Second, Southern Negro newspapers had to rely on advertisements from white merchants for the most part to stay in business because Negro advertisers were few or nonexistent. If white advertisers felt the pressure of discontent from white customers because of something printed in a Negro newspaper, they either applied pressure on the Negro editors to curb their tone or they dropped their ads.[8] And the unmistakable feeling by Negroes that there existed no police protection whatsoever from groups bent on keeping the status quo or keeping the Negro in his place was a third reason for such a widespread lack of editorial aggression.

When further analyzing the lack of aggressiveness by Southern Negro editors, there are several important points which must be considered. Julius Eric Thompson, a researcher of the Mississippi Negro press, made the observation that many editors in that state were ministers who had church-member readers. Those readers, he pointed out, expected a "deep religious emphasis in the press, if not in detail at least in the tone of the publications of the period."[9]

Such a belief in a "deep religious emphasis" must be considered as a viable reason why some editors refrained from reporting the violent news that occurred within their communities. But the fact that the editorial foundation of the Negro press, the militant Negro press, the fighting Negro press, was begun by a minister cannot be ignored. In fact, the Reverend Samuel Cornish, coeditor of *Freedom's Journal*, has been noted as one of the most militant editors in Negro history.

In describing how Cornish replied to those who wished to send free Afro-Americans back to Africa and strengthen the institution of slavery, Lee Finkle, a World War II black journalism researcher, states that Cornish "attacked" his opponents. Finkle reports that Cornish's attacks were "devastating," even "hostile," and it was his goal to "expose" those who thought that no good could come from members of the Afro-American race. Those are not the usual words spoken by the clergy in a Sunday sermon, or any other day.[10] And to reiterate, it was during Cornish's tenure as editor that *Freedom's Journal* "flourished." The "editorials were well written, and the attacks on the Colonization Society were lucid and devastating."[11]

In another instance, the Reverend R. N. Hall, editor of the *Baptist Leader* in Birmingham, Alabama, in the heart of the deep South, received a visit from members of the Ku Klux Klan after he had reported instances of their violence. He was advised to cease publishing articles that involved Klan activities. Not only did Reverend Hall continue to display his mettle by publishing additional stories about Klan activities, he had the effrontery to even run on the front page of the paper a story about the Klan's visit to the newspaper's office. Abbott saw Hall's story and ran it in the *Defender*. Members of the Klan probably could have shut down Hall's paper with little or no difficulty, but they didn't. Shutting down the *Baptist Leader* might silence it, but the *Defender* would not be such an easy target.[12]

There were other instances of assertiveness in the South by Negro editors. It is important, however, to point out that many of these editors used subtleties to survive and get messages to the Negro communities while continuing to maintain a "muted look."

> Many black newspapers contained no identifiable editorial page; others overlooked and camouflaged their responses and coverage of controversial issues. For example, a changed meeting place from one church to another or the announcement of only a speaker's initials and last name probably was insignificant to the white community, but to blacks, it meant an opportunity, in the words of one subscriber, "to go hear something good."[13]

With all the pressures the Southern Negro press faced, none were as powerful as pressures from advertisers. Frederick G. Detweiler, a Negro press historian, discovered that "Negroes did not trust the loyalty of their southern press as much as they did that of the North." A white businessman also mentioned to Detweiler that he was able to influence the expressions used in one local newspaper.[14] Because of that mistrust, the *Courier* and the *Defender* competed successfully for Southern audiences. At one time, in fact, the *Defender* sold more papers to readers on a national level—particularly in the South—than to readers within Chicago.[15]

Percy Greene saw the need to report local and state news, but he stressed corrective action only when the news concerned international situations and the other three-fourths of the nation. In fact, to some readers in Mississippi, the *Advocate* was a relatively "radical" newspaper when compared with others in Mississippi. Pushing for rights to vote as called for by the Constitution earned it that reputation. But Greene was careful to walk a thin line, becoming militant about national problems and inconsistencies but refraining as much as possible from attacking local officials and institutions. As Julius Eric Thompson so vividly pointed out, "fear and intimidation" determined not only what the editors in Mississippi reported but also the tone used in that reporting.[16]

6

WORLD WAR II, 1939–1945

One of the most effective forces keeping an eye on the moves of the United States government during World War II from within the country was the Negro press. Over the years it had earned a reputation for being a "fighting press" and a "crusading press," but never before had it been able to unite editors within its profession nationwide or obtain mass circulation support and solidify its voice against military subjugation practices. Such a unified effort along with mass numbers of subscribers would turn out to be instrumental in the strength and survival of the Negro press.

Throughout its existence, a major problem which had faced the Negro press was how to confront a race issue with some semblance of a united front that would show racial solidarity. The fact that most Negro editors in the past did fight against discrimination directed against Negroes was not the issue. The messages conveyed were too often sporadic, accommodating or moderate at best, and ill-timed, or they were ignored by those who believed that the subscription totals of a newspaper were the hallmark of that newspaper's effectiveness. What the Negro press needed was a combined, organized entity to coordinate major problems, local or national, and report all findings to the public from as many geographical locations as possible at the same time.

Newspaper editors, publishers, and other executives from across the country therefore met in Chicago to develop such a plan. Of immediate interest was the continual problem of low advertising revenue. The disunity among editors on how and when to confront a race problem, particularly when that problem occurred within a newspaper's coverage area, was the next consideration. Another problem which had been festering for decades, the sudden and ill-timed uncoordinated changes of editorial philosophies, was also addressed.[1] Those issues were the foundation on which the organization would be formed.

69

With everyone in agreement, in February 1940 the National Negro Publishing Association (NNPA) became active. John Sengstacke, who had followed Robert Abbott as editor of the *Defender*, became its president.[2]

Prior to the start of the war, as a result of the successful use of sensational journalism by Robert Abbott and his *Defender*, much of the news that covered the pages of the Negro press had emphasized crimes committed by Negroes and the violence committed against them. Some editors may not have agreed with Abbott's philosophy of sensationalizing the news, but at least that practice was paying the bills.

With the approach of World War II, the Negro press faced new and varied issues,[3] including the following:

1. Concern over the U.S. Navy's recruiting policy after the Navy Department revealed that Negro sailors at the end of 1939 numbered only 2,807, out of a grand total of 116,000
2. The lack of Negro enrollment in the Naval Academy, the policy that Negroes could serve in the Navy only as mess attendants, and the fact that they were excluded from service in the Marine Corps and in the Coast Guard[4]
3. The awareness of the Negro faithfulness to the American side of the war, the task of the Negro press to stress that loyalty from time to time, and the need for Negroes to give financial, moral, and physical support to the war effort
4. The need to be prepared to face sedition and disloyalty charges, which were often leveled by the government during times of strife
5. The need for a show of national unity to overcome the opposing forces in the war[5]
6. The rampant use of employment discrimination
7. Military discrimination against Negro troops, the failure to recognize their accomplishment, and abuses in U.S. Army camps and army towns[6]

As the Negro press pondered those new issues, editors of the *Courier*, the *Defender*, and the *Black Dispatch* also faced the same old problems which had lingered throughout their editorial existence. Should they curb their editorial tone, salvage what little advertising base they had, and die a slow and painful death through circulation loss? Unfortunately for Negro editors, they faced many hurdles in their profession that just wouldn't go away. The problems caused by the war only added to those with which they already had to contend. History had already shown, however, that satisfying advertisers through toned-down rhetoric usually resulted in a loss of subscriptions. Losing subscribers did not necessarily appeal to advertisers, so advertisers would soon disappear. Abbott had shown with his *Defender* earlier in the century that militancy when it had a well-meaning purpose was almost certain to increase subscriptions. But there was also a downside to that militancy. He also had proven that such outspoken statements during times of war were certain to bring about a clash with the government. Thus the Negro editors faced yet another problem. Should they curb their editorial tone to survive sedition charges the government often used in an attempt to subdue the militancy of the Negro press during times of war?[7]

The editors must have realized that Negro readers represented yet another side of the picture that could not and would not be ignored. The timely use of militancy, for example, had made them reputable men whose opinions were sought and valued. They recognized the formula for success and believed subscribers should be given serious consideration. Subscribers' response to what editors were saying was quite evident when Abbott delivered the messages they wanted to hear during the Great Migration. Such messages began with Negro reporters:

> The Negro reporter is a fighting partisan. The people who read his newspaper ... expect him to put up a good fight for them. They don't like him tame. They want him to have an arsenal well-stocked with atomic adjectives and nouns. They expect him to invent similes and metaphors that lay open the foe's weaknesses and to employ cutting irony, sarcasm and ridicule to confound and embarrass our opponents. The Negro reader is often a spectator at a fight. The reporter is attacking the reader's enemy and the reader has a vicarious relish for a fight well fought.[8]

But that was not all. Caucasian and Negro newspapers in many instances carried the same news story, particularly when the event involved civil rights or Negro crimes against whites. The white press customarily presented that news from its own editorial point of view. A Negro person reading that story did so to note not only what was being said about Negroes in the white press but also how it was said. And since readers could not envision what was not said in the story, they then looked for a Negro newspaper and searched for that same incident. Once they had found that same story, they expected to see a strong opinion, a strong demand, if appropriate, for equal civil rights. There was no question in these readers' minds that an action which was bad had been left out of the story if a white person had performed it, and an action which was good was left out of the story if a Negro had performed it.[9] If the *Courier*, the *Defender*, and the *Black Dispatch* continued giving their readers what they wanted, circulation would clearly rise.

Percy Greene with his *Advocate*, on the other hand, believed that what the people wanted was inconsistent with his own beliefs and was an imposition that was too forward and too fast. He thought that the race should "look inward" to solve all of its racial problems, rather than seek outside assistance. Instead of providing viable stories that would attract more subscribers, thus attracting more advertising revenue as a result, Greene thought that catering to the wishes of advertisers would keep the revenue coming in.[10]

As far as circulation leadership was concerned, many historians have singled out the *Defender* as the most influential force during the era of the Great Migration and World War I. If any Negro newspaper deserved that same distinction during World War II, it would be the *Pittsburgh Courier*. It was the leader in the fight for Negro civil rights and for fair treatment of Negro soldiers. By the spring of 1942, its circulation had risen high enough that it had become the largest Negro newspaper in the country.[11]

Giving the people what they wanted editorially has always been the key to success in the history of the Negro press. Roscoe Dunjee was noted for his ripping comments, even if they were more appreciated outside the state of Oklahoma. Russwurm and Cornish were successful for a short while with *Freedom's Journal* in 1827, when using that same concept. Their readers abandoned them when Russwurm's contents became contrary to what they had expected. When Ida B. Wells gave her readers what they wanted, they embraced her as their champion. Those who didn't appreciate what she had to say shut her down violently, but not before the *Free Speech* had shown an increase in circulation. And what can be said about Robert Abbott and his use of an aggressive editorial style? He took it to extremes, but the people loved him for it. Whether his editorial style trod upon the sanctity of Negro editors' domain was irrelevant. Abbott revitalized a sagging Negro press and put life into it. But it was Robert Vann who determined that black newspapers could thrive when pursuing stories with strong circulation appeal, even if it meant changing the paper's editorial philosophy or changing its staff. He showed it was possible to survive without a broad base in advertising revenue and without going to the extremes, as did Abbott.

The key was in discovering those stories with race appeal. When those stories were found, the editor had to devote "considerable editorial space to those issues."[12]

It was just before the beginning of World War II when Vann discovered several issues with almost certain circulation appeal: the army had virtually excluded Negroes from its ranks, particularly the officers corps,[13] and the navy only used Negroes "As Seagoing Chambermaids, Bell Hops, Dishwashers," but not as fighting men.[14]

Vann believed that such a policy was demeaning to Negroes and began a drive in 1939 to correct it by recommending that a proportional number of Negroes be allowed to serve in the army. The White House on October 9, 1940, disagreed and issued a statement which declared that "the policy of the War Department is not to intermingle colored and white enlisted personnel in the same regimental organizations."[15]

In 1940 shortly after Vann's death, an incident occurred which placed the new editor of the *Courier*, Percival L. Prattis, in the forefront of Negro civil rights efforts. Thirteen Negro seamen somewhere overseas aboard the *U.S.S. Philadelphia*[16] had written to the *Courier* to voice their discontent with the navy's racial policy.[17] Upon discovering that those sailors had written a letter of complaint, the navy had them arrested. They were scheduled for a court-martial at a later date. But even while in jail the seamen were able to notify the *Courier* of their incarceration. The story of the jailing was printed by Prattis on October 5, 1940.[18] The response from Negro readers was as anticipated. Letters of protest poured in to the *Courier*'s office. Some letters were even sent to the jailed seamen. Prattis then interceded with the navy on behalf of the sailors, a move which led to their release without a court-martial, but the sailors were sent back to the States and released with either undesirable or bad conduct discharges.

That too did not sit very well with Prattis. But even though he insisted, the navy refused to reopen the case, explaining that the seamen had brought discredit upon the navy and had "spread discontent among Negro mess attendants." In response to the question of why Negro sailors were restricted to the position of mess attendants, the navy said that Negro seamen who were elevated in rank superior to that of white men could not maintain discipline. Therefore it was in the interest of efficiency that the policy of restricting Negroes to the mess attendant's position be maintained.[19]

The *Courier* experienced another clash with the navy in 1941 when a Negro mess attendant, Dorie Miller, performed heroics beyond his called-for duties during the attack on Pearl Harbor. Even though his ship was under heavy enemy fire and the bridge had been hit, he dragged his wounded captain out of danger. Miller then found a machine gun and began firing at Japanese warplanes from a burning deck until he had run out of ammunition.[20]

Prattis, believing this incident totally vindicated him for his continual clashes with the navy to enter Negro sailors into combat, pushed for the Congressional Medal of Honor for Miller. Instead, Miller was awarded the Navy Cross. Quite clearly, the circulation figures of the *Courier* during those confrontations with the navy had grown substantial enough that the navy took complete notice of what the *Courier* had to say. Prattis then called for Miller's return to the mainland, as was the usual practice when white servicemen received similar recognition.[21]

It would seem likely that incumbent government officials or those just taking office in 1939 would not only have knowledge of what had occurred between 1917 and 1921 but actually picked up where previous officeholders had left off. "Wartime sedition laws" had been passed near the end of World War I and were still in force at the beginning of World War II. The seated government was also well aware of the "critical attitude" of the Negro press during the first war. As a result, government officials began investigating the Negro press prior to the beginning of the second war. The Negro press, on the other hand, began an assault on the government because it had gained more power through wide circulations as the years passed and was still smarting over the government's refusal to honor its World War I commitment.[22]

P. B. Young, Sr., publisher of the *Norfolk Journal and Guide*, revealed that the FBI had visited some Negro newspapers almost every day before the war. The visits, he said, were a result of the strong anti-discrimination articles being pushed in those papers.[23]

In 1939 the FBI obtained a document titled Report on Japanese Propaganda in the United States that discussed Japanese propaganda among Negroes. This report contained pro–Japanese comments from some members of the Negro press. In particular, the *Baltimore Afro-American* was quoted as stating: "It is plain now that the objective of the Japanese Government is to boot the white races out of China, and set up an Asiatic Monroe Doctrine through which Japan can control the destinies of the Far East. The *Afro-American* fully believes Japan is justified in the foregone objectives."[24]

The FBI was also interested in what the *Courier* was reporting and visited that newspaper in 1940. The agency had received reports that the writers of the paper were "holding America up to ridicule."[25]

In December of 1941, five Negroes in Virginia were asked for their opinions on "what Japan's attitude would be towards blacks if it won the war." The *Afro-American* newspapers printed the results, which read: "The colored races as a whole would benefit.... This would be the first step in the darker races coming back into their own." Although no violations of the law were found, the FBI was asked to investigate the *Afro-American* chain "as well as the 'character and pertinent activities' of its editors to determine if there was a tie-in with 'hostile or subversive sources.'" Since the paper was merely stating what individuals had to say, no laws had been violated.[26]

The FBI also visited the *Courier* and columnist Cliff McKay at the *Atlanta Daily World*. They were interested in whether outside forces "had tried to influence the paper editorially." The FBI also sent letters of complaint to the editor of the *Birmingham World*, who had criticized J. Edgar Hoover, the FBI chief, for not hiring Negroes as FBI agents. The *Courier* and the *Atlanta Daily World* issued editorials condemning such visits as an effort to pressure the Negro press into holding back its attacks. By that time, the *Courier* was riding high with a circulation of about 200,000 and was confident that the government would not try to suppress it. And even if it tried, the *Courier* staff believed that it would be difficult for the government to sway the courts in its favor. The confidence of the staff was evident in an interview given by columnist Frank Bolden:

> The investigation was a farce. They [the agents] never harassed anybody or threatened anybody. They just expressed their dissatisfaction at what we were doing... . They suggested that we protest in another way or wait until after the war. But to my knowledge, they never threatened to arrest anyone or told anyone they had to do something... .
>
> [Executive Editor Percival Prattis] just called them scared white people, Hoover's flunkies. We all said that. We just considered them Nazi strong men. We just ignored them. I guess you could call it contempt.[27]

In mid-1941, the army became very interested in what was being printed in the Negro press. It informed the FBI that "Japanese and

Communist press agents are releasing news in all available negro publications and in some cases, Communists or Communist sympathizers
are employed on the editorial staffs of these papers." As a result, the
FBI visited the office of the *Courier*, one of the papers named as having Communists on its staff.[28]

The *Courier*, of course, was not alone in its attacks on the government, including the military, to obtain better treatment of Negro
servicemen. The government had already exerted pressure on several
other Negro newspapers "to conform and help the war effort while
putting aside until peacetime all efforts to end discrimination." And
five Negro newspapers under the *Afro-American* chain,[29] which apparently had not ceased their efforts to end their militancy, were already
in danger of being suppressed. In the eyes of the government, the
strong civil rights protest tone some editors were using showed disunity
within the country.[30]

Also under review by military intelligence was a particular headline written in the *Black Dispatch* which read, "War Department Aids
Hitler by Letting South Wreck [*sic*] Prejudice on Negro Soldiers."[31]
Dunjee with his *Black Dispatch* did not have the circulation clout that
the *Courier* claimed, but it was substantial enough for the government
to leave him alone for a while.

On the surface, publishers and editors of the black press showed
confidence and a blasé attitude toward government attempts to intim-
idate them. Behind the scenes, however, many were nervous and not
certain what would come about because of their actions.[32] Prattis
thought therefore that revealing the true sentiments of the *Courier*
and its readers in support of the country from time to time would not
be out of line:

> In the march to victory the colored American will be in the
> FRONT RANKS, as he has been in every struggle in our national
> history.
> He will sacrifice and fight and DIE, along with other Americans,
> in order that American civilization shall live and prosper.
> The American Negro has NEVER hesitated to rush to arms in
> the DEFENSE of the Stars and Stripes—and he never will.
> Though national prejudice may for a time discriminate against him
> and compel him to fight in segregated units, he will nevertheless fight
> and die in the knowledge that right and tolerance will ultimately prevail.
> The Negro marches WITH America to victory.[33]

In its January 17, 1942, issue, the *Courier* printed another article
to counter any charges of disloyalty. "The Japanese, Germans, Italians,

and their Axis stooges know that it is futile to seek spies, saboteurs or Fifth Columnists among American Negroes. Every attempt in that direction has been a miserable failure."

In Chicago, Sengstacke also saw no reason why true sentiments should not be shown and announced the *Defender*'s position by stating:

> The Negro press will not blemish its magnificent record of sound patriotism by indulging in subversive advocacy to the impairment of the national will. However, unless and until constitutional guarantees are suspended, the Negro press will continue to use its moral force against the mob in its criminal orgy, against such ultra violences as lynching, burning at [the] stake and judicial murder. It will continue to fight for those legitimate democratic rights that have been denied the Negro. It will insist on the thesis that the best way to save democracy is to extend it to all the citizens without regard to color or race. Such an attitude can hardly be construed as smacking of disloyalty and disaffection... .
>
> We are for national unity. We are for victory. We are for a working democracy. But, no one must conclude that in opposing clear cut discriminations in civilian life or in the army and navy, that the Negro press is disloyal. In this opposition is the essence of loyalty and devotion to democracy—and a free press.[34]

The *Defender* also sent a copy of the editorial to FBI chief Hoover.

Already under careful scrutiny by the government, Roscoe Dunjee, in a typically long editorial, not only asked the country to stand together, but continued his attacks by pointing out the problems and conditions of Negro people that should not be overlooked while standing together.

> The offspring of Crispus Attucks, and those who fought with General Jackson at New Orleans, and those who later shed their blood during the war of the states, on the Western frontier, and who rescued Teddy Roosevelt at San Juan Hill, the sons of men who fought at Sissions and Monkey Mountain are willing again to face death in the trenches, in the air and on the seas, but they asks, as they start towards certain slaughter on foreign battlefields that their white brothers grant them a democratic place at the council tables of state and nation.[35]

Dunjee's counterpart in the South, Percy Greene, announced the *Advocate*'s loyalty about one week after the war had started. Greene also stated that the seemingly "unenthusiastic anti-Hitler" mood of the Negro was a result of economics, not a lack of patriotism. He further stated that:

> In discussing the attitude of the Negro toward war with Japan
> there is bound to be raised the question of the color of the Japanese
> people as affecting this attitude, but we are of the firm conviction that
> the patriotism of the American Negro is not changed by the color of
> the enemy's face, and that his prayers, sacrifice, and loyalty will be as
> fervently American in this war against Japan as they have been in all
> the wars of the United States History.[36]

Unlike the *Courier*, which sought stories with circulation appeal
and ran with them, or the *Defender*, which had reached into the heart
of the South and had given red ink headlines to violence whenever it
occurred, or the *Black Dispatch*, which overtly attacked government
officials regardless of their location or clout, Greene with his *Advocate*
didn't pursue stories with circulation appeal. Instead, he continued to
provide those stories he thought were agreeable and illuminating but
posed no threat to any party, Caucasian or Negro. Some of his stories
were also designed to educate those Negroes still in need of instructions on how to handle themselves when out of Negro neighborhoods.

Greene clearly demonstrated his editorial philosophy by giving
plenty of editorial space to what the president had to say about the war
immediately after the bombing at Pearl Harbor. Greene reported news
of the enemy's atrocities or losses and carried good news on things the
army was doing, but never bad news about its activities. He also provided updates on racial problems around the South, but only in those
areas outside of Mississippi. His editorials were mainly commentaries
about the "universal appreciation of the brotherhood of man," updates
on the war with his own bit of morality attached, news of occurrences
in Africa, and a host of other routine topics not related to the war.[37]

The treatment of Negroes by the military and by the South did
not change because of the efforts of the Negro press. Consequently,
early in 1942 the morale of Negroes across the country began to sag
and was recognized by the government to be extremely low. Immediately after the bombing of Pearl Harbor when Greene had made his
declaration of race loyalty towards the war and the government and
his explanation for the lack of enthusiasm by Negro people, his statements were probably more profound than he had realized. Concerns
over the treatment of Negroes in the military and at home were far
reaching, as the following list of grievances shows:

1. When the United States entered the war, Negroes assumed
   that in an effort to solidify and unite the country against its

foes, all racial barriers would be scrapped, or at least modified.[38]

2. The Marine Corps and Coast Guard did not accept Negroes.
   Although the navy did, Negroes were used only in the mess
   corps.
3. The army used Negroes, but only as long as segregated facilities were available.
4. Even the practices by the Red Cross added to the low morale.
   At first they would not accept the blood of Negroes, and when
   they finally did, even it was segregated just as the soldiers
   were.
5. Riots and mob violence continued to take a large toll of black
   soldiers.
6. Lynching was still rather common.
7. Employment discrimination was also prevalent.[39]

Despite all efforts of the Negro press to convince the government
that Negroes should be treated as equal human beings, such policies
weren't forthcoming. Even Negro readers began to show their discontent.

The January 17, 1942, issue of the *Courier*, for instance, carried a
front-page story which indicated that Negro support of the war effort
was only lukewarm.[40] Prattis was only reporting the mood of the Negro
people at that time. In another story the *Courier* took note of the *Crisis* magazine, which during World War I had called for "closed ranks"
but at the current time had made a statement of "no closed ranks."
After all, the morale of many Negroes had dampened considerably
after W.E.B. DuBois had issued the "closed ranks" statement during
World War I. Apparently, the *Crisis* magazine did not want to make
that mistake again. Prattis also noted: "Black Americans are loyal
Americans, but let there be no mistake about that loyalty. It is loyalty
to the democratic ideal as enunciated by America and by our British
ally, it is not loyalty to many of the practices which have been—and
are still—in vogue here and in the British empire."[41]

But just how low the morale of Negroes had fallen became quite
evident when the *Courier* printed a letter to the editor from James G.
Thompson, a cafeteria worker at the Cessna Aircraft plant in Kansas.
The letter reflected an individual's opinion, but the government must
have taken its appearance in the *Courier* to indicate low morale, which
became subsequently a sign of disloyalty:

> Being an American of dark complexion and some 26 years, these
> questions flash through my mind: "Should I sacrifice my life to live
> half American?" "Will things be better for the next generation in the
> peace to follow?" "Would it be demanding too much to demand full
> citizenship rights in exchange for the sacrificing of my life?" Is the kind
> of America I know worth defending.... Will Colored Americans suffer
> still the indignities that have been heaped upon them in the past?
> The V for victory sign is being displayed prominently in all so-
> called democratic countries which are fighting for victory over aggres-
> sion, slavery, and tyranny. Let we colored Americans adopt the dou-
> ble VV for a double victory. The first V for victory over our enemies
> from without, the second V for victory over our enemies from within.[42]

Adopting this idea, the *Courier* decided to launch a Double V
campaign with its February 7 issue.[43] It was a very careful and low-
keyed introduction, a "feeler," perhaps, with no announcement and no
front-page or editorial-page coverage. The timing of the campaign
was perfect. Even Prattis could not have envisioned the success it garnered. And before it had reached its peak, the response had been so
phenomenal that the government once again became concerned that
such a campaign might result in a refusal of Negroes to support the
war effort at the very moment when support was most needed.[44]

The need for good timing to fend off any moves by the government was important for Prattis. To say he used timing wisely would
clearly be an understatement. He pointed out the success of the campaign to his readers but did not overlook the attachment of race loyalty:

> Our office has been inundated with hundreds of telegrams and
> letters of congratulations, proving that without any explanations, this
> slogan represents the true battle cry of colored America.... . Ameri-
> cans all, are involved in a gigantic war effort to assure victory for the
> cause of freedom—the four freedoms that have been so nobly expressed
> by President Roosevelt and Prime Minister Churchill. We, as colored
> Americans are determined to protect our country, our form of gov-
> ernment and the freedoms which we cherish for ourselves and for the
> rest of the world, therefore we have adopted the Double "V" war cry—
> victory over our enemies at home and victory over our enemies on the
> battlefields abroad.[45]

The Double V campaign was begun by the *Courier* in support of
"victories over totalitarian forces overseas and those at home who were
denying equality to Negroes."[46] With its confidence bolstered by such
a wide show of Negroes supporting its position, the *Courier* beefed up
its coverage of the campaign. Other Negro newspapers, including the

Amsterdam Star-News and the *People's Voice* in New York, the *Chicago Defender,* and the Washington *Afro-American,* began to display the symbol.[47] After word got around concerning what the Double V stood for, more and more people purchased papers to read about what was going on. Other newspapers also gave their support.[48] The campaign became so popular that circulations among Negro newspapers across the country began to soar. The *Courier* became the Negro paper with the largest circulation, 270,812, and the *Afro-American* (Baltimore) wasn't far behind with 229,812, followed by the *Defender* with 161,009 and the *Journal and Guide* (Norfolk) with 77,462. Along with the campaign, the Negro press launched another round of militant attacks against unfair treatment of Negroes.[49] This time it had support and clout in the form of massive circulations.

According to Patrick Washburn, a World War II historian, the government became alarmed over the popularity of this campaign. It viewed the Double V crusade as a prelude to disloyalty and quickly blamed the Negro press for Negro discontent. Pressures and other steps not used before were taken to curb attacks on the government. Unquestionably, this became the most dangerous period in history for the survival of the Negro press, but the editors did not back away from their stance. The *Courier* reminded the government of its unfulfilled promise made during World War I by stating: "It is our duty to submit the injustices and hypocrisies of this nation to the conscience of the Republic. We will remember Pearl Harbor and we will aid in avenging it, but we are not forgetting ourselves."[50] But the government hadn't played all of its cards yet.

It wasn't long thereafter that government officials paid visits to five of the largest Negro weeklies—the *Amsterdam Star-News*, the *People's Voice*, the *Courier*, the *Defender*, and the Washington *Afro-American.* A report which followed those visits suggested that the Double V campaign was being widely used and that the editorial content of those papers emphasized the unequal treatment of Negroes and was "hurting Negro morale."[51]

The Office of Facts and Figures (OFF) also viewed the unity and popularity of the Double V campaign with some concern. In an effort to cut off the present trend and tone down the actions of the Negro press, the OFF invited the editors from major Negro newspapers and the major Negro civic leaders to a five-hour meeting in Washington to clear up misunderstandings and discuss possible solutions. In extending its invitations, however, OFF committed a major oversight.

An invitation had not been sent to the *Defender*, one of the giants of the Negro press. Upon realizing their mistake, OFF officials quickly dispatched an invitation, but it was too late. The *Defender* quietly declined.[52]

During the meeting, the editors stressed that they would not back down on their tone or cease to address unfair practices. They further acknowledged the difficulty the government said it faced in attempting to elevate Negro morale without eliminating some of the nation's discrimination practices. Sadly absent from the discussions, however, were the statements that the editors really wanted to hear—that new race relations policies were being reviewed, that arbitrary killings would cease, and that members of the military would all get the same treatment.[53]

Despite the militant front originally presented by the Negro editors, government officials were so persuasive with their talks that some editors decided to take another look at their editorial philosophies and agreed to approach new opinions with some caution.[54]

Not the *Courier*, however.[55] Just as Abbott had reacted in his *Defender* to the "close ranks" proposal during World War I, Prattis took issue with the OFF recommendations. He published the following report about the government and how it was handling the Negro press:

> The hysteria of Washington officialdom over Negro morale is at once an astonishing, amusing and shameful spectacle.
>
> It is astonishing to find supposedly informed persons in high positions so unfamiliar with the thought and feeling of one-tenth of the population. One would imagine they had been on another planet, and yet every last one of them insists that he "knows the Negro."
>
> It is amusing to see these people so panicky over a situation which they have caused and which governmental policies maintain.
>
> It is shameful that the only "remedy" they are now able to put forward is jim crowism on a larger scale and suppression of the Negro newspapers; i.e., further departure from the principles of democracy....
>
> If the Washington gentry are eager to see Negro morale take an upturn, they have only to abolish jim crowism and lower the color bar in every field and phase of American life.
>
> Squelching the Negro newspapers will not make the Negro masses love insult, discrimination, exploitation and ostracism. It will only further depress their morale.[56]

As the threat of government suppression increased, Walter White, the executive secretary of the NAACP, became alarmed over the intensity of attacks being made by the Negro press and the possibility of press suppression. President Franklin D. Roosevelt, who was also concerned about those attacks, met with White in December 1942 to discuss a possible solution. After the meeting, White called for a conference of editors from 24 of the largest Negro newspapers, including the *Courier,* the *Defender,* and the *Black Dispatch.* White stressed the warning he had received from the president. And though the warning from White was completely understood, Sengstacke was still stinging from the earlier snub by OFF. As far as he was concerned, he didn't need White to tell him how to run his business and he would never again attend another such meeting called by the NAACP's boss. Overall, however, the Negro press did temper its attacks, but not because of White. In fact, most editors had already toned down their editorials even before the conference was held.[57]

It became increasingly clear to many Negro editors just how seriously their position with the government had deteriorated when scare words such as "suppression" and "sedition charges" began to filter into the newspaper offices. But it was in 1943 that this volatile situation reached its peak. The U.S. Post Office had already inspected a number of Negro newspapers for wartime violations. They found the *Boise Valley Herald* (Middleton, Idaho) and a publication called the *Militant* (New York) to be in violation and revoked their second-class permits.[58] Those were small newspapers with little or no editorial clout. When the scrutiny reached the *Negro World,* however, unbridled fear of suppression sifted quickly through all levels of the Negro press. The *Negro World* came under governmental scrutiny because of its November 1942 issue which had published the following editorial:

> What is meant by Subversive and pro-axis activities, when a Negro can be arrested for evading the draft and the same Government has no right to interfere with a white civilian in Louisiana who shoots down a Negro after he becomes a soldier? If the Axis shoot him down, he died in the service of his country, if a Cracker shoots him down no harm is done.[59]

The Post Office wanted to take some kind of action against the *Negro World,* a Negro publication with a sizable circulation but thought it would not get the needed support from the U.S. Justice Department, which was responsible for preventing seditious material from moving through the mail. The Justice Department "was concerned only with those parts of the Espionage Act that made it illegal to give aid to the enemy and to interfere with enlistment and recruiting."[60]

In addition to the Justice Department, at least six other governmental agencies investigated the Negro press during that period: the

FBI, the Post Office Department, the Office of Facts and Figures, the Office of War Information, the Office of Censorship, and the U.S. Army. One other agency, the War Production Board, may have made an illegal attempt to tone down the Negro press by reducing or cutting newsprint supplies to some papers. The White House also had launched investigations concerning what was going on in the Negro press.[61]

Meanwhile, Greene continued in the *Advocate* with his style of reporting the news. He gave big headlines to Roosevelt's messages to the nation, attacked the Japanese, and praised *Fight for Freedom*—a "patriotic organization interested in the attitude of the Negro toward the present world conditions."[62]

In another issue, Greene reported that an execution had been halted in Virginia, an attorney had been run out of town in Tennessee, and some army air cadets had begun training at Tuskegee, Alabama. Also in that issue, he offered the following injunctions: "Love thy neighbor as thyself," "Do unto others as thou would have them do unto you," and "PEACE ON EARTH AND GOODWILL AMONG MEN."[63]

Greene continued to follow this same style into 1942, concentrating his efforts on national Negro history week,[64] placing out-of-state violence on the front page, and confining his editorials to events such as a lynching in Missouri and Negro morale in the face of lynching.[65] In one editorial, Greene praised the Mississippi Power and Light Company for its recognition of the thousands of Negroes "enrolled in the Armed Forces," but he implied in the same editorial that the Negro press was aiding the enemy and lowering Negro morale:

> Having some knowledge of the use of propaganda, we are afraid also that much of what the Negro has been reading both, news and editorial, with its resulting ill effect upon the morale of the American Negro, will find its way into the hands of the skilled German and Japanese propaganda machines, and be used to lower the morale of the millions of yellow, brown and black men fighting the cause of the United States and England in the Philippines, Hawaii, China, Malay and Africa, and to effect our relations with the great countries in South America, like Brazil, where 95 per cent of the people, and the ruling class, are of Negro blood.[66]

Roscoe Dunjee's robust and fierce editorials were long, but he was noted worldwide for keeping the reader's interest. Greene, on the other hand, had developed a style using lengthy sentences with ambiguous meanings. The above editorial paragraph, for example, contains 114 words, all in one sentence. Greene printed other sentences within his editorials containing as many as 175 words.[67] In fact, his editorial concerning the Mississippi Negro schools had a sentence which was even longer, with at least 227 words:

> The N.A.A.C.P., according to news report has seen its suit, filed to speed up integration of local public schools, taken under study by the presiding federal judge whose written decision is to be made sometime in the not too distant future, which would give time for some Negro group in the state to file a "friend of the Court" brief, in the first place to establish the fact that the N.A.A.C.P. legalism of "a class action" in that its suits represents the desires and opinion of all Negroes of the state, is now, and always has been based on a false assumption; that Negro education in Mississippi has been and is not inferior to white education in the state because of the long practiced discrimination in the allocation of public money as between Negro and white students for educational purposes; that the Mississippi Negro is an American and therefore his identity as such cannot be made subject to the presence in his midst in any place of any other American, of any other race or color; and therefore bring to a halt the efforts to force Mississippi Negroes into abandoning their own schools: the efforts being promoted and urged by northern Negroes, who know nothing of, and who care less about the traditional and historic value of Negro schools to Negro life and culture in this state.[68]

With his newspaper, Greene provided his readers with nothing but positive information about what the government was doing and avoided mentioning the ways in which it handled Negroes. By not giving visible support to the Double V campaign, he of course avoided the governmental confrontations some other Negro newspapers were facing.

In some reports issued by the FBI, the Negro press was said to be responsible for much of the low morale in the Negro communities. Some publications were accused of having "alleged Communists on their editorial staff or employees who maintained contacts with Communists ... or they ran articles that followed the Communist Party line." Those publications were the *Baltimore Afro-American, California Eagle* (Los Angeles), *Chicago Defender, Colorado Statesman* (Denver), the *Crisis* magazine (New York, N.Y.), the *Denver Star, Kansas City Call, Los Angeles Sentinel, Racial Digest* (Detroit), *People's Voice* (New York), *Michigan Chronicle* (Detroit), *Black Dispatch* (Oklahoma City), and *Opportunity* (New York). Five other publications, including the *Pittsburgh Courier,* "were cited for running pro-Japanese material."[69] Greene's *Advocate* was not listed, of course, within any of those categories.

To make matters worse, particularly since so many agencies were reviewing the contents of those Negro papers and investigating them, the *Defender, Courier,* and some other Negro papers openly praised the U.S.S.R. as having peace and harmony among its citizens.[70] And the *Jackson Advocate* published a wire service news release titled "Writer Lauds Russia's Treatment of Negroes," although it did not carry the piece as an editorial. The tone of the news release was indicative of how Greene walked the tight rope: "The British Commonwealth of nations is not alone among the capitalist democracies in the refusal to accept racial equality. In the United States, the Negroes, in particular states, are excluded from being full fledged citizens with the right to vote and to become representatives."[71]

Negro newspapers did have frequent contacts with Communist personnel, as Billy Rowe, a *Courier* reporter explained, but the contact was unavoidable: "They were always wanting us to do something for a worthy cause, to help the family of someone who had been lynched or to help someone who needed money. It was never as blatant as doing it for the Communist Party. They didn't announce they were Communists, but you found out after awhile."[72]

Some of the official government reports seemed out of control as the FBI attempted to label some Negro newspapers as Communistic. For instance, the Oklahoma City FBI office reported that the *Black Dispatch* was using well-known Communist phrases such as "civil liberties," "inalienable rights," and "freedom of speech and of the press."[73] Dunjee was also cited when he reported that he had "Communistic leanings."[74]

In a typically long editorial, Dunjee attacked Congressman Martin Dies in Washington, who had previously reported that Mary McLeod Bethune, president of Bethune-Cookman College in Florida, and other individuals had Communist leanings:

> Last week, Congress Martin Dies in Washington announced that three of our outstanding Negroes in this nation were identified with subversive influences. Congressman Dies named William Pickens, Mary McLeod Bethune and E. Franklin Frazier, and he alleged to his astonished colleagues in congress that the Robert Marshall Foundation was being used to promote Communistic causes.... .
> We shall have to report that we personally do have Communistic leanings. We have said under oath in the state capitol of this state that we were not a member of the Communist party, and have never been, and that we are opposed to the economic theories of Communism. That is our statement now; but even so, we do have

Communistic leanings when it comes to the Communistic theory of
the international state and the question of racial equality... .

Communism believes in racial equality and so does this writer.
It may be perhaps that this is the one fault Congressman Dies has
found with Communism, for we note in his talk to the congress last
week the noted Texan said: "I deplore the fact that throughout the
South today subversive elements are attempting to convince the Negro
that he should be placed on social equality with white people."[75]

Upon investigating the *Black Dispatch*, the FBI also learned that
Dunjee "favored interracial marriage" and that he thought the "free
association between black and white people" was not wrong.[76]

Some attempts at governmental suppression of Negro newspapers
continued until 1944. The *Courier*, still leading the way in the press's
fight for race equality, continued to hammer away at the government:

> It becomes clearer and clearer that our white folks simply can't
> take it... . When Negro newspapers print the facts and criticise [*sic*]
> the criminal collusion between officialdom and crackerdom leading to
> treasonable discrimination against the mistreatment of Negro soldiers
> and sailors simply because they are colored ... a cry goes up, not for a
> change of policy toward the Negroes, but for penalization of sup-
> pression of the Negro newspaper.[77]

On the surface, it may have looked throughout much of the war
as if the government as a unit was out to shut down the Negro press.
But not all agencies or departments viewed with alarm the Negro press
or its attacks made in the interest of fair treatment of its people. Even
though some Negro newspapers were suppressed, generally the ones
with small circulations, most of them enjoyed freedom from suppression. Attorney General Francis Biddle, a serious advocate for freedom
of the press, had the final say on any charges filed against the press.
And though he was not able to stem the many investigations launched
by the FBI, he did control the FBI's court actions.[78]

When learning that charges had been filed concerning "a close
link between the Communist Party line and the Negro press' editorial policy," the Office of War Information delivered a strong rebuff. It
issued a report which stated that "the Negro press has never advocated
the overthrow of the present form of government and has never upheld
a philosophy or a policy alien to constitutional formulations of the
American way of life."[79]

Throughout the war, Negro editors and their staff made efforts
to show the government their loyalty to the United States and the war
effort. But Hoover just wasn't buying it. He believed that "The black

press ... was expected to give up its demands for full black rights until the end of the war."[80] Unfortunately for Hoover, history had already recorded the fact that the same scenario between the Negro press and the government had been played out during World War I. The government at that time asked the black press to give up its demands until the end of the war. The message was delivered via the "close ranks" proposal of W.E.B. DuBois. And though many of the editors did not entirely trust such a proposal at the time, they went along with it in a show of unity. After the war, however, the government was blind to the issues of the black press or the Negro people.

By 1945, the Negro press, for the most part, had survived World War II and the efforts made to scare it either out of business or into submission. Throughout the war, there had been much low Negro morale sweeping the country, but the government made no overt move to reward or lift Negro spirits. To have shut down the Negro press and cut off the flow of information, the only bright spot many blacks had in their lives, might have brought about even deeper internal strife. Deception, overt threats, threats through leaks, and investigations of all kinds were tried by some officials. Some tactics worked, some did not. A unified Negro press had formulated a plan, followed it, and was able to survive the pressures throughout the war.

Attorney General Francis Biddle and the Justice Department have been given credit for saving the Negro press from sedition charges. After 1942 the serious threats in those regards diminished. Most of the threats had come principally from the FBI, the Post Office, and the White House.[81] But Biddle could not be convinced that the Negro press was all those things mentioned in the various reports. Many of the charges went beyond what the black editors and publishers were seeking: an equal chance to fight for their country in a war, recognition of their accomplishments the same as all other uniformed personnel, and cessation of abuses, violence, and lynching without the guilty parties receiving judicial punishment.

In following Vann's philosophy by recognizing stories with circulation appeal, changing editorial philosophies as a result, and giving the people what they wanted, the Negro press gained more respect than it had ever had before. And regardless of how militant their editorial attacks on governmental discrimination, the words were aimed at the unfair treatment of people, the Negro people. But the government did not receive all of the criticism. There were some attacks on tendencies that had become a part of the American way of life, attacks that criticized the ease with which some white citizens could raise violence against their Negro neighbors, and sometimes white neighbors, without ever having to answer to the law.

The Negro press was indeed a major problem for the government during World War II. Its belligerency towards governmental policies, although legal under wartime sedition statutes, was severe enough to warrant many investigations. The questions most asked by these investigators were whether this criticism by the Negro press should be allowed to continue, and if not, how the courts would react with regard to the issue of freedom of the press. If Negro newspapers were suppressed, how would Negro morale be affected? Would such an attempt at suppression further anger the Negro population of 13 million? The government, for a change, had to walk a tight rope in that regard because "Everyone agreed that Negro support was necessary to win the war."[82]

After the war, the *Black Dispatch*, one of the newspapers which had survived its ordeal with the government, found itself faced with a lack of financial support, a condition it had faced throughout much of its existence. Dunjee had begun his paper at a time when white advertisers did not seek the services of Negro-owned newspapers, particularly in the South. But now that the war was over and particularly after he had delivered an attack on some politicians, a group of white individuals offered Dunjee financial support if he would curb his editorial tongue. He refused the offer. In another instance, "a white politician offered to buy him an entirely new printing plant if Dunjee would support him for governor." Dunjee was even offered a $400 a month salary by another white politician who wanted to control the editorial philosophy of the *Black Dispatch*.[83] Instead, Dunjee began to rely only on circulation to sustain the newspaper through that unstable period.

It should be pointed out that circulation of the *Black Dispatch* was substantial. Unfortunately, it had grown to the point where out-of-state subscribers far outnumbered those within Oklahoma. Those advertisers who had remained loyal to the *Black Dispatch* until after the war began to voice concern about such a large out-of-state circulation. Realizing that shoppers in Los Angeles or New York would not be interested in items on sale in Oklahoma and seeing that the local circulation was not improving, they too dropped their advertisements.[84] Unless drastic measures were taken, the *Black Dispatch* was in danger of going out of business. This was one instance when an editor had sought stories with race appeal and increased circulation as a result, but found itself in a unique position by having most of its subscribers from outside the state.

Dunjee then sought help from Negro churches, Negro-owned businesses, civic groups, and individuals. They were either financially unable to help or totally disinterested. Roscoe Dunjee, the man who had spent his earnings repeatedly to help others was in trouble.[85]

Dunjee then turned to one last person for help. He went to see his friend, Dr. Gravelly E. Finley, a physician on the northeast side of Oklahoma City, told him of the financial problems the newspaper had encountered, and how long he had been in business. He also said where he had been for help and who had turned him down. Dunjee further stated that if Finley did not invest in the *Black Dispatch*, the newspaper would not reach the streets of Oklahoma City on the following Thursday. Finley invested. Dunjee later sold the remaining stock to his nephew, John Dungee,[86] who was to become editor after Dunjee's retirement.[87]

Dunjee's role as owner of the newspaper that had altered the course of history within Oklahoma had come to an inauspicious end. And though he continued to function in the role of editor and publisher, the aggressiveness he once had, the stirring editorials that had once jumped from the pages, the reliable investigative analysis he was once so noted for were not there any more.[88]

Dunjee retired in 1955 after more than 40 years of service to the Negro community, Oklahoma City, the state of Oklahoma, and the nation. Honors have been bestowed upon him. Schools, parks, and streets are named in his honor. His likeness is the first portrait of a Negro person ever to hang in the official gallery of the Oklahoma Historical Society.[89] The first Negro journalist to be honored by the Oklahoma Journalism Hall of Fame at the University of Central Oklahoma was Roscoe Dunjee. He was a respected man in the Negro community, and though he did not have that same respect in the white community, the people there tolerated him, for Dunjee was a worthy adversary.

Meanwhile, the *Black Dispatch*, now under John Dungee, the *Courier*, under Percival Prattis, the *Defender*, under John Sengstacke, and the *Advocate*, still under Percy Greene, would continue their newspapers and enter the era of the civil rights movement. Within that movement of threats, intimidation, and violence, Negro editors would face new problems, new dangers, and a division between an editor and his readers that forced a Negro civic leader to attempt to run that editor out of business.

7

THE CIVIL RIGHTS
MOVEMENT, 1960–1965

One of the lessons that the World War II era had taught the black press was how it could fight consistently and effectively with unity for a cause by confronting forces—governmental forces, if necessary—head-on without bending and survive. More than that, it had resisted the urge to acquiesce under threats of physical violence, had only flinched under the customary charges of Communist leanings or infiltration, and, for the most part, had ceased publication rather than submit to censorship or allegations of sedition.

With the arrival of the 1960s, the number of black newspapers began to rise again, as it had in the past when former editors and would-be editors surfaced to give their accounts on what was going on in black America. Nationally, 217 newspapers were begun in response to the civil rights movement; California had at least 32 at one time, while Illinois had 28. Mississippi was third with 18 new organs.

Some of the significant journalistic events which occurred during the civil rights movement included the sit-ins which began in 1960, the Freedom Riders in 1961, and the struggles of James Meredith to enroll at the University of Mississippi in 1962. Also of significant note, in 1963 there were demonstrations in Birmingham, Alabama, the murder of Medgar Evers in Mississippi, the "March on Washington for Jobs and Freedom," the bombing of the 16th Street Baptist Church in Birmingham in which four black children were killed, and the death of President John F. Kennedy in Dallas, Texas.[1] In 1964 there were the Freedom Summer Projects in Mississippi which also caught the attention of the nation.

During the civil rights movement, the black press found itself confronted with far different situations than it had ever faced before. In addition to contending with familiar outside forces still threatening

91

the survival of Negroes, it had to struggle with divided support from those within the race who wanted the quest for civil rights to be passive, as was the successful Montgomery, Alabama, bus boycott in 1955, which had been headed by the Reverend Martin Luther King, Jr. At the same time, others did not want to be passive in their quest for civil rights, but wanted to reciprocate violence when confronted with violence. A third group consisted of those who thought that the first two groups were pursuing civil rights in a manner which would clearly alienate members of the Caucasian race, particularly since those groups had been unquestionably infiltrated by Communists. Their desires were to assume the role of accommodation in the expectation that members of the Caucasian race would eventually give first class citizenship to members of the Negro race.

If that wasn't enough, there were those youths who were able to take the initiative away from "the elders" or veterans of the Negro race, whom they believed to be moving too slowly in their quest for equal civil rights. Those youths felt that a name change from *Negro* to *black* was also appropriate since it was a name *chosen* to be used by members of the race. At any rate, the simplicity of reporting events within the Negro race as editors had done during other eras obviously would not exist for the black press during this period.

A controversy even within that controversial name-change effort, for example, occurred over how the new name was to be used: *black*, with a small "b," comparable to the term *white* as used by members of the Caucasian race, or *Black* with a capital letter, thus eliminating the term *Negro* entirely. Unfortunately, those people, white and black, who had fought for so many years to bring some dignity to the name *Negro* had no say in whether a name change was even necessary. In fact, some black people even in today's society still cringe when being referred to as *black*, a term which at one time, particularly during the early years of their generation, was used as an insult. Some still refer to themselves as *colored*. It is interesting, to say the least and considering the number of name changes Negro members have had to endure, that no name change has ever been placed before the race at large for a vote in the history of the United States.

Then there were those editors who "knew their place" in society, though it was inconsistent with their readers' viewpoint, who had to make hard decisions concerning their editorial philosophy. Accommodation was still seen by those editors as the proper and best way for blacks to survive and assimilate in an orderly way into American society. In their news presentation, they walked a very thin line, trying to accommodate those officials and others concerned with maintaining the status quo and those faithful readers expecting the press to come out slugging away at its adversaries.

The goals of the civil rights movement centered around the notion that whatever one citizen of the United States had in the form of civil rights also belonged to another and another and another without regards to race or color or nationality or socioeconomic status or gender or geographical location or political status. There were to be *no* exceptions. Saying that some people in some regions of the United States were not ready for the assimilation of blacks into American society was tantamount to believing that the portion of society that still clung to the idea that some citizens of this country belonged to an inferior class of citizenship had the right to say when that class of people should be elevated to a higher status.

Another goal of the movement was to impress upon the people that some federal laws of the land were not being properly enforced. (The government was already aware of this.) If laws of the land have been enacted for all the people of the land by a majority vote and representation of everyone has been afforded—even when he or she did not agree to that representation—then all states and all peoples, even those wishing for an exception, must abide by those laws without the benefit of supersession. Even when history has recorded a region's distaste for a given law there has been no excuse for ignoring that law. And any embellishments to those same laws should be consistent with the intent of that law instead of attempting to circumvent it.

The civil rights movement adopted five areas of proposed change:

(1) Equal voting rights in every section
(2) Equal access to places of public accommodation
(3) Equal opportunity in employment
(4) Equal and unsegregated education
(5) Equal opportunity to make a home anywhere within one's means[2]

During the middle part of the cold war era in 1954, the battle lines for the overall tone of the civil rights movement, particularly in the South, began to be established. More specifically, Mississippi became the target of attention for civil rights demonstrations when white officials there decided to use legislation and other forces, when they became necessary, to maintain their status quo. They were determined that if a ruling came, one that called for the integration of all schools, it would not be obeyed by the people in that state. Mississippi's lawmakers, feeling far less optimistic about their position than in the past, therefore began preparations for their public schools to continue with the "separate but equal" practice in use by the South since 1896. What they had in mind was to attempt to reduce the disparities between education for blacks and whites under a "school equalization program" which they had enacted in 1953. The separate but equal policies already being practiced by the state would not change, but officials hoped that their *effort* to equalize race facilities might convince the federal government not to intervene.[3]

The Mississippi legislators also established a Legal Educational Advisory Committee to "promote the best interests of both races." That committee was to serve as a planning agency to resist unacceptable federal rulings. The mere planning of programs, however, was not the only responsibility of the committee. It also was required to obtain sanctions of state plans from the black communities in the state—against their wishes, if necessary—plans which were not necessarily in the best interest of blacks, but which were considered by lawmakers to be best for that race of people. The committee had little difficulty in gaining legislative approval of a plan which called for "an amendment to the state constitution permitting the legislature to abolish public education, as a 'last resort'" if federal rulings did not go as hoped. The committee failed, however, to obtain approval of its plans from black Mississippians.[4]

It should be pointed out that in Mississippi voting by the general populace or the state's legislative body lay entirely in the hands of the white citizens of the state. The fact that Mississippi had one of the largest populations of voting-age blacks in the country did not mean that those voting-age blacks were registered to vote. The almost exclusive power of the white vote had been obtained through an "understanding clause" passed in 1890. The idea of the clause on the surface was to place the vote in the hands of those who could read and write and interpret the state's constitution. The would-be voter was also required to give a reasonable interpretation of the constitution when it was read to him or her. However, the registrars or election officials, who were always white, had the unchallenged power to decide if the answer given by an applicant was reasonable .

In 1890 the political power structure of the state was in the hands of the democratic party, which favored the clause, but the Republicans had been able to gather almost enough votes to block passage. Just one more vote for either side would decide the fate of that clause. By coincidence, there was still one vote not yet counted, the deciding vote oddly enough, and it was in the hands of Isaiah T. Montgomery, a black Mississippi delegate. Instead of voting against the clause, which could have stopped, at least for the time being, the attempt to block blacks from voting, he voted in favor of it, thereby locking out much of the black population in Mississippi from the right to vote for approximately 70 years. Ever since that clause was passed, white citizens in Mississippi have had a voting majority and have been able to maintain political power in most counties in the state.[5]

Despite all their preparations in anticipation of bad news, Mississippi officials in 1954 were still astounded when the *Brown v. Board of Education of Topeka, Kansas,* decision by the U.S. Supreme Court barred the de jure segregation of students by race, a ruling which stated that separate schools were inherently unequal.[6] Governor Hugh Lawson White said that Mississippians were "shocked and stunned" and that the state was "never going to have integration in its schools." James O. Eastland, a U.S. senator from Mississippi, said, "the South would not abide by, nor obey, this legislative decision by a political court." And the state's Speaker of the House, Walter Sillers, stated that such a ruling would serve only to push the state "out of the public education business."[7]

There were two more maneuvers Mississippi officials would make to solidify their efforts to obstruct steps being made by the federal government to integrate the races in the state. A Citizen's Council was formed in July 1954. Its membership consisted of militant segregationists, approximately 80,000, who were "legislators, judges, mayors, physicians, lawyers, planters, industrialists, and bankers."[8] A State Sovereignty Commission, established in 1956 "to perform any acts deemed necessary to protect the sovereignty of the state and her sister states from the encroachment of the federal government and to resist the usurpation of rights and powers reserved to the states" was also formed. That commission, headed by the governor and other high-ranking state officials, was also created to "protect the people of the state from subversive influences." The commission was far more secretive about what it would do than the Citizen's Council.[9] Mississippi had now established its defenses. Through the use of state laws and power groups designed to keep things the way they were,

Mississippi was ready to circumvent any unwelcome federal laws and to survive.[10]

All that the state of Mississippi could do now, with its defenses set and ready for attacks from invading forces, was to wait for what it was certain was coming. But as it turned out, North Carolina, rather than Mississippi, was the scene where the civil rights movement began.

The civil rights movement started on February 1, 1960, in Greensboro when four students from North Carolina A&T College were refused service at an F. W. Woolworth department store lunch counter.[11] Upset by that refusal to serve them because they were black, the four students sat at the counter and remained in the store until it closed.[12] Through that simple strategy an idea was born.

The next day, after receiving essential advice from the Greensboro National Association for the Advancement of Colored People (NAACP) chairman, Dr. George Simkins, a veteran civil rights advocate,[13] the four students, Joseph McNeill, Ezell Blair, Jr., David Richmond, and Franklin McCain, along with other students from the college, returned to the lunch counter at the store and sat down during the rush hour. Again they were ignored. Forty-five students appeared in protest the following day. The demonstration was a necessity, the students declared, and they would continue the sit-in at that store until Negroes were served.[14] On the third day, a number of other students from nearby colleges, North Carolina A&T and Bennett College, and three white students from the Women's College of the University of North Carolina had joined the protest.[15] The sit-in movement that was only in its infancy had breached the color line.

It was not by chance that those four men entered the Woolworth store and asked for service. The event had been carefully planned the night before. Joseph McNeill, one of the principal participants in the sit-in protest, had recently returned to the college from his home outside of Greensboro. When he had gone into the Greyhound bus terminal for something to eat, he had been turned away, not because he did not have the money or because he was slovenly dressed or was rude but because he was black. It was when he returned to the A&T campus that he and three colleagues planned to stage an event by asking for a meal at the Woolworth lunch counter.[16]

Some scholars and historians give the starting date for the civil rights movement as December 5, 1955, as far back as the Montgomery bus boycott. But some believe that the date should be May 17, 1954, the date of the *Brown v. Board of Education of Topeka, Kansas,* U.S.

Supreme Court decision.[17] In Oklahoma City, the youth council carried out a successful sit-in-strike in August 1958.[18] That date, too, has
been mentioned as the start of the movement. February 1, 1960, the
date of the Greensboro sit-in, seems to be the most appropriate choice
for the beginning date because the chain of events from that time is
continuous, from 1960 through 1976. This sit-in involved all of the
national civil rights organizations and the media, it had world-wide
attention, including the attention of presidents of the United States,
and its ramifications were felt in almost every state or city within the
country.

At Shaw University in Raleigh, North Carolina, on April 15,
1960, young students, black and white, from all over the country met
to form the Student Nonviolent Coordinating Committee (SNCC).[19]
The students were encouraged by the Reverend Martin Luther King,
Jr., the head of the Southern Christian Leadership Conference
(SCLC); Ella Baker, an executive secretary for SCLS; and James
Farmer, the head of the Congress of Racial Equality (CORE), to form
this organization. Marion Barry was the first chairperson. SNCC's
"Statement of Purpose" was "We affirm the philosophical or religious
ideal of nonviolence as the foundation of our purpose, the presupposition of our faith, and the manner of our action." The sit-ins came
under the control of SNCC in April 1960.[20]

The *Pittsburgh Courier* began its coverage of the sit-ins on February 13. Coverage of the inconsequential beginning of the sit-ins at
that time appeared on page four, among other race-interest stories. One
of the protest leaders was quoted as saying, "Many of our adults have
been complacent and fearful and it is time for someone to wake up and
change the situation and we decided to start here."[21]

In its next issue, the *Courier* reported on the front page: "Student
Protest Marches Spread." Since the *Courier* carried no actual stories on
the front page (just photographs and headlines summoning readers to
venture inside), the story itself appeared on page three. That headline
stated that student protest had spread to South Carolina. During the
first days of protest at Greensboro, no violence or disruptions had been
reported. By the time the movement had reached South Carolina, however, bomb threats, physical violence, and debris-throwing had greeted
protesters. Even so, the protest movement continued to spread to Virginia, Tennessee, and Florida.[22]

During the month of March, the *Courier* carried a story showing
that 200 students had been jailed and that Thurgood Marshall might

be the defense attorney for those students. It also published an article from the sit-in leaders suggesting what the public could do to help. The *Courier* had started a fund-raising drive called Dollars for Dignity. The newspaper also contained a report on how two fair-skinned black women had posed as Caucasians and ate at a segregated lunch counter at a fashionable store in Charlotte, North Carolina. After sitting around for more than an hour, they got up and returned to their other darker-skinned friends while making certain that the manager saw what had happened. Another story described why the original protest students started the sit-in in the first place: they "just got tired of talking about it and decided to do something."[23]

The March 12 issue of the *Courier* was almost filled with various sit-in updates: the violence in Alabama, how the news of the sit-in was being reported overseas, and a host of other reports. The paper also contained an "Action on Sit-Down Front" column with updates from various cities such as Birmingham, Alabama; Chattanooga, Tennessee; Tampa, Florida; and Columbia, South Carolina. Fresh news items appeared, such as reports about the movement spreading to Northern cities and a message from the attorney general urging Negroes to "renew their efforts to register [to vote] in areas where they have been barred."[24] Also included was a listing of commandments "For Southern Students, White and Colored, Fighting Segregation" on how to act when confronted by disrupters:

> Don't strike back or curse back if abused
> Don't laugh out
> Don't hold conversations with floor workers
> Don't leave your seats until your leader has given you
>   instructions to do so
> Don't block entrances to the stores and aisles
> Show yourself friendly and courteous at all times
> Sit straight and always face the counter
> Report all serious incidents to your leader
> Refer all information to your leader in a polite manner
> Remember the teachings of Jesus Christ, Mohandes [sic] K.
>   Gandhi and Martin Luther King, Jr.
> Remember love and non-violence and may God bless each
>   of you[25]

Because many of the demonstrations had occurred in stores of the Woolworth chain, the *Courier* telephoned and spoke with the store's district managers, North and South, for their response to the sit-ins. C. M. Purdy, the Atlanta district manager, said: "We're guest of any community where we do business. As a good neighbor, the local store must abide by local customs."[26]

In Illinois, the *Chicago Defender* had changed its format to a daily newspaper. It also had changed its name to the Chicago *Daily Defender* in 1956, changed its size from standard to tabloid, and carried only large headlines, sub-heads, and photographs, sometimes with captions, on its front page, which was similar to that of the *Courier*. The large letters which splashed across the front page on February 16 announced that a sit-down protest had begun and was spreading to Virginia. The story noted that in an effort to avoid protesters some lunch counters had been converted to sales counters, some managers had removed lunch counter stools, and many students had been arrested on trespassing charges when they demonstrated.[27] The *Defender* also carried an open letter drafted by the students to State Attorney General Malcolm Seawell:

> For the past few days, you have strongly advocated the use of the "No Trespass Law" on the part of the business establishments involved... . It is highly evident that you have failed to realized the vast devastating effect this could have on the State of North Carolina and other states located here in the South.
>
> It is a known fact that industry tends to shy away from those areas where there is racial unrest.
>
> We would like to make it clear ... that this mass movement was not begun to bring economic suffering to the state but to bring to the realization to the citizens of North Carolina that the Negroes, who are also citizens, can no longer remain quiet and complacent and continue to accept such gross injustice from those who desire to see no change in old customs and traditions solely for the purpose of personal gain or because of the warped ideas which have been instilled in the minds of many responsible citizens.[28]

Since becoming a daily, the *Defender* was able to carry some coverage of the sit-ins in each issue, and it carried more routine matters as well. In the feature section of the March 3 issue, it carried a synopsis of the sit-in movement from its beginning. It further indicated that another installment would be printed the next day.[29]

John Dungee took a brief pause in his attacks on local civil rights violators in Oklahoma to pick up the news of the sit-in demonstrations. The *Black Dispatch* of February 26 mentioned briefly that the Reverend King had made a tour of a Woolworth store in Durham,

North Carolina.[30] Dungee further indicated that the demonstrations had spread to 11 cities. Then in the style almost typical of his predecessor, Roscoe Dunjee, he fired off an editorial pointing out what he saw to be a glaring contradiction in what some managers were allowing. Apparently, at some department stores where there had been demonstrations, blacks had been given the right to stand at lunch counters to eat but could not sit. Dungee further chastised management at stores such as Kress, Walgreens, and Woolworth for their use of double standards with regards to the treatment of blacks. They were greeted with open arms in the North yet were rudely rejected by that same chain of stores in the South. Dungee also noted that in most of the North Carolina cities where the demonstrations were underway, the public schools had been desegregated without violence. As he saw it, the big contradiction in that regard was educating the masses and then restricting the locations where they could eat a hot dog when shopping at five and dime stores.[31]

Dungee also introduced a "City-by-city round-up on Sit-Down Strikes" page. Most of the reporting involved strikes in cities which were located in the South, but there were some reports from Lorain, Ohio; New York City, Boston, and Ithaca, New York. And in Princeton, New Jersey, a group of "anti-sit-downers" who were members of the Colonial Club of Princeton University, clashed with sit-downer sympathizers in front of a Woolworth store. The anti-sitdowners were said to be "made up primarily of southern white students and carrying 'Faubus for President' placards."[32]

Within the state of Oklahoma, meanwhile, civil rights developments were more positive than many of those making the national news. The *Black Dispatch* of April 1, 1960, reported that the governor, J. Howard Edmondson, said he did not approve of discrimination against any group and had appointed a Human Relations Committee "to work out eating problems." The governor further said, "In our desire to develop Oklahoma industrially, it is important that we have harmony and lack of strife between different groups."

In response to the governor's action, the mass demonstration which had been planned by the NAACP was called off. Instead, an official of the civil rights group said: "We are calling on all citizens of good will to join with us at the south steps of the State Capitol ... for the purpose of commending the Governor for his public stand and to demonstrate good faith in compliance with Governor Edmondson's request."[33]

By the April 15 issue, the governor's Human Relations Committee had begun work to end the lunch-counter problems. The committee consisted of Negro and white members who had traveled across the state for the first meeting, and they asked the public for patience and cooperation.[34]

The sit-in movement was viewed by Percy Greene in Mississippi as a step backwards for the race. In fact, when Greene reported on the sit-in movement for the first time on March 5, he said that such a protest by students "darkened" the nation's race picture.[35] He further suggested in an editorial:

> Without attempting to distinguish between the inspired agitations of political groups, whether foreign or domestic, and the legitimate aims and aspirations of American Negroes, having already suffered again and again the slings and arrows of those who are espouse the popular opinion of the moment, we again hear risks their darts and spears by expressing our unalterable opposition to the sit protest; to CORE, the Committee on Racial Equality, by whom they are reported to have been instigated, and to the National Association for the Advancement of Colored People, who according to newspaper reports, have given them its endorsement.[36]

Greene made no attempt to disguise his feelings and ended the editorial by suggesting:

> Despite urgings of the militant and impatient, despite the exuberance of our youths as now being exhibited in the sit-down protests, we say that the future hopes of Negroes for enjoying freedom and citizenship in accordance with the high American ideals, without resorting to revolutionary techniques can best await the inevitable actions of the Congress of the United States, and the development of American public opinion.[37]

But those youths were not waiting for Congress to act. They continued to push for integration of lunch counters, beaches, and libraries.[38] As a result, the barrage of demonstrations began to bring about some positive results within 30 days after its start. And even though most of the demonstrations were centered primarily in the South, many other students began demonstrations in the North to show their support.[39]

The *Courier* reported that a restaurant in Xenia, Ohio, for instance, was dropping its race policy after encountering a student demonstration and after visits by government and college officials.[40] In that same regard, in Austin, Corpus Christi, Dallas, San Antonio, and Galveston, Texas; Winston-Salem and Salisbury, North Carolina;

Nashville, Tennessee[41]; and Tallahassee, Florida, students were being served at lunch counters without incident.[42] Store managers, when asked about the ease with which they had acquiesced to recommendations made by community groups for the ending of lunch-counter segregation, said they "merely were waiting for someone to take the lead, but no one had bothered to check their attitudes."[43]

In previous eras the black press had played the role of leader or "champions of the black people." With the start of the sit-ins, however, the black press responded to the civil rights movement only by reporting the news made by the people, editorializing occasionally about the progress of social or moral events, and taking an occasional jab at governments when legislation was not enacted or properly enforced in a timely manner. With the widespread coverage by commercial television, which provided its viewers with a feel for what was going on at a certain location—an erroneous "feel" in many instances— and the attention of the much larger white print press to black affairs, the black press had been relegated from being a "fighting press" to being a conveyor of black community news. Editorial philosophies were still pertinent, survival was still necessary, but the black people had taken it upon themselves to do what was necessary to bring about changes in the civil rights arena. Only a few editors still attempted to sway social policy. In spite of their determined efforts, they did not have the editorial clout to sway public opinion.

While most black editors seemed to be content with their position of conveyor of black community news, some attempted to convince the restless black youths to temper their actions with patience. In fact, the *Atlanta Daily World* in April thought the sit-in movement should be taken from the streets and placed in the courtrooms:

> The city (Biloxi) today is like a dynamite keg which could be ignited and explode into a general race riot at any minute. We believe that all of this could have been prevented by wiser and more mature approaches to solve Biloxi's problem of removing discrimination in the use of recreational facilities.
> The legal test could have been arranged that would have placed the problem in the laps of the federal courts.
> There is no need for any group to take matters into their own hands in misguided attempts to gain civil rights, when these rights have already been guaranteed by the Constitution of the United States and interpreted and confirmed by the courts.
> Such attempts merely create general ill-will and set up situations that endanger the lives and property of everyone. ... The answer is to

be found at the conference table, ballot box, and in the courts of law; to do otherwise is unsound, dangerous, and impractical.[44]

Several other editors seemed almost reluctant to even mention civil rights demonstrations in their news presentations, even when those events happened right in their state or their city. Three of those editors were based in Mississippi.

Jesse Gillespie, publisher of the *Mid-South Informer* (Walls), believed that the situation for blacks had not improved "because we have not taken advantage of the opportunities that have been opened to us."[45]

Over in New Albany, J. W. Jones, editor of the *Community Citizen*, saw the 1961 Freedom Riders as doing all that they could to disturb the peace. He believed that blacks should "continue to support the status quo."[46]

The third editor, of course, was Percy Greene of the *Advocate*. Even though many of the more violent reportable disturbances occurred within Jackson, Greene did not enter into the spirit of news reporting during that period, as did the *Defender*, the *Dispatch*, or the *Courier*.

The direction of Greene and his *Advocate* was just about certain. He was as accommodating as many believed him to be and now made very little effort to disguise it. Look inward for black race progress, Greene continued to stress, and while looking inward,[47] keep in mind that friendly relations with white people were still the Mississippi Negro's greatest asset.[48] He also printed stories, articles, cartoons, and suggestions on how blacks needed to improve and what they should do to improve. Greene also emphasized the negative side of the demonstrations and made efforts to show that Mississippi was ideal for blacks if they knew where their place was in Mississippi's society.

It is interesting to note that when reading the *Advocate*, the reader must be patient and become accustomed to reading a small part of the story on the front page and then jumping to another page for its continuation. That is of course, the way in which newspapers are usually designed. When there are from six to ten stories on the front page, even if all of them continue on another page, that usually does not present a problem. But when a large number of stories are carried on the front page, the process can become tedious. On the front page of the March 5, 1960, issue of the *Advocate*, for example, Greene inserted three decks of skyline headlines, the masthead, one photograph with caption, two mug shots, one with a caption, and 24 short and varied news reports. Each story had from two to five decks of headline. Of the 24 reports, 20 of them jumped to another page, but the only point of reference that led to that same story once you reached the indicated page was simply the page number from where the story began and one or two key words taken from the original headline that might lead one to the correct story. The top skyline headline on the *Advocate*'s front page on March 5, 1960, referred to the sit-down movement: "SITDOWN PROTEST DARKENS U.S. RACE PICTURE." Since Greene did not necessarily cover his stories with the skyline headline or use some other type of lead-in from the skyline headline to the story, readers had to search for the story, for it could be anywhere on the page. Of the 24 story headlines, "Fear More Sitdown Riots in Nashville," "NEGRO STUDENTS MARCH ON ALABAMA STATE CAPITOL," and "HARLEM PICKETS WOOLWORTH IN SUPPORT SOUTHERN STUDENTS" could apply to that day's headline, even though the word *sit-down* is not in the second or third report. Each story, however, did cover the sit-down protest.

Editor and publisher Percy Greene had settled down with a posture which he could not and, perhaps, would not change. And when his mind was made up, he rarely changed it. For instance, Greene could not shake the idea that many of the demonstrations being carried out across the country were plots of the Communist party "to use the Negro issue in the United States to further its worldwide schemes."[49] He had made similar observations during the 1940s but had received little or no notice.

During the civil rights movement, Greene was not the only person who thought the Communists might be backing the black organizations and their activities. The *Defender* had covered a television program, "College News Conference," which was aired on ABC-TV, Sunday, June 12, 1960, in which former President Harry S Truman had made an appearance. He was defending his earlier statement that the sit-ins were backed by the Communists. The *Defender* on June 13 carried a headline story "'COMMIES PUSH SIT-IN'—TRUMAN":

> Former president Harry S. Truman said Sunday he was convinced that southern Negroes involved in sit-in demonstrations were being exploited by communists.
>
> The students instituting the sit-downs ... were "not necessarily Communist themselves.
>
> "I say it was pushed on by a communist program. That's the kind of program they like to put on. That's exactly what happened."[50]

As if that wasn't bad enough, the *Defender* carried on the following day another headline story: "HST Tells Viewers, 'Niggers Must Grow Up.'" Evidently, Truman was alleged to have said that he knew some [Negroes] who had not grown up and that the "issue of segregation ... had been settled in his home state of Missouri and in Kentucky." It should come as no surprise to say that a barrage of protest calls flooded the *Defender*'s office and the television station after the broadcast.[51]

On June 15, ABC-TV issued a reply to the outraged blacks and suggested that Truman's "Missouri Drawl Was Misunderstood." The officials said Monday after playing the tape of the program several times that they decided Truman said "Nigras—Missouri drawl fashion." They also denied he said Negroes "will have to grow up."[52]

The following Monday, the *Defender* carried yet another story concerning the incident. This time Mrs. Eleanor Roosevelt said that Truman was wrong:

> The former first lady said she disliked "differing with Mr. Truman because I'm very fond of him.
> "But in his assertion which he has made a number of times that the sit-ins in the South among the students are entirely communist-inspired, I think he really does not watch very carefully the way in which Communists ordinarily organize."[53]

"Irrepressible Mr. Truman," the *Defender*'s editorial headline read the next day.

> Former President Harry S. Truman—the rustic "sage" of Independence, Mo., is feverishly engaged in the not-so-difficult task of self-demolition. Lately, like a grasshopper, he has been hopping up and down the country making speeches and predictions, attacking the members of his own political party, spouting off his myopic views on world affairs, giving "history lessons" to inquisitive college students, posing as the only unquestioned liberal of the Democratic party, giving off-the-cuff misinterpretation of the objectives and meaning of the Sit-in demonstrations, America's only grass roots students' movement for human equality, and assuming more and more the role of a buffoon.
> So unpopular has he become with Negroes that mere mention of his name brings prolonged boos. This occurred last Friday, when speaking to a meeting of the local unit of the NAACP, Thurgood Marshall ... referred to Mr. Truman's observation that the Sit-in demonstrations in Dixie were led by Communists.
> Truman could be the most venerated elder statesman who has ever left the White House. He participated in one of the most important phases of world history—the concluding period of the Second

World War—the era that ushered in the atomic bomb that fell on Hiroshima and Nagasaki.... He had, proverbially, the world in a jug and the stopper in his hand. But he fumbled the act and does not know yet that he is a dead duck.[54]

It was on June 28, 1960, that the *Courier* reported on the Truman incident. In its report: "Truman Said 'Nigras' Not 'N-----s,' Claim TV Chiefs." According to the same report, Marion Barry, leader of SNCC, said, "Social change, by nature, creates tension and irresponsible charges of Communist influence, rather than diminish these tensions and incorrectly credit the Communists with movements towards social justice." Former New York governor Averell Harriman also disagreed with Truman's "attitude on the situation."

Four years later J. Edgar Hoover, the director of the FBI, still hadn't altered his belief from World War II that Communists were behind the outspoken efforts of blacks. Greene printed that report and gave it a skyline headline, "HOOVER SEES REDS PUSHING NEGRO MOVEMENT," and a front-page story: "We know that Communist influence does exist in the Negro movement and it is this influence which is vitally important. It can be the means through which large masses are caused to lose perspective on the issues involved and, without realizing it, succumb to the party's propaganda lures."[55]

Greene then issued an editorial call, "Wake-Up Mississippi Negro Wake-Up":

> From up in Washington this week the word came that J. Edgar Hoover, the director of the Federal Bureau of Investigation (FBI), now says without equivocation, that Communist influence is behind the Negro movement, a fact that we have been trying to convey to responsible white and Negro leaders in the state since back in the early 1940's when we began to observe, at first hand, how these influences were being used to seduce some of the ablest Negroes in the United State; that led to, and was responsible for the NAACP Civil Rights Mobilization in Washington in 1950, and saw that organization change its policy and begin demanding integration, instead of equality under the law for Negroes in this country, which by any standard of judgment has already proven to be the greatest mistake, under the cunning of Communist influence attributed to Negro leaders, in the entire history of the Negro struggle in this country.[56]

In addition to thinking that the sit-ins were plots of the Communist party, Greene also thought that the black press should change its editorial philosophy and its pursuits. He believed that fighting for causes such as the equalization of civil rights for all races and integration should no longer be pursued by black editors. Instead, according to Greene, black editors should have more concern for the views of advertisers, whom he thought the black press had to get along with and satisfy "if it expects to gather in any substantial advertising revenue."[57]

When reviewing the fighting spirit for which Greene has been given credit or the militancy for which he showed during World War II, it should not be argued whether such fighting spirit and militancy were apparent. In fact he did show good spirit in his editorial pursuits, but it was in support of the United States as a nation against Japan and Germany. On the other hand, he showed no overt support for the unification of the black press or any of its pursuits and stayed away from reporting those violent events against blacks that made national headlines on television and in many newspapers, particularly when those events occurred within Mississippi.

When blacks in Mississippi during the 1950s began to speak out against racism in the state and to ask for the state to enforce the recent U.S. Supreme Court school desegregation law, Greene, rather than showing support or even maintaining an objective viewpoint, displayed exactly how he felt:

> The time has come, in the light of recent developments affecting race relations in Mississippi for every Negro preacher and teacher, and for Negro citizens of responsibility in all walks of life everywhere in Mississippi who feel a true sense of responsibility for the welfare of the Negro masses in the state to challenge the ridicule and criticism of the new would be leaders of the race in the state by proclaiming anew and at every opportunity that a friendly relations with the white people is still the greatest asset of the Mississippi Negro.[58]

Greene's disagreement with Medgar Evers, a race leader in Mississippi, about how school desegregation in that state should be handled apparently had had a very profound effect. He had come to dislike Evers, a local citizen who had insisted on moving too fast, as far as Greene was concerned, for changes in Mississippi. Because Evers did not think that the advice of "wait and see" was appropriate because segregation in schools was illegal in the state, the fire was lit under Greene and the water was just beginning to boil. Much to the chagrin of Greene, blacks in Mississippi had not listened to him.

Efforts to discredit Evers and to pointing out what he saw as flaws in his leadership soon became evident in Greene's reporting. Unfortunately for Greene, other organizations bent on erasing segregation from schools and other social locations also began to surface around the country. One of those organizations was the SCLC. Greene found that he now had another black leader with which he had to contend, and the man looking at Greene's domain as a desegregation testing site was the Reverend Martin Luther King, Jr. As far as Greene was concerned, there clearly was no role for the Reverend King in the affairs of Mississippi blacks:

> Now comes the Reverend Martin Luther King, magnified far beyond his wisdom, foresight, experience, and dability following the Montgomery Bus Boycott, which, all things considered, has brought nothing but grief and hardship to an increasing number of Negroes in Montgomery and the rest of Alabama, talking about if Negroes in this country are not soon given full rights as American citizens, they will forsake democracy and turn to some other ideology.
> Since it is the only other ideology challenging democracy in the world it appears obvious and logical to assume that the other ideology illuded too by Rev. King is communism.[59]

The *Courier* apparently had already noticed Greene's accommodating editorial philosophy and his open conflict with Evers. Prattis sent Trezzvant Anderson, a *Courier* reporter, to Mississippi to interview the *Advocate*'s editor. Anderson reported that Greene and the NAACP had had a strong difference of opinion after the May 17, 1954, U.S. Supreme Court school decision.[60] Evers and the NAACP had wanted to push for an all-out effort to integrate the Mississippi schools. Greene, with little reservation, believed that such a pursuit "would lead to bitterness between the races and do more harm than good." Greene was also convinced that the NAACP "started a war on me and my paper" that caused his circulation to be reduced significantly.[61]

So deep was Greene's division with the NAACP that he continued to attack Evers, who was the State Secretary of the Mississippi Conference of Branches of the NAACP, by reporting what he saw as the negative side of Evers' appointment. In one editorial he pointed out that Evers' attempts "to organize a Mau Mau Society among the Negroes of the state" was an alliance which "deferred" and "delayed" the full freedom and emancipation of the American Negro. While suggesting that Evers had "marked himself as both a fanatic and a fool," Greene called for new race leadership.[62] He believed that with the absence of black leaders sensitive to the accommodating policies of Booker T. Washington and with the unfortunate adaptation of W.E.B. DuBois's school of thought, "one may readily understand why relations between Negro and white Americans had dropped to the lowest level in years." He went on to add that "the majority of Negroes and their white allies who engaged in agitating and stirring up racial unrest, have been or are now engaged in advancing the cause of communism."[63] Greene, in an overt show of support for accommodation, then ran a full-page ad with a large photograph of Booker T. Washington and his Atlanta Exposition address of September 18, 1895.[64]

In that interview with Anderson of the *Courier*, Greene did not mention whether he was on the payroll of the State Sovereignty Commission as many black Mississippian's believed. However, Erle Johnston, author of *I Rolled with Ross, A Political Portrait of Former Governor Ross Barnett, 1980* and *Mississippi's Defiant Years, 1953-1973*, pointed out exactly how the State Sovereignty Commission had financed Greene's convention trips "because he was an offsetting voice to those who could find only racial wrongs in Mississippi." Johnston also suggested to one of Greene's associates "that he promote a special edition of the *Advocate* with photos and stories about industries and their black employees. I told him I knew the industries would be glad to pay for space and the Sovereignty Commission would spend $250 for an advertisement in the edition and spend an additional $250 for 500 copies we could use ourselves in our public relations effort."[65]

As for the sit-in movement, it was moving right along. One noteworthy demonstration took place in Atlanta, Georgia, where students from Clark, Morris Brown, Spelman, and Morehouse colleges took out a full-page ad in the *Atlanta Constitution* on March 9:

> Today's youth will not sit by submissively, while being denied all the rights, privileges and joys of life. We want to state clearly and unequivocally that we cannot tolerate, in a nation professing democracy and among people professing Christianity, the discriminatory conditions under which the Negro is living today in Atlanta, Georgia. ... We do not intend to wait placidly for those rights which are already legally and morally ours to be meted out to us one at a time.[66]

On April 15 the *Courier* carried comments made by the mayor of Atlanta:

> The mayor of Atlanta has issued a stern warning that his city will not tolerate interference with peaceful school and lunch-counter desegregation next fall.
> In a stinging attack on Southern "rabble rousers" who "Robert E. Lee wouldn't even spit on," 71-year old Mayor William B. Hartsfield declared that racists causing trouble in Atlanta "are going to get their heads knocked together."[67]

As the sit-ins progressed, results were becoming more favorable as racial barriers began to fall and lunch counters opened their businesses to all citizens. The next major problem for the South would be the Freedom Riders. Whether he liked it or not, Greene was now in the center of the arena where the demonstrators were heading—Jackson, Mississippi.

The Freedom Riders began their movement in 1961.[68] CORE, a civil rights organization which began in 1942, loaded two buses with black and white passengers in Washington, D.C., for a trip through the South to test desegregation practices by passive resistance.[69] The idea was not to break the law—segregation on interstate travel was already illegal—but to compel the federal government to enforce the law in Southern states.[70]

James Farmer, who had become the national director of CORE on February 1, 1961, had already received complaints from black travelers who were disturbed about their treatment on interstate travels throughout the South: "When they sat on a front seat of an interstate bus or tried to use waiting room facilities other than those consigned to blacks, they were beaten, ejected, or arrested. 'What do decisions of the United States Supreme Court mean' they asked."[71]

In fact, a Supreme Court decision in 1946 "outlawed segregation on interstate bus and train travel and in 1960 had extended the ban to terminals as well."[72]

On his first day in office, Farmer and his staff pondered their next step for the organization. A journey into the deep South, from Washington, D.C., through Virginia, North and South Carolina, Georgia, Alabama, Mississippi, and Louisiana, to test interstate bus seating and interstate bus facilities was suggested. They would leave on May 4, and they hoped to arrive in New Orleans on May 17. Everyone was in agreement, so plans were made. Farmer then wrote letters to the Kennedy administration and to all of the officials involved with interstate travel and gave them notice of the group's itinerary and intent. To test Southern facilities and see if they were following federal law, CORE would use black and white passengers, blacks to sit in white sections, when appropriate, and whites to sit in black sections, when appropriate. They expected to encounter violence along the route. After recruiting seven black and six white volunteers for the trip, they trained them in Washington D.C., where the trip was to begin. On the departure date, half of the group took a bus from the Trailways bus terminal and the remainder rode a Greyhound bus.[73]

As expected, the Trailways passengers experienced little or no difficulty through Virginia and North Carolina. In Rock Hill, South Carolina, they experienced their first violence. John Lewis, a black student from the Tennessee Bible Institute in Nashville, and Albert Bigelow, who had been a navy captain during World War II, got off the bus in Rock Hill. As they started towards the "white waiting room" door, they were told by a group of men to get to the other side (the "for colored" side) of the terminal. Lewis told the group that he had a right to go on either side, according to the Supreme Court decision in the Boynton case. As he attempted to walk past the group, he was struck and knocked down. Bigelow stepped in and tried to intervene but was also struck down.[74] The two black men were then beaten and left unconscious on the sidewalk. After a few minutes had passed, a Rock Hill police official came up and asked if they wanted to press charges against the attackers. No charges were filed.[75]

The trip through Georgia to Atlanta was about the same as the one through North Carolina. The officials knew the riders were coming but did not enforce Georgia's segregated laws, even though their signs depicting segregated facilities were still apparent.[76]

On May 14, just before leaving Atlanta, the group called their host in Birmingham to find out what the situation was there. They were advised that the Ku Klux Klan had been preparing a reception for them for a full week.[77] With that disturbing bit of news, Birmingham was on their minds as they left Atlanta:

> When the first bus had crossed the Alabama state line, a half dozen young white toughs had boarded with their weapons in sight— pieces of chain, brass knuckles, blackjacks, and pistols. Shortly thereafter, the driver pulled the vehicle off the road and brought it to a stop.... The thugs then got up and began beating the black Freedom Riders who were seated in the front.[78]

When the white Freedom Riders tried to intervene, they were also beaten. One man was "hit with an uppercut that lifted him off the floor and deposited him unconscious in the aisle." The second man "was knocked down and repeatedly kicked in the head."[79]

James A. Peck, the rider who had been knocked unconscious on the bus, said that when they finally arrived in Birmingham, they saw a group of men with pipes standing around the terminal. They saw no policemen. When they reached the terminal and got off the bus, they were attacked by the mob.[80]

The *Black Dispatch* reported the Birmingham violence and some reactions on May 26, "YOUNG FREEDOM RIDERS SET SOUTHERNERS AFIRE." The story contained calls for FBI probes and Department of Justice action and told of editorials which condemned the violence. In a related story, reactions from Alabama officials were also carried. Democratic representative George Huddleson, Jr., said,

> Their sole purpose in trespassing upon the South and its well established and understood customs ... was to create a deplorable and disturbing situation.
> The Negro and white riders had made it clear they were not seeking good will and racial understanding but had set out to violate the laws if Alabama instead.[81]

Alabama Governor John Patterson called the Freedom Riders "agitators" and "rabble rousers." He added that "the citizens of the state are so enraged I cannot guarantee protection for this bunch of rabble rousers."[82]

In a story carried by the *Pittsburgh Courier* on June 3 concerning the beatings at Birmingham, Patterson is quoted as saying, "We have always upheld law and order in Alabama and we intend to keep on doing so."[83]

The Birmingham police commissioner, Eugene "Bull" Connor, earlier had stated "he would never use his authority to enforce integration laws 'even if passed by God.'" He further stated that "these out of town meddlers were going to cause bloodshed if they kept meddling in the South's business."[84]

By this time, the second vehicle carrying the Freedom Riders, the Greyhound bus, had left Georgia, crossed into Alabama, and arrived at the Anniston bus terminal:

> There was a mob of white men standing there at the bus terminal. The members of the mob had their weapons—pistols, guns, blackjacks, clubs, chains, knives—all in plain evidence. The Freedom Riders made a decision on the spot that discretion was the better part of valor in this case, and that they were not going to test the terminal facilities at Anniston.[85]

The bus driver tried to leave the terminal but was stopped by members of the mob as they pounded on the vehicle and jabbed and slashed the tires with sharp objects. When the bus was finally allowed to proceed, members of the mob jumped into cars and trucks and started following the Freedom Riders. On the outskirts of Anniston, the slashed and punctured tires finally went flat, disabling the bus.

The mob pulled up, surrounded the bus, held the door closed so that no one could get out, smashed a window, and threw a firebomb into the vehicle. Fortunately, as one newspaper reported, "The riders managed to escape the bus before it was totally engulfed in flames."[86] Although uniformed policemen were at the scene throughout the entire ordeal, they did not interfere until the Freedom Riders had managed to force open the emergency door and were trying to leave the vehicle. One of the policemen then fired his gun into the air, and the mob dispersed.[87]

On May 16 the Chicago *Daily Defender* ran pictures of the mob blocking the terminal in Anniston, the burned-out hulk of the bus with passengers milling about, a picture of James Peck being attacked by the mob, and a picture of Peck after he had been treated for his injuries.[88] It also ran an editorial on the following day condemning the Alabama mobs for their brutality and the Alabama law enforcement authorities for their apathy:

> It would be idle to ask, how can such gory scenes take place in a supposedly civilized country? It is equally futile to argue the point with Southern racists who are bereft of the capacity to understand the harm their brutal acts inflict upon America's soul and reputation.
>
> What is still more revolting is the posture of indifference of the local authorities under whose very eyes the disgraceful drama was enacted. Here you have police officers sworn to uphold the law, to keep peace and order, yet they chose the role of disinterested, impassive spectators while peaceful men were being assaulted and slammed almost to death. Some of the victims may die from injuries sustained at the hands of the Alabama hoodlums.[89]

The initial Freedom Riders who had begun the bus trip were older veteran members from CORE who had been badly beaten, battered, bruised, hospitalized, or laid up and were not physically fit for any more violent abuse. Members of the Nashville SNCC had been following CORE's progress and, with permission, stepped in with their young, student-age members. SNCC, SCLC, and CORE leaders decided to continue the freedom rides despite the violence and other pressures to discontinue.[90] The new riders were sent to Birmingham to continue the trip as replacements.[91] Upon their arrival in the city however, they were arrested by the Birmingham police and thrown in jail. After a one-night stint, they were released but were escorted by policemen back to the Tennessee line. Undaunted by their arrest and escort from Alabama, the SNCC members made their way back to Birmingham, where they eventually boarded a bus for the next leg of the trip.[92]

With another racially mixed group of Freedom Riders on board, the trip was continued; this time the destination was Montgomery. There was, however, a welcome and comforting change on that leg of the trip. The Justice Department had sent two high-ranking officials to Alabama in an attempt to avoid a continuation of the violence which had occurred in Birmingham. John Seigenthaler, Robert Kennedy's administrative assistant, and John Doar had arranged for some kind of police protection which was to stay with the bus while it was in the state of Alabama.[93] The city police would patrol the area while the bus was in cities, and the state police would patrol while the bus was between cities. Also there would be an airplane flying overhead to warn authorities of problems at overpasses and bridges and any other possible surprises. Such was the case throughout most of the trip from Birmingham until the bus neared the city of Montgomery. Then their highly visible patrol car escort, sixteen cars in the front and sixteen behind the bus, even the airplane flying overhead, without warning pulled away from the bus route and were not seen again. As at the beginning of the trip, the bus and its travelers were on their own. The riders reached Montgomery and traveled through the streets without any difficulty. As the vehicle entered the terminal, however, the passengers noticed that the facility was empty of people and was suspiciously quiet. Since there didn't seem to be any overt reason for them not to do so, the passengers started to depart from the bus. As they emerged, mobs of people suddenly came out from their hiding places, "men, women, children, with baseball bats, clubs, chains," and rushed the bus and the riders trying to get out. With so many people trying to get out of the bus while so many converged on them with swinging tools, the violence spilled out into the street, where two of the traveling women had fled to escape the beatings. But the mob was not particular. All of the disembarking riders were beaten, Freedom Riders and women and other passengers who just happened to be on the bus, in the wrong place at the wrong time; even John Seigenthaler was beaten. He had just driven up in his car, saw what was going on, and rushed in and tried to rescue the women who had fled into the street:

> My colleague John Doar and I ... arrived at the Federal Building in Montgomery, which adjoins the bus station, about two or three minutes after the bus. As John got out of the car, you could hear the shouts and screams from across the way. Doar ran for the Federal Building and I drove up the street and quickly through an alleyway on the back side of the bus station. As I came down the far side, I saw

this almost anthill of activity. The Freedom Riders emerging from the bus were being mauled. It looked like two, three hundred people just all over them. As I drove along, I saw two young women who were Freedom Riders being pummeled to one side. A woman was walking behind one of them. She had a purse on a strap and she was beating the young woman over the head, and a young skinny blond teenager in a T-shirt was sort of dancing backward in front of her [the Freedom Rider], punching the young woman in the face. Instinctively, I just bumped up onto the sidewalk, blew the horn, jumped out of the car, came around, grabbed the one who was being hit, and took her back to the car. The other young woman got into the backseat and I opened the door, pushed this young woman … and said 'Get in the car.' And she said, 'Mister, this is not your fight. I'm nonviolent. Don't get hurt because of me.' I almost got away with it. If she had gotten into the car, I think I could have gotten away, but that moment of hesitation gave the mob a chance to collect their wits. One guy grabbed me by the arm, wheeled me around, and said, "What the hell are you doing?" And I said, "Get back, I'm a federal man."

I woke up half an hour later. Beside me was a police officer. "Well, you've had some trouble, buddy. Is there anybody I can call for you?" I had enough wits about me to say, "Yes, if you would call Mr. Kennedy." "Which Kennedy would that be?" he replied. And I said, "Either the president or the attorney general," and he said, "Who the hell are you, buddy?" And I said, "Well, I'm the attorney general's administrative assistant." He said, "We've got to get you to a hospital."[94]

The mob members had asked no questions and had taken no names. They beat Siegenthaler because he was trying to help the Freedom Riders.[95]

On June 3 the *Pittsburgh Courier* carried an analysis of what might come as a result of the beatings of Seigenthaler and the two women: *Was Beating of Whites Racists' Big Mistake?*

When they beat John Seigenthaler into unconsciousness and left him lying in the street after he had tried to aid a white girl the mob was after, that did it.

The thugs overstepped their bounds when the Freedom Riders came in and brought with them two young white girls students [*sic*] from Nashville.

Normally, beatings and floggings of Negroes in Alabama is a routine thing, generally going unpunished with no arrests, if any, being made.[96]

President Kennedy had been trying to avoid a confrontation between a state and the federal government, but with the beating of one of the administration's top aides, he now felt justified in sending in the federal marshals.[97] The Justice Department reacted quickly: "Robert Kennedy felt betrayed by Governor Patterson's failure to protect the riders. Kennedy ordered six hundred federal marshals into Maxwell Air Force Base at Montgomery. The next day, May 21, groups of angry whites continued to roam the streets of Montgomery."[98]

"Send 200 More Marshals to Ala." the headline of the May 23 *Defender* read. Robert Kennedy said there "would be 600 there by Monday night and another 100 will be sent today."[99] Evidently, some of the citizens of Alabama resented the "interference" by the federal government in their state. The grand wizard of the Alabama Ku Klux Klans, Bobby Shelton, said: "Due to the suppression of the people of the South by the Federal government ... preparations were made for a merger of the bodies under a single banner. This action was necessary due to the concerted efforts on the part of Negro and other integration groups to force upon the people of Alabama and the South an untenable situation."[100]

Shelton said that "he joined C. F. Craig, grand dragon of the United Klans of America, other KKK officials and segregationists in an all-night discussion meeting at Rome, Ga., Saturday." Shelton further stated that "while the klan did not condone violence, it would 'take all measures necessary' to preserve Alabama customs."[101]

On its June 2 editorial page, the *Black Dispatch* carried some comments from other newspapers around the South and the remainder of the country on Alabama's treatment of the Freedom Riders. The *Atlanta Constitution* reported:

> This group passed through Georgia without incident. There are mobs in Georgia. Their instincts warned them that trespasses against the law would be punished here. They were right. For this all Georgians—and we mean all Georgians—can be eternally grateful.[102]

From the *Nashville Tennessean* came:

> For this is the kind of thing which makes the United States an object of criticism throughout the world and undermines its reputation for equal law enforcement. It proves that the Ku Klux Klan mentality still prevails in some areas, and in this respect it should serve as an alert to good citizens.[103]

The Louisville *Courier Journal* used sarcasm to deliver its editorial:

> Oh, well. One cannot expect too much. In race relations, Alabama makes haste slowly. From outright lynching to lead pipe beatings is

progress of a sort. On the other hand, the switch from cross-burning to bus-burning represents a degree of backsliding. But that's the way it goes. One cant ask for miracles. After all, these things take time, and it has been only 100 years since the Civil War, not quite that long since the 14th Amendment to the Constitution, and only seven since the U.S. Supreme Court called for school desegregation with all deliberate speed.[104]

One of the reporters for the *Courier* during the civil rights movement was the Reverend Fred Shuttlesworth. Since he was right at the heart of much of the violence in Alabama, he had firsthand information in many of his reports. On June 3 the headline for one of his stories read: "Cool Off? ... For What? 'The Mob Must Not Win.'" The Reverend Shuttlesworth was reporting that Attorney General Kennedy had asked for a cooling-off period with a suspension of the freedom rides: "If we are willing to go to jail, stay in jail, keep on riding, have our brains bashed out by mobsters, then it would appear unwise, un-American to ask us ... being right ... to call off our quest for freedom."[105]

The Urban League, usually not so active when it came to altering social policies, said that Robert Kennedy's remarks calling for a cooling-off period had been unfortunate. Henry Steeger, president of the Urban League, went on to say, "This is no time for the nation to compromise with freedom."[106]

Regardless of which civil rights situation was taking place at the time, the *Jackson Advocate* did not alter its response. As far as the Freedom Riders were concerned, it did not find anything favorable to report.

> Those who have been observant of development in American and World history during the past two decades will find it easy to recognize the fact that the come lately groups such as CORE and the Southern Christian nonviolent resistance organizations have not contributed a single original thought or idea to the field of race relations in the South nor in the rest of the country. Every movement and technique endorsed and promoted by these groups being foreign and communist importations.[107]

The *Atlanta Daily World*, which previously called for taking the sit-ins away from the streets and taking the lunch counter matter to the courts, still thought that was the correct way to address civil rights issues. The editorial staff evidently had not changed their minds as the Freedom Riders traveled through the South:

An interracial group called CORE came into the South last week. They were to travel from Washington to New Orleans testing the segregation practices. Everyone knows what happened now as a result of this planned test. The persons responsible for the violence were wrong and should be dealt with by the police and the courts. Even though the riders knew that they might be attacked, this action could have triggered a reaction that could have caused many innocent persons to suffer physical injury.

Calm, quiet, intelligent approaches are the best way to solve complex problems of this sort. Fanatical emotionalism on the one part, only beget fanatical extremism as a reaction.

The courts have decided the issue of interstate transportation and use of facilities. Dramatizing the lag between the legal rights and the social fact, it seems to us, only gives the communist adversary additional propaganda weapons to use in furthering their cause of capturing the undecided area of the world.[108]

The *Daily World* was started in 1928, at the beginning of the Great Depression era, when the economic situation was dismal. It has had a history of trying to be objective in its editorial philosophy, even when it hurts. Objectivity is necessary to avoid making enemies. The newspaper was located in the heart of the South, in the Confederate South, in a state where segregation was a way of life and in a city where businesses were primarily white. It was also a business, a business which depended on circulation to obtain advertising. Staff members were totally aware that without their faithful readers, the advertisers would soon look to other sources. Even less palatable for the *Daily World* was the need for advertisers on a daily basis, rather than a weekly basis as in the case of the *Jackson Advocate*. By writing that editorial, was the editor protecting the paper's advertising revenue in an effort to survive?

Nevertheless, in Alabama the *Birmingham World*, a part of the *Daily World*'s chain, did not denounce the Freedom Riders, even when they were receiving some of their most vicious beatings. Instead, the newspaper remained cautiously silent regarding the trip through the South. While it was true that William Monroe Trotter with his Boston *Guardian* attacked those of his race who did not verbally support the cause of Negroes by saying, "Silence is tantamount to being virtually an accomplice in the treasonable act,"[109] silence was in this instance at least understandable. But when the riders were jailed and placed "in protective custody," those same riders who had stayed within the guidelines of the laws of the United States, had not injured anyone, and were the receivers of the violence, the *Birmingham World* remained silent no longer: "In Birmingham a few days ago, some freedom travelers were placed in jail for protective custody. If this were truly protective custody, why not take them to a hotel, why treat them as law breakers? Mob leaders were not arrested. Why were they not arrested for the protection of the good community?"[110]

What made that editorial so special? What was it about that editorial that made the *Atlanta Daily World* deviate from its editorial philosophy and print it in its newspaper on May 23?[111] Whatever the reason, it was printed in the Atlanta newspaper, but it did not have an Atlanta dateline.

As for the bus trip from Montgomery to Jackson, martial law had been declared. Six Alabama National Guardsmen rode in the vehicle with fixed bayonets; U.S. marshals patrolled all along the highways, and helicopters flew overhead. There were also police cars patrolling up and down the highway and all other types of law enforcement personnel could be seen just about everywhere.[112]

As the Freedom Riders approached the Alabama-Mississippi state line, it became increasingly clear that testing Mississippi's defiance of the law was particularly meaningful to their leaders because Mississippi was a state "where so many of their constituents have been jailed and are now serving time." When learning that the Freedom Riders were determined to test whether the interstate laws would be obeyed, Mississippi's governor said, "they [Mississippi's law enforcement] have plenty of room in the jails." Reverend Wyatt Tee Walker, executive director of the SCLC, responded to that comment by saying, "We'll fill them up."[113]

At the Alabama-Mississippi state line, the bus pulled over to the shoulder of the highway, and the driver and guardsmen departed the vehicle. Then, another group of guardsmen and a new driver entered. Also entering the bus was the Alabama director of public safety, who whispered a message to the reporters who had been traveling with the riders. All but one of the reporters then left the vehicle. It seemed that word had been received by the director that once the bus entered Mississippi, it would be "ambushed and destroyed." With that disconcerting bit of news, the bus with its new crew continued its trip, crossed the state line, and entered Mississippi. Mississippi guardsmen were standing on both sides of the road, rifles pointing away from the bus and towards the trees lining the highway. The trip continued without incident. When the bus reached the Jackson terminal, all of the Freedom Riders were escorted off and arrested. Eventually they were sent to the state prison:

Robert Kennedy had struck a deal with James O. Eastland of
Mississippi, chairman of the Senate Judiciary Committee. The U.S.
attorney general had agreed not to enforce the Supreme Court decisions desegregating interstate travel. Mississippi authorities, in turn,
had guaranteed there would be no violence.

The certainty of a jail sentence did not stop the Freedom Riders. By summer's end, 328 had been arrested in Jackson. More than
half were black. One quarter were female. Most were college students
and from the South. Most served time in the state penitentiary.[114]

Although the Freedom Riders had intended to disregard the Mississippi laws regarding segregation and interstate travel intentionally,
they did not expect to receive any help from the federal government
or the Mississippi authorities in the manner which it came:

National Guardsmen aboard the bus got off first. Newsmen followed. Then the "freedom riders" stepped down.

A sign in the bus terminal said the Negro area was closed. The
nine Negro men filed into the men's rest room reserved for "white
only" and were arrested—seven minutes after arrival.

The one white man and the two Negro girls with the group also
were arrested. They were ordered into a black police wagon and rushed
to city jail where they were held in lieu of $500 bond each on charges
of inciting a riot.[115]

The *Defender* had a report four days later which stated that the
Freedom Riders had been hijacked in Jackson. The judge at the trial
said the riders were traveling through the South "for the avowed purpose of inflaming public opinion." They were given $200 fines and 60-
day prison terms, which they chose to serve. During the trial, however, the Freedom Rider's attorney, Wiley Brandon, a Pine Bluff,
Arkansas, "veteran of the legal battle of the Little Rock nine," raised
the "planned arrest" question to the first witness for the defense. The
Reverend James Lawson from Tennessee

testified that the bus on which he was a passenger bypassed Meridian, Miss. a scheduled stop, and the military official in charge of the
vehicle refused to permit passengers to get off and relieve themselves.

The witness also testified that upon arrival at the bus terminal in
Jackson the "Freedom Riders" were "funneled" into the waiting room
labeled "white" and arrested.[116]

The *Defender* also followed up those stories with an editorial:

Just as we were applauding Attorney General Robert F. Kennedy
for his forthright stand and definitive action in the Freedom Riders'
encounter with the blood thirsty mobs in Alabama, he reverses his

position and tosses the whole fat in the burning pile of Southern race prejudice.

What we had expected from the Justice Department was a warning to the Governor of Mississippi that any violations of the riders' constitutional rights will be met with prompt Federal action.

But to ask for an indeterminate cooling off period in so vital an issue as freedom of choice and movement strikes us as being a timid plea for suspension of human rights.[117]

On another front, the *Courier* reported two interesting stories in July of 1961. One concerned what the Georgia governor had said about the law in his state:

Georgia rabid segregationist Gov. S. Ernest Vandiver has publicly vowed to maintain law and order in the state capitol when public school integration begins here in four previously all-white high schools.

In a statement that amazed most Negroes in the state, Governor Vandiver acknowledged that the Federal court order telling Atlanta to integrate is the law "like it or not."

Vandiver said he didn't believe in integration, but "unless the state of Georgia wants to secede from the United States and fire on Fort McPherson out here, we'll have to obey that court order."[118]

The second story concerned what former president Harry Truman and Governor Nelson Rockefeller had to say about the Freedom Riders during a taped radio broadcast:

Former President Harry S. Truman, during one of his morning "constitutionals," was approached by James Peck, a CORE "Freedom Rider" who was severely beaten by a Birmingham mob.

When Peck introduced himself as a "Freedom Rider from the North," Truman commented "Well, you'd better stay there."

After Peck made an impromptu speech asserting that "racial segregation—more than any other single factor—besmirches the U.S. in the world's eye and aids the Communists propaganda machine," the elder statesman snapped, "That's just what you're doing helping the Communists."

Meanwhile, New York's Governor Nelson Rockefeller ... praised the "Freedom Riders" and their efforts at integration in the South, calling them "an evidence of vitality in our system."[119]

When he addressed the U.S. Senate, Senator James Eastland expressed his belief that the Freedom Riders movement was Communist inspired: "The agent provocateurs who have descended upon the southern states, in the name of 'peace riders' were sent for the sole purpose of stirring up discord, strife and violence. "Peace riders" is a revered Communist term, an old Communist technique."[120]

The Baltimore *Afro-American*, on the other hand, was more concerned over the country's image as seen by other nations when the government continued to worry about politics and ignored or condoned the human suffering and countless instances of lawlessness which were rampant in the South:

> If the tragic events incident to the Freedom Riders have proved nothing else, they have shown that the Federal Government no longer can afford the luxury of permitting defiant state officials to disobey the law of the land.
> Too, it clearly illustrates the moral shame that ill becomes the world's leading democracy at the very moment we are trying to convince millions of persons to close their ears to the siren song of the Communists and follow us.[121]

And though the violence encountered made the front pages of the *Defender*, the *Courier*, the *Black Dispatch*, and just about every other news gathering media all over the world with large headlines and photos of the injured, the burned-out bus, and other descriptions of the violence in Alabama, Percy Greene with his *Advocate* continued to present the news in the way he thought best for his readers.

One of the favorite tools the media uses from time to time to emphasize a point or to make viewers aware of a local situation or civic problem is repetition. In some geographical areas, for example, the media emphasizes the necessity to abandon the unsafe structure of a mobile home during a tornado. Members of the reading and viewing public generally are sophisticated enough to take seriously the repetitious showing of mobile homes being blown over and destroyed during a tornado, and they may act accordingly when warranted.

Another tool the media sometimes uses to emphasize a point is omission. Unlike repetition, which is overt and up front, omission is a quiet tool, not readily apparent, but it is just as effective as repetition. The reading and viewing public might be sensitive and sophisticated enough to determine eventually what has been omitted, but it takes a far longer time to make that detection.

Omission was another tool that Greene used in an attempt to convince black Mississippians that the status quo was essential for the well-being of Negroes. Rarely did he carry any local news concerning violence between the races. Even when the Freedom Riders arrived in Jackson, Greene did not report their arrival or that at least 25 of the travelers had been jailed there on May 24. By contrast, the *Defender* not only carried the story but even provided the names of those who had been jailed.[122]

With so much news of the Freedom Riders on television, in other black newspapers, and in the white press, surely Greene must have realized that omission from his newspaper did not mean omission from the other media. The airwaves were inundated with news of the civil rights movement and a host of other movements going on at the same time. If Greene had a role to play, an agenda he had to follow, he was following the script quite well in that regard. Eventually, however, even he had to acknowledge what was going on and report the Freedom Riders' presence in Jackson.

Once again Greene did it in his own way. His May 27, 1961, issue, for instance, carried a skyline headline that read: "POWERFUL VOICE RAISED AGAINST BAPTIST SPLIT," which apparently was a far more important lead story as far as Greene was concerned than the Freedom Riders. Furthermore, Greene also carried two more headlines which did not acknowledge the Freedom Riders: "387 To Get Degrees From Jackson State College" and "AFRICAN DIPLOMAT SAINTS JUNIOR COLLEGE COMMENCEMENT SPEAKER." And though the front page of the *Advocate* did carry five reports about the Freedom Riders, each one failed to tell what the Freedom Riders were doing in Jackson or trying to accomplish. Instead, Greene told that the Freedom Riders planned to continue, that they had requested support from U.S. marshals, that a warning from the Jackson mayor had been issued, how the state of Mississippi was ready for them, and how their ride was causing problems for the Kennedy-Khrushchev meeting. There was no mention of the motive for the Freedom Riders' trip, the violence being encountered along the way, or why they were being jailed there in Jackson.

Meanwhile up at Oxford, Mississippi, James Meredith had attempted to transfer from Jackson State College, an all-Negro institution, to enroll at the University of Mississippi (Ole Miss) in 1961 but had been denied because "Jackson was not a member of the Southern Association of Secondary Schools and because he did not have letters of recommendation from five alumni of the university." The university returned his admission papers and room deposit fee. In May of that year, the NAACP Legal Defense and Educational Fund, a legal services organization which handled civil rights cases, filed suit on Meredith's behalf in U.S. District Court. The suit charged that Meredith had been denied admission "solely because of his race."[123]

On June 30 the *Jackson Advocate* carried a skyline headline which read: "MEREDITH WINS UNIVERSITY OF MISS. SUIT." It appeared that the U.S. Circuit Court of Appeals had ordered the university to accept Meredith's enrollment. The court said that Meredith had been "turned down solely because he is a Negro."[124]

That was a story with a Mississippi flavor, but it was not necessarily supportive of the state itself. Greene was quick to report the story, however, and gave it a very prominent place on his front page. On the surface, it would appear that he was eager to announce a civil rights victory. Yet on Greene's editorial page in that same issue, it was as if another person had surfaced and taken his place. In response to a report that the court's action was the first "'integration decision' aimed at the state of Mississippi," Greene was quick to fire off a rebuttal:

> We completely reject the idea that the action of the court is an "integration decision" aimed at the State of Mississippi. On the contrary we see the action of the court as furthering the opportunity of the state to give Negro students that equality of education, long promised and talked about, but never yet attained. We can conceive of nothing that is doing more to hold back the broad general progress of the state that the use of the cry "integration" to prevent every effort at Negro advancement.
>
> As regards the appeal to the United States Supreme Court, in a state where so many needs are going unmet because of the lack of sufficient money, there are far better uses to which the money necessary for such an appeal can be put to, instead of an appeal to a court which has already given every manifestation of its determination, as far as lies within its power, to use the judicial decree, as far as concerns segregation and discrimination because of race or color, allowing the law to bring about those changes not only in Mississippi, but throughout the nation, to meet the uncompromising challenge of world Communism.[125]

Was Greene walking the line here? First, the fact that he even reported the story, a story contrary to what state officials desired, suggested that he thought it was worthwhile to report. Education was important to him, equal education for everyone, but it need not be integrated. In exploring the second issue, giving the story such a position on the front page with such a prominent headline would suggest that he was glad about the decision and wanted others to see how well the state was doing, in an offhanded sort of way. The third point to be considered is that he chastised Meredith for wasting money, money which was used for his appeals, money which Greene said could have been used for far better things. It didn't seem important that the money used did not belong to the state, to Greene, or the Citizen's Council. Greene showed joy over the legal decision, but believed that the money used to obtain that legal decision should have been spent on other things. Fourth, it appeared that he didn't like the use of the word *integration*. In fact, it almost seemed that he was upset by its use. Was this an attempt to placate some of the eyes which were keeping watch over his editorial direction?

Two weeks later Greene reported that Meredith had lost his bid to enter Ole Miss during the summer semester.[126] It appeared therefore that Meredith would be registering at the university during the fall semester. In Greene's eye, was this revelation a plus for the state or another setback for the civil rights movement?

On September 10, 1962, ten days before the fall registration date, the U.S. Supreme Court "upheld Meredith's right to be admitted to Ole Miss."[127] The governor of Mississippi went on television and declared: "There is no case in history where the Caucasian race has survived social integration. The state will not drink from the cup of genocide." State officials then made two maneuvers reminiscent of the 1950s that were designed to impede Meredith's enrollment. Governor Barnett appointed himself as university registrar so he could block Meredith's entry to the university. The second maneuver was to establish a law that would allow officials to bar anyone entry to a state school who had been "convicted of a state crime and not pardoned." Meredith had not been convicted of a state crime, but according to Henry Hampton, a civil rights historian, "While he attempted to register at the campus in Oxford, Meredith was tried in absentia by a justice of the peace in Jackson and convicted of the crime of false voter registration."[128]

Burke Marshall, the Mississippi assistant attorney general who played a major role in the negotiations between the federal government and Governor Barnett, had very few kind words to say about the governor:

> Governor Barnett was intransigent and he was also stupid. He had a narrow political vision. He knew that Meredith was going to the University of Mississippi, he just didn't want it to be his fault. So that if you could give him a way of acting like a governor and performing a governor's duty and at the same time say, I couldn't help it, then Governor Barnett's very narrow, short-range, stupid political values and political goals would have been achieved. What we were

trying to do in the negotiations between President Kennedy and Governor Barnett was to try to give him an out of that sort.[129]

After the negotiations had been concluded, Meredith was flown in to the Ole Miss campus and secretly registered on September 30. To protect him while he was on campus, the federal government had 536 law enforcement personnel standing by. When white Mississippians heard that Meredith had been enrolled, a riot broke out. The federal marshals, overwhelmed by the mob, were under orders "not to shoot back." So while being fired upon with live rounds by several thousand members of the mob, the marshals could only fire back with tear gas. That drama continued throughout the night until the arrival of additional federal troops sent in by the president. The results of the confrontation: "Two people were dead.... Twenty-eight marshals had been shot and 160 injured."[130]

"Would the Justice Department ... ever have done it that way again?" John Doar, an attorney in the Justice Department who served as Meredith's escort during the confrontation, answered, "No, they wouldn't have." Doar went on to answer additional questions:

> Did the state of Mississippi have any justification for the way it behaved? Absolutely not, there was total lawlessness. The people that came up there to get into the riot, did they have any right to come up from halfway across Mississippi, or halfway across Alabama, to get into that thing? No. But I suppose that with power and authority you have to take the responsibility for doing it right, and I'm sure that everybody in the Justice Department believed that if you were going to be confronting something like this again you had to do it with a lot more force than two or three hundred marshals, and you couldn't depend on the state police force of Mississippi.[131]

William Simmons, a chief spokesperson and editor of the newspaper published by the Mississippi Citizen's Council, was at the office when the riot broke out. He said he kept abreast of the events through radio reports:

> There was a lot of excitement because rumors were flying that Governor Barnett would be arrested by United States marshals. Many people, probably several thousand, surrounded the governor's mansion in downtown Jackson and stood there. It was very orderly, not too excitable, but they stood there as a sort of human barrier, to protect the governor and to simply show solidarity with him in support for his position in trying to protect the integrity of the university.
> We thought the use of marshals was pretty bad. We viewed the whole episode as an attack on the authority of the state.[132]

Percy Greene published an editorial in the *Advocate* on October 13. Throughout the civil rights movement, his fixation over the possible return of the post-reconstruction period continued to surface:

> According to the historians and students of the south, the ill manners and intemperate conduct of Negroes, urged on by the carpetbaggers and other adventurers who had entered the south to exploit the Negro issue, largely for their own benefit without any sincere regard for the Negroes future, was largely responsible for the tragedy of the Post Reconstruction Era. The Era which saw the Hayes-Tilden Deal and the Un-written Compromise, which brought about the withdrawal of the Federal Troops from the south, took away all the gains that had been made by Negroes during the Reconstruction Era, and made possible the total disfranchisement of Negroes, made possible the one-party system of politics in the south, and put upon the Negroes all of the handicaps of segregation and discrimination....
>
> It is important for us, the Negro citizens of the state, in the light of the above brief sketch of southern and Negro history that we make sure that nothing in our conduct and manners, and in our attitude and relations with our white neighbors will contribute to another tragic era following the withdrawal of the troops and the end of the Meredith crisis at the University of Mississippi. To us this is the challenge of history.[133]

By the end of 1962, members of civil rights organizations had encountered a barrage of violence across the country in their efforts to gain equalization of citizenship for black Americans. Violence had been encountered with the sit-ins, the Freedom Riders, a parade in Albany, Georgia, and attempts to register and vote at different locations around the country. Many civil rights members had been fined or jailed or both. Many were still serving prison terms as 1963 arrived. Interestingly enough, many were serving jail terms for violating unconstitutional state laws, while others were serving jail terms for taking a bus trip from the Mississippi-Alabama state line to the city of Jackson without a rest stop. On their faces and on other parts of their bodies, many still showed deep scars. There were scars in their eyes as well. Some were still in hospitals going through slow mending processes, and some have injuries so severe that they will be wheelchair-bound for the rest of their lives.[134] But despite the wide ranges of violence that had occurred, the injuries, the deaths, the scars inflicted had been one-sided, that is, the demonstrators had been peaceful, they had endured what had been dished out to them.

With the arrival of the new year, which started with some

menacing warnings from the state of Alabama, civil rights leaders found some new faces on the political scene. It didn't take long for them to find out who Alabama's new governor was, and they learned of the new methods of brutality that had been planned for them by the governor in concert with Birmingham's old commissioner of public safety, Bull Connor.

"I draw the line in the dust and toss the gauntlet before the feet of tyranny ... and I say segregation now ... segregation tomorrow ... segregation forever." Those were the words spoken by Governor George C. Wallace at his inauguration ceremony. Changes also had been made in the governmental structure at Birmingham. The commission form of government had recently been replaced by the position of mayor. Bull Connor, who previously had had a very strong power base as one of three commissioners in the city, now faced a power struggle within the city's new political structure that could decide whether his commissioner's position would be eliminated. The blow for Connor was twofold. First, he had seemingly lost his position of commissioner, a position he thought he held with the blessings of the people of Birmingham. Next, after sensing that his former position of commissioner was in jeopardy, he ran for the office of mayor, but lost that election to Albert C. Boutwell, a former member of the Citizen's Council but still a bit more moderate than Connor.[135] Reverend Shuttlesworth, who did not agree with that assessment, remarked that "The only difference between Bull Connor and Albert Boutwell was that Bull was a bellowing bull and Boutwell might have been a crying, trembling bull."[136] Because Bull Connor was no longer a commissioner and was on the losing end of the mayoral race, Birmingham businessmen thought they had finally gotten rid of the highly visible police officer. But they hadn't seen the last of Bull Connor.

In charge of the planned civil rights activities at Birmingham was the Reverend Shuttlesworth, minister of Bethel Baptist Church and one of the founders of the Alabama Christian Movement for Human Rights (ACMHR). He realized that the Birmingham-based civil rights organization had had successes within the city's boundaries, but it had had losses there as well. What the black people needed in Birmingham was a resounding victory of some kind to break the string of successes against the black people and the grip the segregationists had clamped over the city. The best man for the job, Shuttlewworth thought, was the Reverend King with the SCLC. Many others thought, however, that King had not done very well with his demonstrations in Albany and might not be right for the job. But Shuttlesworth believed that Birmingham could be the success King needed to get back on the winning track. At the same time, the ACMHR also needed a lift in Birmingham, "to confront segregation in a massively nonviolent way, with our bodies and our souls."[137]

In the opinion of Wyatt Tee Walker, the executive director of the SCLC, Birmingham was a good target for the next civil rights demonstration because it was "the biggest and baddest city of the South."[138] The Ku Klux Klan had gotten so bold with its activities there that members used no robes or hoods to conceal their identities. They burned crosses with little or no need for discretion because law enforcement officials did not seem concerned about their actions when blacks were the victims. The use of explosives in the Negro district was on the rise but no one had gone to trial for the bombings.[139] Shuttlesworth had been chain-whipped by angry whites not for breaking the law but for trying to enroll his child in a white grammar school, and his home had been bombed twice thereafter. In addition, those blacks who were bold enough to protest what was going on or those who introduced legislation or civil rights recommendations usually had to face a "three-tiered" civil process designed to guarantee that blacks come out on the losing end: "If the Klan didn't stop you, the police would stop you. And if the police didn't, the courts would."[140]

Walker's theory when he began planning for the Birmingham demonstration was to develop a "strong non-violent movement" with marches, sit-ins, and boycotts:

> I targeted three downtown stores. Since the Sixteenth Street Baptist Church was going to be our headquarters, I had it timed as to how long it took a youngster to walk down there, how long it would take an older person, how long it would take a middle-aged person, and I picked out what would be the best routes. Under some subterfuge I visited all three of these stores and counted the stools, the tables, the chairs ... and determined what the best method of ingress and egress was.[141]

For all the planning that went into the agenda for the demonstrations at Birmingham, the idea of demonstrations was not overwhelmingly embraced by black people. Those who wanted to hold things in abeyance believed that there had been new leadership in Birmingham, fresh political officials who had been recently voted into office and had not been given a chance to work at a peaceful solution to the race problem. Others, white and black, particularly those who

were members of the Birmingham reform movement, believed that
"progress could be made without forcing a racial confrontation."[142]
Meanwhile, neither of the three candidates who had run for mayor on
March 5 had won a majority of the vote. A runoff between Bull Connor and Albert Boutwell had been scheduled for April 2. The reform
movement had therefore asked King and the SCLC for more time to
solve some of the city's problems before activists resorted to demonstrations.[143]

Prior to the elections, it appeared on the surface that the city's
politicians could not or did not want to address the race problems in
the city, and since blacks were determined to demonstrate in an effort
to obtain desegregation of public facilities, the inevitable destruction
of the business industry was the price to pay for maintaining the status quo. It had been the business managers of the city, still recovering
from their bout with the violence during the Freedom Riders episodes
in 1961, who took political matters into their own hands. They formed
biracial committees and began a dialogue on city integration in an
effort to avoid further demonstrations, violence, and further national
embarrassment to the city. Since their recommendations, which had
to be submitted to the incumbent city leaders for approval, were
rejected, those business leaders "felt that their other only remaining
option in settling black demands without disrupting economic development objectives was to elect more conciliatory public officials."[144]

A.G. Gaston, a successful black motel owner in Birmingham, was
one of the businessmen who thought that King's presence was not
needed: "We didn't anticipate the need for Martin King at that time.
We had a fellow named Shuttlesworth that was raising sand around
here. Shuttlesworth was a leader. I got him out of jail many a time. He
was a brave young man. He was the one who led the organization that
brought King over here from Atlanta."[145]

Despite the recommendations by local business officials and by
the Kennedy administration to hold off the demonstrations, King and
the SCLC went ahead and started the sit-ins on April 3, 1963. Many
of the city's internal problems still had not been resolved. Most important, the officials who had been voted out of office had issued a challenge to the legality of the new political structure and refused to vacate
their offices. One of the old politicians still in place was Bull Connor,
whom the business leaders had worked so hard to oust. He was still
entrenched as the police boss.[146]

What the business leaders needed was time, but King and the

SCLC had delayed as long as they thought they should. There were two city governments—the old administration and the newly elected one—trying to function in office at the same time, a law suit had been filed by Bull Connor which the business men had to consider, and the Easter shopping season was at hand. On the other hand, members of the business sector were trying to enhance their businesses, not destroy them. Since they had not been successful at getting the Reverends King and Shuttlesworth to hold off on the demonstrations, the business leaders went to the courts and obtained an "injunction against further demonstrations," a step which could buy them some time. King refused to obey that injunction, however, and was jailed.[147]

Another call by Attorney General Kennedy for a cooling-off period and delay in the demonstrations did not escape the eyes of Percy Greene. His skyline headline read "Attorney General Kennedy Calls for Negro Cooling Off Period," but the accompanying story read "Negro Leaders Rejects Call of U.S. Attorney Gen. Kennedy." In the story, Greene pointed to King and Shuttlesworth as leaders who rejected Kennedy's call.[148] Greene's agenda for keeping up the attacks of negative news concerning the Reverend King was on schedule.

Meanwhile, the demonstrations in Birmingham continued throughout April and into May. At first, Connor, still at the helm of his old job, exercised some degree of restraint in handling the demonstrators. Eventually, however, he got tougher and released his dogs and turned high-pressure fire hoses on groups of school children who were being used in the marches.[149]

> As the children marched out of Sixteenth Street Baptist Church, Bull Connor arrested more than six hundred, ranging in age from six to eighteen. The next day, as another thousand children gathered at the church, an angry Connor called out the police canine units and ordered his firemen to rig high-pressure hoses. At one hundred pounds of pressure per square inch, the fire hoses were powerful enough to rip the bark off trees.[150]

It was bad enough for the police to use German shepherd dogs and high-pressure hoses on the demonstrators, but they were not careful about who was in their line of fire, demonstrators or onlookers. With such indiscriminate use of the fire hoses, tensions in on-lookers mounted higher than ever before.[151]

So horrified and distressed had the adult on-lookers become as they watched the black children being tossed about by the high pressure hoses that they just charged across the street, waded in, and began to attack the police with "guns and knives and bricks." It was the Reverend James Bevel, an SCLC organizer, who stepped to the police side of the confrontation and faced the angry brick-throwing mob to remind them that despite the violence they were witnessing and experiencing, they should respect the police. The Reverend Bevel afterwards said he was trying to avert a riot and was surprised at how quickly the people obeyed his "orders."[152]

The *Pittsburgh Courier* and the *Black Dispatch* carried reports on the reaction of Bull Conner when he learned that the Reverend Shuttlesworth had been injured by a high-pressure water stream from a fire hose:

> The ingrained hatred that Eugene "Bull" Connor, Birmingham's racist lame-duck police commissioner, harbors for the man who has defied him over the years, was expressed callously here last week when Rev. Fred Shuttlesworth was injured by a blast of water from a high pressure fire hose.
> Connor, informed that the minister had been taken away in an ambulance after the blast hurled him violently against the stone wall of the 16th Street Baptist church and had to be carried away in an ambulance said: "I wish they had carried him away in a hearse."[153]

Robert Kennedy, who had been trying to reach an understanding between the federal government and the state of Alabama on the need to maintain law and order and protect all citizens within that state, including those in pursuit of equal rights, held a 90-minute conference with Governor Wallace. A report in the *Courier* on May 4 suggested that Kennedy was less than satisfied when the conference was over and was reported to have said: "It's like being in a foreign country. There's no communication."[154]

Bull Connor, Alabama, Birmingham, and violence against Negroes had become synonymous since the Freedom Riders rode through the South. It was believed that the people of Alabama encouraged Connor's actions, spurred him on, and pushed him to act for them vicariously. It was also believed that other Southern states applauded his actions. The *Black Dispatch* ran comments from other Southern editors about the Birmingham commissioner. Within the state of Alabama, the *Birmingham News* wrote:

> Birmingham should appreciate the efficiency with which its Police Department has handled the demonstrations which have been going on here.
> Those who come to a city to direct such demonstrations feed on

disorder. They count on serious incidents to generate big, black headlines for them. Birmingham has had the good sense to disappoint them.

From Public Safety Commissioner Bull Connor and Police Chief Jamie Moore on down, the department has acted smoothly and calmly and with great determination to handle both potential white troublemakers and Negroes who have refused to obey lawful authority.[155]

Across the northern Alabama state line, the *Nashville Tennessean* wrote:

Mr. Connor, it seems, succeeded in depicting Mr. Boutwell as an integrationist and drove practically all of the city's 11,800 Negro voters into Mr. Boutwell's corner. The winner amassed a majority of 8,000 in a record vote of 51,000.

Mr. Connor thus can take major blame for his defeat because of the needless excess in frightening the Negroes in order to convince the whites of his towering bigotry.

Though the Negroes found no advocate of their cause in Mr. Boutwell, both races in Birmingham can be thankful they didn't put Mr. Connor in city hall.[156]

To the northwest, in Arkansas, the *Little Rock Gazette* stated:

Developments in Alabama on segregation issues offer reasons to hope that Alabama, even under a demagogue like Governor George Wallace, will not blindly follow the "Oxford example" in the showdown on school desegregation.

Eugene (Bull) Connor, a rampant segregationist and veteran city commissioner at Birmingham has been beaten decisively at the polls in a race for mayor. His conqueror is, by Alabama standards, a moderate. The mayor-elect is Albert Boutwell, a former lieutenant-governor who stood up for law and order in his mayoralty campaign. If a large Negro vote in Birmingham was influential in Mr. Connor's defeat, it only underscores once again that Negro voting is one of the keys to the Negro's attainment of his other rights under the law.

Birmingham is Alabama's largest city. The Connor defeat is only one of several signs pointing towards the possibility, at least, that Alabama will meet school desegregation, when it comes, without substantial public disorder and violence.[157]

Over in Georgia, the *Atlanta Constitution* wrote:

On Tuesday, the people of that great Alabama city spoke. In a runoff between Connor and the more temperate and progressive Albert Boutwell for the office of mayor in a new mayor-council system, Boutwell won by 8,000 votes in record balloting.

And no matter what the outcome of the commissioner's sour-grapes lawsuit, no matter how the Boutwell administration deals with the challenges it has accepted, the important turning point for Birmingham came Tuesday.

That was the day the people spoke.

They said no to any further management of their city by a man whose acts had linked its name with reaction and racial injustice.[158]

Throughout most of the violence in Birmingham, Greene was able to keep the Reverend King's name prominently displayed in the *Advocate*. "Rev. Martin L. King's Criticism of President Kennedy Result Of Grants [from] Rockefeller Foundation," was a story published on April 13 in which an Atlanta dentist charged that the SCLC had sold out to the Rockefeller Foundation. An editorial in that same issue called for new Negro leaders because the Rev. King "and his cohorts are not nearly as much interested in Negro civil rights as they would have most Negroes believe, but are playing both ends against the middle." The story "Martin Luther King Still in Jail After Pres. Kennedy Phone Call" appeared on April 20, and "SAY SOUTHERN CHRISTIAN LEADERSHIP CONFERENCE WILL ABANDON NON-VIOLENCE AND TURN TO REVOLUTION IN DRIVE FOR DESEGREGATION appeared on April 27, and "Martin Luther King Turns Deaf Ear to Billy Graham" appeared on May 11.

The state of Alabama was clearly having more than its share of violent and nefarious activities since the civil rights movement began. Greene was therefore able to divert his attention to other states for his major headlines, thus urging upon his readers the belief that everything was going well between the races within Mississippi. Unfortunately for Greene, while he concentrated primarily on events in other states, other states were concentrating on events in Mississippi.

One of those events was alluded to by the *Courier* in a 1961 report which revealed that "More Negroes Leave Miss. Than From Any Other State." The report went on to show that "the State of Mississippi continues [to be] the least liked, and probably worst state in the union for Negroes." In the ten-year period from 1950 to 1960, Mississippi lost 70,715 persons. The information for the story was obtained from the 1960 census by the U.S. Census Bureau. Arkansas was second on the least-liked list. It lost 37,852 blacks during the same period. The report also showed that although blacks faced the possibility of segregation in the South more than in the North, Florida increased its black population by 277,085, Texas went up by 209,667, and Louisiana's increase was 156,779.[159]

Aside from the Freedom Riders, an occasional shooting here and there when someone tried to register to vote, and other missing black persons infractions, the state of Mississippi had managed to keep a lower news-related profile than expected. In fact, Alabama and North Carolina—the latter only briefly—so far had taken the spotlight away from Mississippi. In March, however, Mississippi's violence began to accelerate and was not only noticed by the national media but gained international attention as well. On March 9, 1963, for example, the *Jackson Advocate* began its coverage of a story about the shooting of a black man, a shooting which caused Greene to splash a skyline headline across the top of his paper: "CIVIL RIGHTS GROUPS INVADE LEFLORE COUNTY." Although the report carries a dateline of Atlanta, Georgia, the shooting took place in Greenwood, Mississippi. That story was not written in the typical manner for which Greene had become so known:

> Four of the nation's leading Negro civil rights organizations have announced an immediate drive to make Leflore County Mississippi a testing ground in an all-out campaign to register every eligible Negro of the county in retaliation for the last Thursday, Feb. 28th shooting of James Travis, 20-year-old Voter Registration worker for the Student Non-Violent Coordinating Committee, in Greenwood, principal Leflore County City, and headquarters for the Committee's Negro Voter Registration work. [160]

The remainder of the story consisted of a statement made by Wiley A. Branton, a Negro lawyer and director of the Voter Education Project. He indicated that the latest shooting was another incident which pointed to the intolerable conditions under which voter registration people had to work and said that people of this land did not need to be "afraid to be free."[161] Branton stated:

> We are, therefore, announcing that the full resources of the agencies cooperating with us in the Voter Education Project will be immediately concentrated in Leflore County, Mississippi. Mr. Roy Wilkins of the National Association for the Advancement of Colored People, the Rev. Martin Luther King, Jr., of the Southern Christian Leadership Conference, Mr. James Forman of the Student Nonviolent Coordinating Committee, and Mr. James Farmer of the Congress of Racial Equality, have agreed with us today to put all necessary support at once into a concerted campaign to get every qualified Negro in Leflore County registered to vote, if he or she has any desire to do so.
> Our methods will, at all times be peaceable and lawful and will be conducted in the best traditions of American democracy.[162]

Once again Greene seemed to be walking the line in voicing disapproval of the violence against the efforts of black Mississippians to vote. The story originated in Atlanta, and the words spoken were from an NAACP official from that office. And though an accompanying editorial on the same subject was primarily in Greene's words, he conveyed his message through the use of quotes from the *Christian Science Monitor*. What made this all the more interesting was his frank admission that he agreed with the *Monitor's* editorial.[163]

One week later the *Advocate* again reported another shooting incident in Greenwood. Also once again the SNCC voter registrations workers were the targets for some "white men in a station wagon without license plates."[164]

Greenwood, a small inauspicious town that was nestled among the tall pine trees in southeast Leflore County, Mississippi, shared the media's attention with Birmingham. Greene no longer followed the philosophy of reporting the news as though everything was going well between the races in Mississippi. Perhaps it was the attempt to deny black Mississippians the right to vote or the fact that four of the major civil rights groups were now quartered just a few miles north of Jackson, but Greene was reporting about Greenwood flare-ups as they occurred, even though the undertone of a need for harmony in race relations was still present.

The week of March 30 was no exception as the number and seriousness of incidents escalated. A story titled "SNCC Drive Seen Worsening Race Relations In State" clearly placed the blame for the deteriorating conditions not on the people who would use any type of violence to disrupt voter registration and maintain the status quo but on members of SNCC, an outside group. In that story the *Advocate* reported that on Monday a fire had been set in the SNCC office. On Tuesday of that same week, someone fired a shotgun into the home of a black student attempting to enroll at the University of Mississippi. Greene also pointed out that James Farmer had "demanded" that President Kennedy send in federal troops to protect SNCC workers and those black's attempting to register there.[165] Mississippi had begun to occupy front-page positions in black newspapers almost weekly.

Reports within Mississippi noted that state officials had said that they had no objections to blacks registering to vote, they just didn't condone the demonstrations. The mayor of Greenwood, C. E. Sampson, stated: "We warned them we were not going to have it, but they're trying to incite a riot. We haven't stopped them from registering to vote but we aren't going to let them march two abreast down the street."[166]

The voter situation in Mississippi, though not as explosive as the Freedom Riders or the sit-ins or the Birmingham demonstrations, continued to draw not only state and national attention but international attention as well. Russian correspondents stationed in the United States had heard about the "political terror in the South." The correspondents wanted to visit Mississippi to see for themselves exactly how the black people were being treated there. The *Daily Defender* reported the story:

> Russian correspondents stationed in the United States are protesting because the U.S. State Department will not allow them to travel in the South to view the racial situation, the Soviet newspaper Tass revealed.
>
> Realizing that political terror in the South of the United States contradicts the attempts of American propaganda to present the United States as a country of equal opportunities and a model democracy, the American authorities do not permit Soviet correspondents to visit the Southern states.
>
> The U.S. State Department said it had canceled the travel privileges of two groups of Soviet correspondents going from New York to Mississippi because of the "tense situation" there.[167]

Approximately one year later, the *Jackson Advocate* carried a report stating that a Russian reporter did visit Mississippi and found that black people believed that white people "means something unkind." When the Russian, N. Kurdyumov, tried to photograph a black woman and child, he felt that they were afraid of him because he was white.[168]

For whatever reason he chose to become involved with the civil rights movement, comedian Dick Gregory went to Greenwood to try and encourage blacks there to register and vote. While waiting at one of the demonstration sites for some assistance to help him return to voter registration headquarters, Gregory was confronted by a policeman and told to move away from the Leflore County Courthouse. When Gregory refused to move, the policeman twisted Gregory's arm behind his back in a hammerlock and moved him across the street from the courthouse. In an editorial, Greene suggested that Gregory go back to Chicago and leave Mississippi's problems to Mississippians. Greene also had a brief story on the front page and a news photograph showing Gregory as he was being grabbed by the policeman.[169]

Up in Chicago, the *Daily Defender* also covered how the Greenwood police were treating Gregory. It suggested that he was manhandled.[170]

On the other hand, the *Black Dispatch* concentrated its reporting on Greene's reactions to Gregory:

> A Negro editor, once a national board member of the NAACP, declared last week that Comedian Dick Gregory could do more to help the cause of race relations by remaining in Chicago where some conditions are worse than those in Mississippi.
>
> Percy Greene, editor and publisher of the Jackson Advocate, said that Gregory's presence in Mississippi can have "only the direct effect on Negro voting and political participation."
>
> Greene, once regarded as a militant in the civil rights field in Mississippi, is now looked upon by Negro leaders as an "opportunist" who has found it financially expedient to echo white sentiment regarding Negro rights in the state.
>
> His paper has continuously condemned the NAACP and CORE as "outside agitators." Greene opposes law suits, sit-ins, marches and boycotts. He argues that while full Negro rights are desirable, it is best to await the willingness of the white man to hand them over. He is a strong advocate of "education" and a "change of heart" as necessary implements of social change.[171]

In another similar report, the *Black Dispatch* on May 31, 1963, reported, "2 Negro Editors Make 'Uncle Tom' Appeals to Negroes to Reject Civil Rights Drive." Greene again made the headlines. On that occasion he was quoted as saying "that Negroes face a 'long era of suffering' if they don't change current methods of demanding equality." Echoing Greene with the same rejection of demonstrations was Willie J. Miller, editor and publisher of the *Mississippi Enterprise*.[172] The *Enterprise* was also located in Jackson, was started about the same time as the *Advocate*, consisted of from six to eight pages, standard size, and followed the philosophies of Booker T. Washington.

While events were intensifying in Birmingham, Greene reported that the mayor of Greenwood, Charles E. Sampson, stated that "his administration is pleased that a vast majority of local Negroes took no part in 'The silly, noisy demonstrations that have lately disturbed the people of this city.'"[173] Yet two weeks later Greene carried a front-page story in which Hodding Carter, a Pulitzer Prize–winning Mississippi editor, called Jackson, Mississippi, the least civilized spot in the state. Carter went on to add: "The non-violent position taken by Negroes cannot be eternally maintained.... It takes an angel to get his face slapped a dozen times and not fight back."[174] Greene had straddled the fence on many occasions, trying to satisfy his benefactors and keep his readers happy, but in that instance, it was not a matter of fence straddling but of mixed signals.

The *Advocate* on June 1 reported that sit-ins had begun in Jackson and that violence had flared up as a result. Local leaders then met with city officials in a meeting at Jackson's city hall. Percy Greene also attended. While addressing the meeting, he advised the "Mayor and Commissioners to take some action now in removing some of the areas tension less he continue to play directly into the hands of the Communist who are using the southern racial tension and violence to further world communism."[175]

Also on June 1, the *Pittsburgh Courier* reported that "Sit-ins Now Have 'Green' Light—Jack." Jack Greenberg, director-counsel of the NAACP's Legal Defense Fund, said "the ruling culminated 'the legal manifestation of the most important social movements in America....'" He further stated that this ruling meant that "cities that make segregation a policy either by ordinance or official statements can not prosecute Negroes for attempting to use such facilities as lunch-counters in privately owned establishments." Greenberg also stated that "The recent Supreme Court ruling back the right of 'sit-ins' to seek service" and "has been heralded as the go-ahead sign for increased peaceful demonstrations throughout the nation."[176]

One week later the *Courier* reported that violence had occurred at a Jackson sit-in demonstration. It also reported that the NAACP's Roy Wilkins had been jailed in what he called a "Nazi State."[177]

The national sit-in movement which had begun in 1960 was now well into its third year. All over the country laws of desegregation were being contemplated or passed. One of the last bastions still clinging to the racial separation concept was Mississippi. It had made its preparations during the 1950s to avert or divert all efforts of integration, and so far it had made them work. Mississippi had drawn a line in the sand. Those who had dared to step across had been viciously repelled. To keep things the way they were, officials had said they would use force, if necessary. And as strange as it may sound, also assisting Mississippi's officials in keeping that line in the sand was Percy Greene with his *Jackson Advocate*.

Greene had been calling for "outsiders" to stay out of Mississippi and Mississippi's business. But officials from CORE, the SCLC, SNCC, and the NAACP, which had already stepped on Mississippi's line, were now ready to step across. They had feinted and probed and prodded Mississippi's defenses. They knew the going would be a harrowing experience to relate to others, if they survived. Now they were ready to challenge those who ignored changes. And whether state officials or Greene liked it or not, those groups were entering the state and focusing upon Mississippi's "business."

In 1962, Medgar Evers and Aaron Henry of the NAACP, Dave Dennis of CORE, and Bob Moses of SNCC reorganized the Council of Federated Organizations (COFO), a group of volunteers from all around the country who went to Mississippi to encourage blacks there to register and vote. Such a combined effort of the major civil rights groups, it was believed, would provide unity and boost the strength of COFO's influence in the state.[178]

Of all the voting-age blacks residing in Mississippi in 1962, only five percent were registered. In fact, in some of the 83 counties of the state, no blacks were registered at all. Unfortunately for the black people there, going down to the courthouse to register took more than just courage. The power of the vote belonged to white Mississippians, and they wanted it to stay that way. With the arrival of COFO in the state, more and more blacks were appearing at the courthouses and attempting to register. It was a slow and arduous process because so many blacks could not be convinced that voting was one of their rights as a citizen of the United States. Some also thought their one vote made no difference. And others believed the trouble they would encounter from making the effort was not worth it. As one Mississippi Delta woman stated: "I had never heard until 1962 that black people could register to vote…. I didn't know we had that right."[179] The county registrars and voting officials still had the power to decide who got to vote, but the increase in the number of blacks attempting to vote could not be ignored. Other measures were therefore used to dissuade blacks from making trips to the courthouses. Blacks were intimidated more than in the past. They were harassed and beaten, and their headquarters and homes were burned. They were riddled with bullets or bombed. They were jailed, charged with bogus crimes, shot at or even killed when they showed serious interest in the voting process.

Fannie Lou Hamer, who worked for many years on a Delta plantation, went to Indianola to take the literacy test when she learned that voting was one of her rights, something she hadn't known throughout most of her life. That evening after she had returned to the plantation, her boss fired her because she had made an effort to vote. Several days later her bedroom was sprayed with bullets. Fortunately, she was not at home at the time of the incident.[180] Another instance of violence against those blacks who attempted to vote occurred when a group of blacks in a Southern Mississippi town went to register; there were people outside the courthouse taking down license numbers of cars driven by blacks. When a local black SNCC field worker reported that he had seen those who were taking down license numbers, he was killed. The state legislator who killed him said he had been attacked by the black man. The legislator, who was supposedly the most powerful man in the county, was absolved of all charges.[181] In a third instance, COFO workers drove some would-be voters to a courthouse to register. While they were at the courthouse, a highway patrolman who happened to be in the room at the time stood around watching the efforts of the small group. Later when members of the group left and were en route to the SNCC office, they were stopped by that same highway patrolman who had been at the voter registration office. After speaking with the local passengers briefly, the patrolman arrested the COFO worker when he tried to intervene on their behalf. The COFO worker spent two days in jail.[182] On yet another occasion, three COFO workers were out driving when three white men pulled up alongside the car and fired a gun at them. One COFO member was hit twice.[183]

On May 28, 1963, after talks with Mayor Allen C. Thompson had broken off, Medgar Evers, a Decatur native, made another attempt to move Mississippi forward by leading an NAACP boycott of the stores practicing segregation in downtown Jackson.[184] The boycott obtained national media attention. It was an economic success because it hurt the businesses being boycotted, and Evers was given credit for that success. According to Myrlie Evers, wife of Medgar, "because of that success … our home was firebombed; we received threats on almost an hourly basis at home."[185]

Death threats or violence to civil rights advocates and workers were routine in Southern states, whether that person was man or woman, white or black, child or adult, or young or old. Still, it was a shock to the nation when hard-working Medgar Evers, who had just come from a rally, was shot in the back on June 12, 1963.[186] The bullet passed through his body and crashed into his house. Myrlie, who was in the house at the time, rushed out to see what had happened:

> I rushed out and saw him lying there, and people from the neighborhood began to gather, there were also some whose color happened to be white. I don't think I have ever hated as much in my life as I did at that particular moment anyone who had white skin. I screamed at the neighbors, and when the police finally got there, I told them that

they had killed Medgar. And I can recall wanting so much to have a machine gun or something in my hands, and to stand there and mow them all down.[187]

The *Daily Defender* carried the news of Evers's death the following day, "Kennedy Shocked By 'Barbaric' Murder Of Evers." It also carried comments from Mississippi members of congress, Attorney General Robert Kennedy, and other U.S. congressional members. In another story, reactions from the children of Evers were carried. His wife and three children, Darrell, 9; Denise, 8; and Vandike, 3, were in the house when the bullet crashed through a window.[188]

"State NAACP Secretary Is Shot To Death" was Percy Greene's headline. The story reported that police believed "that the fatal shot was fired from a rifle in the hands of a sniper hidden in a vacant lot across the street in front of the home" and that Roy Wilkins, the NAACP executive secretary, had posted a reward. Comments from Jackson's mayor, Allen Thompson, were included, and it was stated that Governor Ross Barnett was expected to have comments in four days.[189]

Over in Oklahoma, the *Black Dispatch* carried a story with a Chicago dateline on June 21, featuring comments made by Charles Evers, Medgar's brother. The headline read: "EVERS' KILLER WAS EXPERT SHOT." That was the opinion as given by Charles who speculated that the killer used a telescopic lens on the rifle. Governor Barnett assumed that the killing was done by outside agitators, an assumption some NAACP officials labeled as "ridiculous."[190]

When the *Pittsburgh Courier* ran its story: "Bury 'Tall Quiet Man' from Decatur, Miss." on June 22, it also had a related story: "Jackson's Police Holding 'Suspect.'" Since the investigation was ongoing, the report said, the name of the suspect was being withheld.[191]

Also on June 22, the *Advocate* covered the burial rites for Evers which were held in Jackson. In attendance were Dr. Ralph Bunche, assistant secretary general of the United Nations, the Reverend King, Congressman Charles C. Diggs, Jr., Detroit; and comedian Dick Gregory. Roy Wilkins was the principal speaker. The *Advocate* also reported that Charles Evers had been named to the NAACP field secretary post.[192]

Although Percy Greene appeared to have put aside his differences when covering the death of Medgar Evers, he was back to his old tricks shortly after the burial. The *Black Dispatch* continued to keep an eye on his old tricks, however, and reported in a story on June 28, with a Jackson dateline:

> Negroes here were shocked and revolted by an intemperate state-
> ment credited to Percy Greene, editor of the Jackson Advocate, the
> city's oldest Negro newspaper.
> Greene, dubbed an "Uncle Tom" and a "quisling" by most Negroes
> here, and one of the slain Medgar Evers' severest critics, was quoted
> as telling two Washington newsmen:
> "No nigger in New York or Washington is going to run down here
> and in 20 minutes tell me what I'm going to do."
> Greene's outburst came while he was being interviewed recently
> by Laurence Stern and Wallace Terry of the Washington Post. Terry
> is a Negro.
> "I'm opposed to all demonstrations," Greene continued, "because
> we must have public opinion on our side to get these rights."
> Greene's use of the word "nigger" was regarded by Negroes here
> as an affront that even Mayor Thompson avoids using in public.[193]

From assessing some of the stories contained on selected front
pages of the *Advocate*, it is clear that the progress of the civil rights
movement, as far as Greene was concerned, was not going very well.

In the July 7, 1962, issue of the *Advocate*, Greene reported the
dissatisfaction of black students in Charlottesville, North Carolina,
while attending integrated schools. One story noted that a Black Muslim was in a Belleville, Illinois, jail "awaiting trial for his life on
charging of killing a … farm couple." Another report from Philadelphia, Pennsylvania, stated that "Dakota Staton well known singer
charges the Black Muslim Movement with being a discredit to Islamic
faith one of the principal religions of mankind." The reports continued from New Orleans, where a soldier was arrested for "looking
into parked cars." He was later shot in the back when he tried to
escape. There was a noted absence of stories with Mississippi datelines.

"VIOLENCE FLARES AS NAACP BACKED SIT-INS
START HERE," was the headline in the June 1, 1963, issue. The Reverend King was back in the news, from Los Angeles where he
"attacked" President Kennedy. Other stories mentioned that President
Kennedy "ignores" King's demands for the escort of students attending the University of Alabama, and that Secretary of State Dean Rusk
"says U.S. racial conflicts force U.S. diplomats to conduct foreign policy like sprinters with one leg in a cast." In other stories with out of
state datelines, a black lawyer from Oakland, California, said "that
Negroes have gotten nowhere with their drives to abolish segregation,
and that civil rights campaigns like the one in Birmingham 'destroy
rather than create pride and dignity in the Negro.'" Also on the page

was a report that a federal judge refused to order the public schools in Birmingham to be integrated because "Negroes had not exhausted administrative remedies."

The June 29, 1963, issue showed basically the same kind of civil rights gloom: a federal judge had dismissed a federal lawsuit seeking desegregation, Congress was moving slowly "towards the debates on civil rights," Senator Barry Goldwater had only slightly modified his stand on civil rights, and demonstrators had been arrested during a speech made by Governor Carl Sanders of Georgia. In other reports a shotgun blast from unknown assailants had disrupted a voter registration meeting, the Baptists had called for a "halt in demonstrations," and "Rev. Martin Luther King ignores President call to stop demonstrations while Congress considers civil rights legislation." Greene also carried a headline which read: "NATION'S ONLY NEGRO DAILY NEWSPAPER JOINS PRESIDENT KENNEDY IN CALL TO STOP ALL PUBLIC DEMONSTRATIONS." Greene chose to quote the *Atlanta Daily World*, a daily newspaper with a very conservative and anti-demonstration stance in the civil rights struggle but forgot or just ignored the presence of the *Daily Defender* and the *New York Amsterdam News*. Also in that issue, the *Advocate* reported that "Accused Slayer Of Medgar Evers Awaits Action [of the] Hinds Grand Jury." It appeared that the suspect in the murder of Medgar Evers was Byron De La Beckwith, and the *Advocate* announced: "A Marine Corps Veteran, reputedly a gun collector and a member of the White Citizens Council was arrested by agents of the Federal Bureau of Investigations after he had been identified as the owner of the telescope-sight used on the high-powered rifle found in a field adjacent to the Ever's home following the slaying."[194] The *Advocate* also mentioned the fact that Attorney Hugh Cunningham, a law partner of Mississippi's Governor Ross Barnett, was one of four legal counselors for Beckwith.

In the July 13, 1963, issue of the *Advocate,* there was a story headlined "BYRON DE LA BECKWITH" PLEADS NOT GUILTY." The newest development in the case showed that a group of white businessmen were reported to be raising money for Beckwith's defense fund.

In an interesting turn of events, the *Advocate*'s July 20, 1963, issue reported that District Attorney Bill Waller had filed a motion to have Beckwith undergo a psychiatric examination because the defense had not done so. If the motion was approved, the suspect would be sent to the mental hospital for 30 days. Greene also commented in an

editorial on how the plans for the March on Washington were progressing better than it had originally appeared.

The November 30, 1963, *Advocate* reported that a trial date for
Beckwith had been set for Monday, January 27, 1964. No other new
developments were reported.

On February 15, 1964, the *Jackson Advocate* and the *Pittsburgh
Courier* reported on Beckwith. The *Advocate* reported that the trial
circuit judge, Leon Hendrick, had ordered a mistrial because the jury
"after sitting through 11 days of testimony and argument, failed to
agree on a verdict." The *Pittsburgh Courier* wasn't as objective in its presentation and began its report with a bit of contempt:

> At least five people in the State of Mississippi believe that it is a
> crime to kill a Negro.
> This possibility loomed last week when an all-white jury was
> unable to reach a verdict in the trial of Byron De La Beckwith accused
> slayer of NAACP Field Secretary Medgar Evers. After hearing testi-
> mony for 10 days and deliberating for 11 hours, five of the 12 jurors con-
> tinued to vote for Beckwith's conviction, against seven favoring acquit-
> tal even on the 20th ballot.[195]

"La Beckwith Free on Bond" was the headline of the *Courier*'s next
report on the trial. Once again the reporter made no attempt to disguise the contempt for the jurors' decision:

> The "unwritten law" of the Mississippi Delta, which permits a
> white man to kill a Negro who strays from his "place," apparently con-
> tinued to hold sway, here, when a second all-white jury failed to agree
> on a verdict against Byron de la Beckwith, accused slayer of Medgar
> Evers....
> When the jurors still were deadlocked, eight to four, for acquit-
> tal of Beckwith, after 18 hours of deliberation, Circuit Court Judge
> Leon Hendricks declared a mistrial, commenting: "I have never been
> in favor of forcing a verdict ... of wearing out 12 men such as you."[196]

Since the date for the March on Washington was getting closer,
newspapers began to report on its progress. The August 17 issue of the
Pittsburgh Courier reported that 2,000 buses and 14 special trains had
been set up to carry marchers. Since the event was supposed to be
peaceful and was not expected to be unruly in any way, the *Jackson
Advocate* also reported on the transportation of the marchers on that
same date, stating that "A massive 'Freedom Fleet' of buses, trains and
airliners was being assembled." It also stated that at least 2,173 park-
ing spaces would be needed at the Washington Monument.[197]

The *Black Dispatch* reported on the March on Washington preparations on August 23, 1963, when it said that the "Urban League Endorses March on Washington; August 28." While the Urban League planned to become involved in the march, it made it clear that picketing was not its policy and that it would not engage in the meeting of senators or congressmen, since they do not "lobby for legislation."

The March on Washington took place on August 28, 1963. In the *Daily Defender* for that day, there was but one word in the front-page headline: "MARCHING!" It also carried a photograph of marchers boarding a train and a picture of the nation's capitol. The headline in the caption read: "The Key To The Civil Rights Struggle." An editorial inside the paper told specifically why "the Negroes and those who believe in their cause" were marching.

The front-page headline on the *Daily Defender* the following day, August 29, 1963, continued with a report of the march: "300,000 MARCH! GREATEST DAY IN U.S. HISTORY." Inside the paper, President Kennedy commented that the "March Advanced Mankind." Many other reports from all around the country applauded the march and what it stood for.

When the *Black Dispatch* reported on the March on Washington on August 30, 1963, it reported how eager the marchers were, so much so that they began to march down Constitution and Independence avenues before the planned leaders were in place. The leaders had "to run like the devil to catch up and keep up with those whom they are supposed to lead." The *Dispatch* also reported no evidence of violence and noted that twice as many as had been expected showed up and that good, not gloom, "will come as a result of the March." The inside stories also told of the physical conditions of the marchers and how they fared in the warm 80-degree-plus weather, noting that "many marchers suffered hunger and thirst because warnings were not heeded." The headline read: "CITY GROUP IN WASHINGTON MARCH."

Once again the *Black Dispatch* carried on September 13 some comments from other newspapers around the South and the remainder of the country on the March on Washington. The *Record* of Columbia, S.C., noted: "It aroused much latent anti-integration sentiment in the North. ... It is doubtful that it won a single vote for the civil rights program advanced by the Kennedys. The pressure campaign might have caused some acquiescent Congressmen to recoil."[198]

North to Chattanooga, the *Free Press* wrote: "The marchers were not primarily seeking to gain these civil rights for themselves but to deprive others of their civil rights so that the demonstrators might have what belongs to others."[199]

Westward across the Tennessee hills to Memphis, the *Press Scimitar* stated: "The demonstration, we think, is bound to have a favorable effect, both on Congress and the country. It is time for Americans to get over their terror of Negroes. The polite crowds discipline themselves. And their speakers for those who still think of Negroes in terms of 'Yassah, Boss,' were dignified and articulate."[200]

In Philadelphia, the *Inquirer* noted: "What has set it apart ... from all mass demonstrations of the past was the incomparable good nature, the superb dignity and unflinching sense of responsibility with which vast numbers of closely packed people conducted themselves in the face of an emotional strain which is beyond imagining by all except those born to contend against centuries old injustice."[201]

The *Courier*'s front-page headline read: "DECADE'S BIGGEST STORY IS 'MARCH.'" The August 31, 1963, story emphasized that "We march together, Catholics, Jews, Protestants, for Dignity and Brotherhood All Men Under God. Now!"

Down in Jackson, the *Advocate*'s front page of August 31, 1963, instead of announcing that a local group had been involved in the march as had the *Dispatch*, read: "LOCAL GROUP LEAVES— MARCH ON WASHINGTON." The article reported that some Mississippi delegates had decided to end their participation in the March on Washington before its completion. In another related story, "Congress Remains Unmoved by March on Washington," Greene still did not mention the success of the march. Instead, he reported instances of massive traffic jams, buses being stranded miles away from the march site, confusion at the site, and the arrest of a Nazi party member. In another story he reported that "not all of the nation's five Negro Congressmen are convinced of the advisability of the March on Washington as are the leaders of the six major civil rights organizations sponsoring the march." In other news he reported that three white workers complained of racial bias; that Dick Gregory, the comedian who led some civil rights groups and who was arrested in Chicago in a civil rights demonstration, was released from jail; and that the managing editor of the *New York Times*, Turner Catledge, saw no solution to the race question. It was interesting to note that in one of Greene's front page stories, the headline read: "Demonstrations To Honor Those Who Have Lost Their Lives." Greene was referring to the March on Washington. One of the men who had lost his life was Medgar Evers.

The *Courier*, the *Defender*, the *Dispatch*, and the *Advocate* had clearly emphasized in their early reports the march and its consequences, a much larger and more encompassing event than just the speeches being made. On September 7, 1963, however, the *Courier* finally got around to the Reverend King's historic speech: "I HAVE A DREAM ... TODAY!" Once again the front page was filled with a large photograph and several reports of the march. The lone report on the standard-size front page not concerned with the march reported on the funeral of W.E.B. DuBois, who had died earlier in the week.

One newsworthy incident concerning the march was not mentioned by the *Advocate*, even though it occurred in Mississippi. The incident was reported, however, by the *Black Dispatch*, which was still keeping an eye on Greene and Mississippi. Some members of the March on Washington delegation from Mississippi whom Greene had reported as leaving Washington apparently had traveled south safely as far as Meridian, Mississippi, on their way back to Jackson. On August 29 while delegates Bernard Hubbard and Will Palmer were waiting for bus transportation, they were confronted and severely beaten by several whites, with one man requiring medical attention.[202] Greene had been interested in these members of the delegation and had pointed them out as a show of disunity when they left the gathering in Washington. The violence they encountered in Greene's own state, on the other hand, did not fit his standard theme that everything was going well in Mississippi.

Up to this point, being black, living in Birmingham, and being an active participant in the civil rights movement had exposed one to violent retaliation in many instances. Since the occurrence of recent demonstrations, being black, living in Birmingham, and being a non–civil rights participant was just as dangerous. Four young Negro girls, Denise McNair, Addie Mae Collins, Cynthia Wesley, and Carole Robertson, attending a Sunday school class were killed on September 15, 1963, when a bomb was thrown into the Sixteenth Street Baptist Church.[203]

The September 16, 1963, edition of the *Daily Defender* carried that report and also mentioned that two other children had been killed. A 16-year-old boy had been killed by a policeman when he refused to follow police warnings and another boy had been shot and killed while riding his bicycle in the suburbs. Whether these shootings were connected to the bombing is not known since no further information was given.

John Sengstacke was back at the center of things in the September 17, 1963, issue of the *Defender*, as he announced a fund drive to help rebuild the active church. The paper also gave residents of Chicago an opportunity to express themselves about the Birmingham bombing.

The *Black Dispatch* applauded the fact that there had been only one exception to the restraint shown by Negro leaders. Bishop C. Ewbank Tucker of the African Methodist Episcopal Zion church in Louisville, Kentucky, had urged his parishioners to take up arms and protect themselves from "intrusions." In its September 27, 1963, issue, the *Black Dispatch* also carried comments from some of the white children in Birmingham who had been asked to express themselves about the bombing. Some urged Negroes to fight back, some thought Negroes should throw rocks, some thought the bomber should be tried and sentenced to life, while some thought Negroes should have the right to go to integrated schools.

While from almost every corner of the nation, leaders and other officials were condemning the killing of children in Alabama, Greene issued an editorial. He did not, however, condemn the act itself or the persons responsible for the tragedy. Nor did he call for better protection of buildings housing religious services or even for a cooling-off period to assess the damage and draw the line when it came to killing children. Instead, he declared:

> While accusing fingers have been pointed at the Governor of Alabama, and the President of the United States among thinking Negroes in Alabama, and throughout the nation, outside of the ranks of the professional Negro race leaders, and civil rights crusaders, there is the possibility that somber thoughts are causing many fingers to be pointed at the professional Negro race leaders and civil rights crusaders.[204]

With the death of Medgar Evers still echoing through the ranks of civil rights advocates and anger still simmering at the brink of boiling over into a national uprising over the death of the four children in Birmingham, it was a devastating shock for the nation when John Fitzgerald Kennedy was assassinated on November 22, 1963.

In its November 29, 1963, issue, the *Black Dispatch* carried a black-bordered, empty picture frame on its front page with the name of the president centered. The report concerned Kennedy's record, but the headline read: "WILL JOHNSON CARRY TORCH OF FREEDOM?"

Many black civil rights leaders firmly believed that President Kennedy had not moved as fast as they would have liked and had not done as much as they thought he should have, but as the *Dispatch* reported, he was the "greatest loss to Civil Rights and Reform." The *Dispatch* further reported, "We know only that President Kennedy died of the same disease as did Medgar Evers of Mississippi and the four little girls who died in the bombing of a church one Sunday morning in Birmingham."

There were three major headlines on the front page of the *Jackson Advocate* on November 30. "MILLIONS VIEW FUNERAL OF PRESIDENT KENNEDY," "Nation's Negroes See Kennedy Martyr To Their Cause," and "PRESIDENT JOHNSON URGES CIVIL RIGHTS BILL PASSAGE-NOW." Greene also provided an editorial in which he said:

> The nation was shocked and the entire world surprised and dismayed as the news came from over in Dallas, Texas, the other day, that John F. Kennedy, the President of the United States had been felled by an assassin.
> Among the 34 occupants preceding him in the office of the Presidency, more than any of those who preceded him, with perhaps singular exceptions, John F. Kennedy displayed qualities that won the admiration of friend and foe alike in the American political arena, and brought him to the magnitude and aura of an exception [sic] personality among the leaders of the world.[205]

As did the *Black Dispatch* and the *Jackson Advocate*, the *Pittsburgh Courier* in its November 30 issue also emphasized the new president, Lyndon B. Johnson, writing in its headline: "EYES OF ENTIRE WORLD ON LYNDON B. JOHNSON." The entire front page was devoted to reports on Kennedy's death and reactions to it. Inside was an editorial which stated:

> All of this means that the nation must take up where President Kennedy left off and "carry on" under the leadership of President Lyndon B. Johnson, who, by his actions in the office of Vice Presidency, has proven himself ably fitted to take up the task.
> America is fortunate to have had President Kennedy as a leader. America is fortunate to have a man like Lyndon B. Johnson ready to step into the late President's shoes.[206]

Unlike the other three newspapers, the *Daily Defender* of November 25, 1963, did not place much emphasis on President Johnson's new office but referred to Kennedy's death with the headline: "The World Weeps As JFK 'Goes Home,'" on page two. There was no detailed account of Kennedy's death, but a round-up of reactions from Paris, Rome, and London was inserted.

With the arrival of the year 1964, the Civil Rights Act, which had been pushed by President Kennedy before his death and President Johnson thereafter, was passed by the House on February 10, 1964, passed by the Senate on June 19, 1964, and signed by the president on July 2, 1964.[207] The law became known as the Civil Rights Act of 1964. The stranglehold Mississippi and its sister states had been using to deter blacks from voting had technically lost its bite. Title I, Section 101 (2), of that act states:

> No person acting under color of law shall (C) employ any literacy test as a qualification for voting in any Federal election unless (i) such test is administered to each individual wholly in writing; and (ii) a certified copy of the test and of the answers given by the individual is furnished to him within twenty-five days of the submission of his request made within the period of time during which records and papers are required to be retained and preserved pursuant to title III of the Civil Rights Act of 1960.[208]

As a result, voting officials could no longer legally control would-be voters, members of the black race in particular, who wanted to go to a courthouse and register. For those Mississippians who still wanted to maintain the status quo regardless of existing laws or new ones, the next step, then, would be to coerce blacks into staying away from the polls. Such a practice was unfortunately not repugnant to many.

The Mississippi Freedom Summer Projects were begun in the fall of 1963, in preparation for the summer of 1964. To undertake the massive job of registering blacks to vote, COFO issued a nationwide appeal for out-of-state student volunteers to come join the Freedom Summer Projects. Approximately 700 students of all colors and races arrived to operate freedom centers and to assist in urging local blacks to register and vote.[209] Many of the volunteers for the projects were from out of state; most were students from good homes and families, most were not poor, and most were white. Orientation for the new activists was required and necessary for their safety and well-being. There were several out of state orientation centers being used. One was at the Western College for Women in Oxford, Ohio, where participants were given background information and instructed how to survive while living in the state.[210] Among other things, they learned:

> Fifty-one percent of the people in the Delta earn less than a thousand dollars a year.... Mississippi is not just a closed society. It's

locked and the vote is the key that will open it.... In Bolivar County the superintendent of schools forbids teaching foreign languages and civics in Negro schools—also American history from 1860 to 1875.... The schools are a kind of brain-washing. The Negro child is trained to accept without question. Teach him to ask why and the system will fail.[211]

Project participants were cautioned about carrying pocket knives, even small ones, guns, or anything else that might be considered a weapon. To move around the state, they needed their own transportation because nothing in the local areas would be available for them.[212] They were also taught how to react (or not react) if they were attacked by police or members of the Ku Klux Klan.[213]

When the instructional period was over, the group departed for Mississippi. The first bit of news many of them heard upon their arrival was that three of their co-workers had disappeared. On June 21, Andrew Goodman, a 21-year-old white student from Queens College, Flushing, New York; James Chaney, a 21-year-old black Mississippi CORE worker, and 24-year-old Michael Schwerner, a white social worker from New York, had apparently driven to Mount Zion Methodist Church in Neshoba County in eastern Mississippi. They wanted to look over a burned-out church which had been slated to be used as one of their headquarters. On the way back to Meridian, the young men drove through Philadelphia, Mississippi, where they were arrested by the highway patrol. After being detained for several hours, they were released later that night, but they were never seen again.[214]

"Find Them: LBJ Orders FBI in Miss. Mystery," the June 24, 1964, issue of the *Daily Defender* reported. The report stated that the president was concerned about law and order across the nation, that he was sending former Central Intelligence Agency (CIA) director Allen W. Dulles to meet with state officials, and that the police had discovered near Jackson the burned-out station wagon in which the three COFO workers had been riding.

The next day the *Daily Defender* placed a question before its readers: "Was Trio Killed? Miss. Invasion Set." The report stated that 200 law enforcement officers were searching the area around Philadelphia, that the car was discovered through a tip from an informant, and that lab reports showed no bullet holes in the vehicle or signs of a struggle. In an editorial carried in the same issue, the editors said:

> Lawlessness whether it explodes in Brooklyn or in Mississippi can never be condoned. Brutality whether it is practiced by young Negro

hoodlums or middle-aged red-necked Mississippians can never be ignored. Every fiber of our minds and bodies must be mobilized to stamp out, as we would stamp out a disease, the sickening sore of race hate that still infests the body politic of this country.[215]

From Oklahoma City on July 3, 1964, the *Black Dispatch* reported that CORE's director, James Farmer, believed the three workers to be dead and that CORE members were forming picket lines at federal buildings in key cities "urging full federal protection for civil rights workers involved in the Freedom Summer project."

Two mutilated bodies of other missing Negroes were discovered during the search for the three COFO members, according to a report in the July 31 issue of the *Dispatch*. The dismembered bodies of Charles Moore and Henry Dees "were found in the Old River swamp near Tallulah, La." The Mississippi NAACP field secretary, Charles Evers, sent a letter to the governor "requesting that he call upon state lawmakers to enact special legislation to guarantee the safety of Mississippi Negro citizens." He also indicated that "Most of these murders were committed by local police officers." Concerning the FBI and their performance, Evers also asked the question: "You really begin to wonder, 'what good are they? What are they doing here?'"[216]

By the time the *Pittsburgh Courier* printed its report on the three missing COFO members, the car had been discovered. On July 4, 1963, the report stated: "STUDENT RIGHTS GROUPS FEAR FOR LIVES IN MISS." Also on the front page were mug shots of the three missing workers. The report went into greater detail on Chaney's background and carried a review of the concerns of the FBI and Attorney General Robert Kennedy.

When the bodies of the three missing COFO workers were finally found, the *Jackson Advocate* did carry a report. The skyline headlines, however, read: "Aaron Henry Urges Safety of Summer Project Workers" and "WHAT HAS BECOME OF $375,000 OF AME CHURCH MONEY?" The actual story of the discovered bodies appeared under the headline "Find Bodies of Summer Project Workers." The report was brief: "The bodies were found in shallow graves at the site of a newly created pond six miles from the town of Philadelphia, and some 20 miles from the place where their burned out station wagon was found on June 21st."[217]

"Will Killers of Civil Rights Trio Be Brought to Justice?" That was the question the *Black Dispatch* asked in a report on August 14. In that report, Charles Evers answered that question: "No. They will be tried by local authorities and a local judge, and a local jury with the aunties and uncles on it, and turned loose."[218]

COFO's goal in concentrating its activities on Mississippi was to enlighten the black people all across the state.[219] It was an awareness program designed to assist Negroes in learning about the Mississippi constitution in preparation for taking the required literacy test conducted by the state. The system of education for black children in Mississippi's schools was, in fact, largely responsible for the lack of literacy among some potential black voters. But intimidation was also a hurdle that some just didn't want to challenge, and some blacks believed that it was useless to vote. In fact, in 1920 Roscoe Dunjee had tried to reason with the apathy shown by Oklahoma Negroes of that era: "The most disgusting and senseless Negro that we know is the fellow who stands around and says, 'Oh I never vote; I'm not registered.'"[220] Unlike those who knew about the vote but not about its power, many of the blacks in Mississippi, for whatever reasons, were not even aware that voting was one of their rights.

It was not until 1962 that Fannie Lou Hamer, for instance, found out that black Mississippians had the legal right to vote. She found out at the age of 47, but only after COFO had reorganized in 1962 and had gone around from door to door attempting to get people to go down to the courthouse to register.[221]

Not at all happy with the influx of strangers who came to Mississippi to help register voters, the State Sovereignty Commission "termed the project 'a massive attack on Mississippi customs.'" Many other whites claimed that subversive elements were among the ranks of COFO members. Senator Eastland spoke to the U.S. Senate and advised that "the Communist Party is the cancerous force behind the biracial Mississippi Summer Project."[222]

At the same time, the black people of Jackson and those in other parts of Mississippi shook their heads in disbelief when the *Advocate* also opposed the role of COFO and openly rejected its functions. After all, Greene had always supported the right for blacks to vote. Now, however, he reported that COFO was causing "the breakdown of Negro confidence in the American democratic elective system."[223] If Greene had ever been consistent about an issue before, giving the Negro the right to vote was at the top of the list. Even during the beginning of the civil rights movement he still supported that position. And though the *Advocate*'s March 9, 1963, headline read as though the state had been invaded by a foreign enemy force, Greene's voting rights support was still clearly visible, although he resented the idea that outside forces were entering the state to do what he thought was "his job."[224] "There never will be a healthy political climate in Mississippi that will contribute to the development, and all around progress of the state as long as Negroes are denied the right to vote," he said. Evidently Greene believed that giving blacks the right to vote in Mississippi was all right as long as it was given freely by white Mississippians.[225]

Despite the violence encountered by members of the Freedom Summer Projects, the apathy of many of the black people in Mississippi was the hardest hurdle to surmount. Anne Moody, a young Mississippi civil rights worker who had seen and encountered some of that violence in her efforts to register blacks, remembers how difficult it was to get some of the black people interested in voting. They were looking for handouts (an inducement used to draw the black people from remote rural areas), she remembers. As long as someone was giving something away, they would show up at the center:

> The minute I saw them there, I got mad as hell. Here they are ... all standing around waiting to be given something. Last week after the church bombing they turned their heads when they passed this office. Some even looked at me with hate in their eyes. Now they are smiling at me. After I give them the clothes, they probably won't even look at me next week, let alone go and register to vote.[226]

Percy Greene continued to look inward, continued to feel that if blacks would just have more patience, wait a while longer, everything would be all right. The beatings and other violence in Mississippi and the murders of civil rights workers Andrew Goodman, James Chaney, and Mickey Schwerner near Philadelphia, Mississippi, were regrettable, as far as Greene was concerned, but would not have happened if "Twentieth Century Carpetbaggers" had not come to town.[227]

It was for good reason that Greene didn't like the idea of so many newcomers showing up in town. One of them turned out to be his new competition. His one sentence, 175-word editorial of February 2, 1963, voiced part of his feelings.

> The news of a few days ago about a white man from up north in Ohio who recently came here and took over the editorship of a local Negro Newspaper, The Free Press, originally backed principally by a group of Negro business and professional men, which subsequently ran into financial difficulties that caused it to suspend publication, having gone up north to Chicago and other places where he was given

> assurance of enough financial aid to resume publication of the paper
> which is dedicated to the more militant approach the cause of Negro
> civil rights; the continuing news about groups of whites and Negroes
> from outside the south, principally from New York and Chicago, com-
> ing into Mississippi to work for Negro civil rights; the advent into
> Mississippi, last week, of Dick Gregory, the Negro comic to talk to
> James Meredith on the eve of his probable discontinuance as a stu-
> dent at the University of Mississippi, leads us to the consideration of
> this subject: The Mississippi Negro, his civil rights, and the Twenti-
> eth Century Carpetbaggers.[228]

It should have come as no surprise to Greene that outside influences would eventually come to Jackson to provide a different point of
view. After all, his concern was not for giving the black people what
they wanted, as did Abbott, Vann, Sengstacke, Prattis, Dunjee, and
Dungee. And since the black people of Jackson no longer sought the
wisdom of Greene, any businessperson with enough daring to venture
into Mississippi could obviously take advantage of that black journalistic void.

The "carpetbagger" to whom Greene referred who started the
competitive newspaper called the *Mississippi Free Press*[229] didn't hesitate to announce the newspaper's role:

> Our purpose is to promote education and enlightenment in the
> principle of democracy to encourage all citizens to participate fully in
> their government. Until Negroes in Mississippi gain the power of the
> ballot and until all the people exercise the rights of citizenship, the
> needs of Mississippi will continue to go unmet; legislation to promote
> the social welfare and encourage economic growth will continue to be
> non-existent. In Mississippi, the fear of economic reprisal and the lack
> of vital knowledge make even registering to vote an extremely difficult
> task.[230]

Those were strong words for a newcomer's first venture into the
stronghold of Mississippi. To the black people of Jackson, the new
publication was an offsetting voice to the *Advocate*, a voice which was
a welcome relief. They previously had had to rely on outside sources
for their news, the *Defender* or the *Courier* or anyone else with some
believability. The White Citizen's Council and the State Sovereignty
Commission, on the other hand, viewed the new publication as an
upstart troublemaker, an ill-timed nuisance, a pest which should be
controlled, if not eliminated.[231] So powerful were the influences of the
Commission and Council that they flagrantly used the police force to
disrupt the *Free Press*'s circulation. They also used the police to harass

and observe the paper's staff. More importantly, the editor of the Lexington *Advertiser* had lent support to the *Free Press* by allowing it to use that paper's printing facilities. The Commission and Council threatened the *Advertiser*'s editor, even though she was white, with ruin for supporting the *Free Press*. When it came to keeping someone in his or her place, no lines were drawn as to gender or color or age.[232]

Offering something other than "a discouraging word," the new voice, the alternative point of view which had come roaring into Jackson in the form of the *Free Press*, had run into the wrath of the State Sovereignty Commission and White Citizen's Council. It did not close down, but its initial roar to the people was reduced to a soft purr after it was placed under such tight scrutiny by Mississippi's established powers.[233]

Despite the widening gap between Greene and his targeted readers, he managed to keep publishing. That was understandable because his advertisers did not lend their support based on circulation. Unfortunately for Greene, however, his position with his readers and advertisers began to deteriorate dramatically. It started when he received a letter from one of his advertisers who discontinued his ad in the *Advocate* because "a recent editorial expression differed so far from his thinking that he, in good conscience, could no longer support his paper."[234] Greene's problems in that regard were just beginning. To the citizens of Jackson, the paper had become well known as a pro-segregation organ. Rather than look towards its contents for guidance and counsel, blacks avoided or ignored it. Subsequently, because the number of paid subscriptions was low and he was eager to spread his advice, Greene resorted to giving the paper away to those who would read it.[235]

As for the Reverend King, Greene wouldn't cease in his efforts to discredit the civil rights leader and continued to call for new Negro leadership:

> Negroes are being led into a repetion of the history that led to the post-Reconstruction's "Unwritten Compromise" the total disfranchisement of the southern Negro, the south's one party political system, the enactment of the segregation laws, and the discrimination that has been the southern Negro's greatest handicap during the one hundred years since emancipation.[236]

Throughout the civil rights movement, Greene had been critical of the Reverend King. That most recent editorial, however, caused Charles Evers, NAACP field secretary and brother of the slain civil rights advocate Medgar Evers, to take some kind of action to put the

Advocate out of business. Since he could not attack the paper directly, Evers threatened Greene's advertisers with a boycott of their stores or products if they did not drop their ads from that publication. Such a bold proposal by Evers apparently was very effective and caused Greene to issue another editorial:

> Our right of freedom of speech, and our right to use and prac-
> tice the right of freedom of the press is now being challenged, and
> attempts are being made to destroy the medium through which we give
> expression to our right of freedom of speech, and the freedom of the
> press by Charles Evers the state NAACP Secretary, who disliked the
> subject of, and the content of, a recent editorial in our medium the
> Jackson Advocate and he has now launched upon a new campaign to
> destroy the Jackson Advocate, interposed upon the campaign that has
> been going on for the past ten years, only this time threatening the
> merchants who advertise in the Jackson Advocate.[237]

Medgar Evers had always been a thorn in the side for Greene. Charles Evers had taken up where Medgar had left off and was just as sharp a thorn.

By the time the year 1965 had arrived, Greene's front page had shown very little change. His March 13, 1965, issue, for example, carried stories about a feud betwen the NAACP and COFO leaders, that COFO planned to move its headquarters, and that the Mississippi Economic Council "called upon Mississippians to keep the race issue out of future political campaigns ... and to oppose candidates who use the issue to get elected." Greene also carried a short notice on the former *Black Dispatch* editor, Roscoe Dunjee, who had passed away at the age of 82.

The heart of a newspaper's existence, its subscribers and advertisers, no longer sought the services of Greene's newspaper. The black people refused to listen to the editor, but the *Advocate* refused to alter its position. What was even more interesting, Percy Greene kept up his attempts to slow down the civil rights movement and convince Mississippi blacks to accept the status quo. With all of his losses—his subscribers, his advertisers, and the black people's faith in his word— Greene was still able to stay in business, wounded and sinking but still going to press each week. In that regard, he was much akin to his hero, Booker T. Washington, who also continued to push for accommodation despite the increasing death and violence around him, countenanced the absence of civil rights for blacks, and perpetuated the theme of keeping the Negro in his place.

CONCLUSIONS

It has been suggested that no two people doing the same thing will react in the same manner to the same kind of pressure under the same set of circumstances. When survival of the race was not an immediate factor but the survival of emboldened Afro-Americans was, John Russwurm and the Reverend Samuel Cornish stepped forward to become founders of the Afro-American press. Unfortunately, they were also the first to succumb to internal pressures caused by direct outside intervention. They, as well as Willis Hodges and Thomas Van Rensselaer of the *Ram's Horn*, dissolved their partnership when problems from within could not be resolved, problems which may or may not have been caused by pressures from without.

Ida B. Wells also broke up with her partner, the Reverend Taylor Nightingale. In that instance, outside occurrences caused internal dissension when the original function of the paper was disregarded to satisfy personal grievances. With the absence of a partner, Wells stuck by the original function, became fearless when carrying out her editorial philosophies, and told the truth as she saw it, rather than reverting to the use of subtleties and diplomacy as other editors had done in the past. She also saw the need for investigating an account of an incident prior to releasing it in her publication. No longer was it plausible in her eyes to report or believe a story simply because someone else had published it before or someone said it had happened. As a result, she added credibility to her reporting, and she didn't hesitate to use statistics, even when the truth placed her personal survival in jeopardy and caused the violent destruction of her business.

When it came to handling pressures or fearless reporting, Robert Abbott must be placed near the top of the list. He was almost fearless in pursuit of Negro civil rights, attacking the federal government during World War I and calling for an end, with a shotgun, if necessary, to lynching.[1] And, as was Ida Wells before him, he was effective in encouraging blacks in the South to leave their homes. Wells recommended that black people should go to Oklahoma or Kansas, but Abbott said, "Come North," where at least there was a reasonable chance for making a living and a better chance of surviving. He would have preferred Southern officials to reduce their mistreatment of blacks. After all, the South was not only his home but also the home of millions of other blacks. But if those officials would not relent and let the black people live in peace, then blacks should live somewhere else.

In response to Abbott's actions, the South then made overt efforts to suppress the *Chicago Defender's* circulation in that region, an attempt that indicated that Abbott's efforts were successful. Abbott responded to those pressures with successful countermoves to maintain circulation and his business. He was an effective editor and never altered his course for justice even when faced with bodily harm. And despite the fact that he used sensationalism in his news presentation, it was a successful move that illustrated that such an editorial philosophy, despite the scorn of many editors, essentially gave the people what they wanted. Even the pressures from his peers could not dissuade him.

Robert Vann, the careful lawyer from Pittsburgh, and Percival Prattis steered the *Pittsburgh Courier* on a course that made it a leader among black newspapers. Vann did not completely follow Abbott's lead in news presentation, but so effective was this editor that presidents sought his counsel, though sometimes superficially. His reputation for accuracy in pointing out the injustices inflicted upon members of the black race followed this newspaper into World War II and beyond, even though Vann passed away in 1940.

It was during World War II that the *Courier* reminded the government of its failure to follow up on promises made during World War I. The militancy Prattis showed in the face of sedition charges from the federal government was backed up by some of the largest circulation figures ever achieved by a black newspaper in the United States. The government, keenly aware of those circulation figures and the need to keep morale among black military personnel from sinking further, sought other means to quiet this organ rather than the use of sedition charges. The strength of the editor even under such massive governmental pressures was evident. And though there were no known bodily threats made against Prattis, he survived the threats of being run out of business or being incarcerated for his editorial philosophy.

At the helm of the *Black Dispatch* was Roscoe Dunjee, a hero in the eyes of many Oklahomans and many other editors. Publishing a newspaper in the South during this period was a significant pressure in itself. Expressing editorial content under the umbrella of freedom of the press, a sacred canon for many but not necessarily for those of the black press, was almost a certain avenue to a short life span, business and editorial. But Dunjee knew the penalty if he practiced his brand of journalism in Oklahoma. And because Dunjee was almost always militant in his pursuit for justice for members of the black race and because he did not temper the content of his newspaper under pressure, he, like Prattis, came under the scrutiny of the Federal government during World War II. So determined were some government officials to change the tone of his editorials that certain words Dunjee had used, even those contained in the Constitution of the United States, were considered to be Communistic in tone.

Dunjee also faced financial problems within the state of Oklahoma. Circulation was adequate, but most of it was from out of state. Nevertheless, advertisers felt the sting of his editorials through disgruntled consumers, but not necessarily those who actually subscribed to the *Dispatch*. With his persistence in calling for equal rights, Dunjee struck a chord of truth about the unfair treatment of blacks, a guilt which many did not want to face. They therefore pressured the *Black Dispatch*'s advertisers to drop their support of the paper and run it out of business.

Some local officials offered Dunjee gratuities for his cooperation that were similar to those offered to Greene and his *Advocate*. Many believed that Dunjee should tone down his militancy and temper his editorial philosophy. The accusations the editor made were too often correct and too often pointed out facts some officials found to be embarrassing when so blatantly put into print. They could not reach Dunjee with the bribes, but so effective was the advertising boycott against the *Dispatch* that despite its large circulation base, Dunjee was forced to turn over the paper to a board of governors. But he had shown himself to be a man of unwavering integrity who never yielded to pressure or the temptation of the dollar. He survived the threats of the government and maintained his editorial philosophy, but he succumbed to pressures wielded by merchants.

Temptation, on the other hand, did reach out and grab Percy Greene. The fact that a disagreement, regardless of the depth, on how to integrate Mississippi's schools was so overwhelming that it would stain his views about those who disagreed with him and how the race should progress seems surprising. Rather than merely rejecting the civil rights organization with which he had had the disagreement, he rejected every attempt at race progression and the black leaders who authored these attempts if they disagreed with the way in which he thought the race should advance.

The eyes of the world became centered on Mississippi because of its staunch segregation background and because of its violent efforts to keep it that way. That clearly was not the time for Greene to join in overtly with his accommodationist side. But rather than support the people who had supported his newspaper by providing national, state, and local coverage of the nation's civil rights struggles, Greene instead displayed his deep fondness for Booker T. Washington and his accommodating editorial philosophy by advising Mississippi blacks to follow that path. He was somewhat militant in his editorial pursuits, the point could be argued, but was very careful that his militancy was directed towards foreign countries, not towards the aggression in his state. And though his pursuits will be clearly seen by historians as misguided and misdirected, he had the courage of his convictions and perhaps a boost by state-supported gratuities as well to stand alone with his editorial philosophy in the midst of the very people who eventually came to despise him.

The fact that the Mississippi State Sovereignty Commission praised Greene and his paper for service to the state may or may not justify the charge that Greene sold out the race under state pressures.[2]

The findings which show that the *Advocate* and several other black newspapers in Mississippi were on the state's payroll cannot be ignored. What is more important, it was even more disturbing to learn that after the disbanding of the State Sovereignty Commission, the legislature sealed the Commission's records in 1977. Those records, which could validate various charges, are to remain sealed until 2027. Papers that should have been a part of the public domain have been sealed by a legislative act that was never legally enacted.[3] Such action has stirred the juices of researchers and civil liberty groups across the country. How could a state that could so easily enact laws for its own purposes fail to do so in that instance? How could a state that prides itself on embracing the law and law-abiding citizens justify its own unlawful practices?

Unfortunately for Greene, he was said to have turned in reports to the State Sovereignty Commission and to those designated by the commission on how he spent the money received. It should not be argued whether Greene, like Dunjee, who refused to accept subsidies when his advertisers abandoned him, would have gone out of business had he not accepted the Commission's offer. Blacks in Jackson, as those in Oklahoma City, had no major businesses. Most of the advertisers were therefore white. It would take a man of strong editorial convictions to ignore pressures under those conditions, but Dunjee did.

It must remain a part of the record that black newspapers in the South were for the most part muted during turbulent times throughout history. The *Black Dispatch* and the *Memphis Free Speech*, far more outspoken than most newspapers, must stand apart from that muted group. The *Jackson Advocate*, on the other hand, initially tried to walk the line by practicing militancy outside of its geographic area. That line was dissolved when gratuities convinced the editor to openly pursue a role of accommodation, a role in which he apparently had always believed.

There are not many recorded instances in history where a black editor accepted gratuities from members of the Caucasian race to impart accommodationist reporting to his or her black readers. John Russwurm with *Freedom's Journal* is said, however, to have accepted money from the Colonization Society in order to leave the United States because he felt not wanted. Dunjee with his *Black Dispatch* was offered bribes that he did not accept. But the conditions Dunjee faced in Oklahoma, though not ideal, were far better than those Greene faced in Mississippi. Within the state of Mississippi, blacks faced pressures to which perhaps only Mississippians can relate. It must be remembered that the tendency to make an assumption without attempting to verify it is one of the curses of American society. Assuming that Greene did sell out his race does not make it so. Greene is said, however, to have accepted the money with instructions to reverse his editorial philosophies and show that all was well among blacks in Mississippi. The *Advocate* did take a firm stand for blacks to better themselves, stay out of national issues that upset the status quo, and bring about equalization of the races through subservience to the majority race, a typical position for accommodationists. It may not have been the most accepted or effective way for blacks to gain equal status, and Greene may have sold out, as some researchers have suggested, but the moral philosophy of the editor—which may have been to survive, to stay alive regardless of the cost—must be viewed with empathy before judgments become final.

It is important to note that throughout history when black civil rights successes have been obtained, eras of specific unfair treatment, turmoil, and violence generally have come to a close. During the antebellum period, black editors were active in the antislavery movement, for example. The black press played a major role in ending the institution of slavery and must be given credit by historians for its efforts. It is also important to note that the black press and its roles throughout history can be measured not only by effectiveness and successes, but also by how the editors survived.

Another overt example of the effectiveness of the black press occurred after Ida Wells had seen too many black people lynched. Wells advised blacks to move west, where a world free of lynching could be found. Many blacks, sensing her to be a champion for their cause, simply packed up and left their homes in Memphis. This was a prime example of editorial influence.

Later, during the Great Migration and World War I, much of the credit for advising blacks to move north has been given to the *Chicago Defender*. Was it simply a call from an ordinary black editor that caused people to pack up and move, even under the threat of violence? Was it merely the idea of better working conditions or better pay? Or was it the idea of freedom from lynching that caused such a massive move? And what about housing, wasn't there a promise that the condition of housing was far better in the North? Whatever the reason chosen for the move, the black press aided in relaying the information to the people. And as Wells was during her time, Abbott was effective in influencing people to move even when they were threatened with violence. What is equally amazing is that both editors survived their eras without abandoning their roles.

The importance and effectiveness of the black press should not be discussed without mentioning Percival Prattis. Although he was not the only black newspaper editor fighting against injustices during World War II, the *Courier* was the leader in this struggle. The unity and effectiveness of black editors against governmental opposition gave hope to the black people, who shed their despondency and became united behind the press. Such unity enabled Prattis to survive a use of militancy rarely tolerated by the government during wartime.

The year of 1963 was one of the bloodiest in American civil rights history. The number of injuries and deaths in Mississippi and Alabama will probably never be known, and one can only speculate about the numbers killed in the name of civil rights that year throughout the country. Many of those killed were unknowns, but they were important enough for someone or some group to see fit to remove them from society. But being unknown means being uncounted, being missed for such a short time and then forgotten by all but friends and relatives, and it means no media attention. Medgar Evers and John Fitzgerald Kennedy have been remembered each year since they were killed. But who remembers the names of the four girls killed in Birmingham? Who remembers the three students killed in 1964 during the Freedom Summer Projects? Who remembers that 100 years earlier in 1863, the Emancipation Proclamation had been enacted? And who remembers that the Emancipation Proclamation's centennial year was one of the most violent during the civil rights movement? Wouldn't it be fitting if all the people killed during 1963 and the other years of the civil rights movement could have their names listed somewhere?

American history is a curriculum requirement in schools across the United States. Although slavery is discussed, the essential details of the harshness, the brutality, and the efforts of the black and white people to end that suffering are missing in many instances. Names such as W.E.B. DuBois, Booker T. Washington, Frederick Douglass, or Ida B. Wells may be mentioned in historical discussions but are treated with such brevity that their deeds appear insignificant. Unfortunately, the deeds of Robert Abbott, Robert Vann, Roscoe Dunjee, Percival Prattis, and John Sengstacke have obtained little or no attention, but they were also heroes, those black editors and those who were white who faced overwhelming odds for expressing their editorial opinions for the survival of a race of people. In doing so, they, too, had to survive and they did.

Educators have come to learn that repetition is the key to retention. But it can also be said that high visibility is another key to retention. Those black editors, indeed, did have high visibility. Their high visibility simply occurred during inauspicious times in the history of the United States. But even though those inauspicious times have passed from the American scene, the critical deeds of those editors should not continue to be buried, ignored, or forgotten. Their work should be allowed to surface in great detail and should be explained to students as carefully as is the Teapot Dome scandal. Doesn't it seem appropriate that all heroes regardless of their time in history should share some place in American history books along with those parties who made history by way of some scandal?

NOTES

Chapter 1

1. John Hope Franklin: *From Slavery to Freedom: A History of Negro Americans*, 3d ed. (New York: Alfred A. Knopf, 1967), 238.

2. Bella Gross, "Freedom's Journal and the Rights of All," *Journal of Negro History* 15 (July 1932): 243.

3. Lee Finkle, *Forum for Protest: The Black Press During World War II* (Cranbury, N.J.: Associated University Presses, 1975), 18.

4. Armistead S. Pride, "A Register and History of Negro Newspapers in the United States: 1827–1950" (Ph.D. diss., Northwestern University, 1950), 309.

5. Gross, "Freedom's Journal," 241.

6. Romeo B. Garrett, *Famous First Facts About Negroes* (New York: Arno, 1972), 49.

7. I. Garland Penn, *The Afro-American Press and Its Editors* (1891; reprint, New York: Arno and the *New York Times*, 1969), 27.

8. The Editors of *Ebony*, *The Negro Handbook* (Chicago: Johnson Publishing, 1974), 418–19.

9. Gross, "Freedom's Journal," 248.

10. Edgar A. Toppin, *A Biographical History of Blacks in America Since 1528* (New York: David McKay, 1971), 410.

11. Martin E. Dann, ed. *The Black Press, 1827–1890: The Quest for National Identity* (New York: G.P. Putnam's Sons, 1971), 17.

12. The Editors of *Ebony*, *The Negro Handbook*, 1974, 420.

13. Pride, "Register and History of Negro Newspapers," 309, 311.

14. The Editors of *Ebony*, *The Negro Handbook*, 1974, 419.

15. Penn, *Afro-American Press*, 61.

16. Ibid., 61–62.

17. Ibid., 62.

18. Ibid., 63.

19. Ibid., 64.

20. Ibid., 65.

21. Ibid., 68.

22. "Titles of Negro Newspapers Often Have Significance Born of Challenges Faced by Race," *Black Dispatch*, 10 November 1955, sec. 2, 1A.

23. Finkle, *Forum for Protest*, 23.

24. Langston Hughes, Milton Meltzer, and C. Eric Lincoln, *A Pictorial History of Black Americans* (New York: Crown, 1983), 188.

25. The editors of *Ebony*, *The Negro Handbook*, 1974, 386, show that the *Baptist Review*, 1841, and the *Southwestern Christian Recorder*, 1848, religious newspapers with limited circulation, were begun in Nashville, Tennessee, before *L'Union*.

26. Pride, "Register and History of Negro Newspapers," 404.

27. Thomas J. Davis, "Louisiana," in *The Black Press in the South, 1865–1979*, ed. Henry Lewis Suggs (Westport, Conn.: Greenwood, 1983), 151.

28. Ibid., 152.

29. Pride, "Register and History of Negro Newspapers," 97.

30. Davis, "Louisiana," 154.

31. Ibid., 155.

32. Ibid.

33. Ibid.

34. Ibid.

35. Garrett, *Famous First Facts About Negroes*, 143.

36. Hughes, *Pictorial History*, 215.

37. Ibid., 214–15.

38. Samuel Shannon, "Tennessee," in *The Black Press in the South, 1865–1979*, ed. Henry Lewis Suggs (Westport, Conn.: Greenwood, 1983), 325.

39. Toppin, *Biographical History*, 446.

40. Shannon, "Tennessee," 325.

41. Ibid.

42. Ibid., 326.

43. Penn, *Afro-American Press*, 408.

44. Shannon, "Tennessee," 326–27.

45. Ibid., 327.

46. Ibid.

47. Ibid.

48. Ibid.

49. Alfreda Duster, ed., *The Autobiography of Ida B. Wells* (Chicago: University of Chicago Press, 1970), 63.

50. Ibid.

51. Ibid., 61–62.

52. Ibid., 63.

53. Shannon, "Tennessee," 327.

54. Hughes, *Pictorial History*, 256.

55. Gunnar Myrdal, *An American Dilemma* (New York: Harper & Row, 1962), 566–67.

56. August Meier, "Booker T. Washington and the Negro Press: With Special Reference to the *Colored American Magazine*," *Journal of Negro History* 38 (January 1953): 74.

57. The Editors of *Ebony*, *The Negro Handbook*, 1974, 420.

58. Toppin, *Biographical History*, 168.

59. Ibid.

60. August Meier, *Negro Thought in America, 1880–1915* (Ann Arbor: University of Michigan Press, 1969), 198.

61. Meier, *Negro Thought*, 198; Roland E. Wolseley, *The Black Press U.S.A.* (Ames: Iowa State University Press, 1971), 34.

62. Francis L. Broderick, *W.E.B. DuBois: Negro Leader in a Time of Crisis* (1959; reprint, Stanford: Stanford University Press, 1966), 66.

63. Penn, *Afro-American Press*, 408.

64. Toppin, *Biographical History*, 168.

65. Meier, *Negro Thought*, 224.

66. Booker T. Washington, *Up from Slavery* (New York: Dodd, Mead, 1965), 138–43.

Chapter 2

1. Langston Hughes, Milton Meltzer, and C. Eric Lincoln, *A Pictorial History of Black Americans* (New York: Crown, 1983), 262.

2. Jessie Parkhurst Guzman, ed. *Negro Yearbook: 1941–1946* (Tuskegee: Tuskegee Institute, Department of Records and Research, 1947), 385.

3. Gunner Myrdal, *An American Dilemma* (New York: Harper & Row, 1962), 194.

4. Roland E. Wolseley, *The Black Press U.S.A.* (Ames: Iowa State University Press, 1971), 27.

5. Mable M. Smythe, ed, *The Black American Reference Book* (Englewood Cliffs, N.J.: Prentice-Hall, 1976), 853.

6. Edgar A. Toppin, *A Biographical History of Blacks in America Since 1528* (New York: David McKay, 1971), 244–245.

7. Wolseley, *Black Press*, 36.

8. Ibid., 37.

9. Smythe, *Black American Reference Book*, 853.

10. Frederick G. Detweiler, *The Negro Press in the United States* (1922; reprint, College Park: University of Chicago Press and McGrath, 1968), 20–21.

11. National Association for the Advancement of Colored People, *Thirty Years of Lynching in the United States, 1889–1918* (1919; reprint, New York: Arno and the *New York Times*, 1969), Introduction.

12. Lee Finkle, *Forum for Protest: The Black Press During World War II* (Cranbury, N.J.: Associated University Presses, 1975), 44–45.

13. Metz T. P. Lochard, "Robert S. Abbott—'Race Leader,'" *Phylon* 8 (Second Quarter 1947): 124–32.

14. Finkle, *Forum for Protest*, 44–45.

15. This newspaper was first founded as the *Christian Herald* in 1848, but it had a name change in 1852.

16. Founded in 1875.

17. Dewitt C. Reddick, *The Mass Media and the School Newspaper*, 2d ed. (Belmont, Calif.: Wadsworth, 1985), 20–21.

18. Detweiler, *Negro Press*, 97.

19. Booker T. Washington, *Up from Slavery* (New York: Dodd, Mead, 1965), 29.

20. Roland E. Wolseley, *The Black Press, U.S.A.* (Ames: Iowa State University Press, 1971, 37.

21. Finkle, *Forum for Protest*, 45.

22. Lawrence D. Hogan, *A Black National News Service: The Associated Negro Press and Claude Barnett, 1919–1945* (Rutherford, N.J.: Fairleigh Dickinson University Press, 1984), 49.

23. Florette Henri, *Black Migration: Movement North—1900–1920* (New Garden City, N.Y.: Anchor Press/Doubleday, 1975), 57.

24. Ibid., 52.

25. Smythe, *Black American Reference Book*, 858.

26. Henri, *Black Migration*, 56–57.

27. "Our Part in the Exodus," *Chicago Defender*, 17 March 1917, editorial page.

28. "Getting the South Told," *Chicago Defender* 25 November 1916, editorial page.

29. Detweiler, *Negro Press*, 73.

30. Henri, *Black Migration*, 59.

31. Detweiler, Negro Press, 72–74; Allan H. Spear, *Black Chicago: The Making of a Negro Ghetto, 1890–1920* (Chicago: University of Chicago Press, 1967), 134–135.

32. "Freezing to Death in the South," *Chicago Defender,* 24 February 1917, 1.

33. Detweiler, *Negro Press*, 72–74; Spear, *Black Chicago*, 134–35.

34. "Farewell, Dixie Land." *Chicago Defender,* 7 October 1916, editorial page.

35. Henri, *Black Migration*, 65.

36. Detweiler, *Negro Press*, 15.

37. Henri, 63, 65–66.

38. Ibid., 65–66.

39. Ibid.

40. Ibid.

41. Ibid.

42. Ibid., 67–68.

43. Spear, *Black Chicago*, 137.

44. Smythe, *Black American Reference Book*, 858.

45. Spear, *Black Chicago*, 137.

46. Henri, *Black Migration*, 66.

47. Spear, *Black Chicago*, 137.

48. Wolseley, *Black Press*, 53–54.

49. Henri, *Black Migration*, 64.

50. Detweiler, *Negro Press*, 154–155.

51. Smythe, *Black American Reference Book*, 857.

52. "Freezing to Death in the South," *Chicago Defender*, 24 February 1917, 1.

53. Smythe, *Black American Reference Book*, 857.

54. Detweiler, *Negro Press*, 72.

55. Ibid.
56. Spear, *Black Chicago*, 135.
57. Henri, *Black Migration*, 72.
58. Ibid.
59. Ibid., 73.
60. Ibid., 63.
61. Spear, *Black Chicago*, 82.
62. Finkle, *Forum for Protest*, 45.
63. Toppin, *Biographical History*, 173.
64. Hughes, *Pictorial History*, 262.
65. Robert Goldston, *The Negro Revolution* (Toronto: Macmillan, Collier-Macmillan Canada, 1968), 169.
66. Finkle, *Forum for Protest*, 46.
67. Ibid.
68. Andrew Buni, *Robert L. Vann of "The Pittsburgh Courier"* (Pittsburgh: University of Pittsburgh Press, 1974), 105–7.
69. Smythe, *Black American Reference Book*, 858.
70. Ibid.

Chapter 3

1. Andrew Buni, *Robert L. Vann of "The Pittsburgh Courier"* (Pittsburgh: University of Pittsburgh Press, 1974), 42.
2. Ibid., 43.
3. Ibid., 43–44.
4. Ibid., 42–45.
5. Ibid., 3.
6. Edgar A. Toppin, *A Biographical History of Blacks in America Since 1528* (New York: David McKay, 1971), 433–434.
7. Eugene Gordon, "Outstanding Negro Newspapers, 1927," *Opportunity* (December 1927): 358–59.
8. Buni, *Robert L. Vann*, 53.
9. Mabel M. Smythe, ed., *The Black American Reference Book* (Englewood Cliffs, N.J.: Prentice-Hall, 1976), 859.
10. Buni, Robert L. Vann, 49.
11. Ibid.
12. Ibid., 52–53.
13. Ibid., 62.
14. Ibid., 61–69.
15. Ibid., 74.
16. Ibid., 102.
17. Ibid.
18. Ibid., 77.
19. Ibid., 74.
20. Ibid., 104.

21. Ibid., 107.
22. Ibid., 108.
23. Ibid., 138.
24. Ibid.
25. Ibid., 138–139.
26. Langston Hughes, Milton Meltzer, and C. Eric Lincoln, *A Pictorial History of Black Americans* (New York: Crown, 1983), 270.
27. How that force was to be carried out was never explained.
28. Hughes, *Pictorial History*, 270.
29. Ibid., 271.
30. Ibid., 270–271.
31. Buni, *Robert L. Vann*, 138–139.
32. Ibid., 140.
33. Hughes, 123–124.
34. Toppin, *Biographical History*, 434.
35. Gordon, "Outstanding Negro Newspapers," 358–363.

Chapter 4

1. Jimmy Stewart, personal interview, 10 May 1982.
2. Ibid.
3. Kaye M. Teall, *Black History in Oklahoma: A Resource Book* (Oklahoma City: Oklahoma City Public Schools, 1971), 271.
4. Stewart interview.
5. Ibid.
6. Ibid.
7. Ibid.
8. Ibid.
9. It is not certain exactly when this newspaper was founded. Dunjee, in an editorial "Freedom for All Forever—Editorial," *Black Dispatch* 2 January 1920, 4, stated the paper was founded on November 4, 1914. On a television program "Freedom for All Forever, Roscoe Dunjee Story," KOCO, Oklahoma City, August 28, 1981, he said he founded the paper in 1914. But in a front-page news story, "Sanford and Dunjee Form Partnership in Publication of the Black Dispatch," September 14, 1940, a founding date of November 8, 1915, is carried.
10. Armistead S. Pride, "A Register and History of Negro Newspapers in the United States: 1827–1950" (Ph.D. diss., Northwestern University, 1950), 138.
11. Stewart interview.
12. "Our Policy," *Black Dispatch*, 28 June 1918, 4.
13. Stewart interview.
14. "Freedom for All Forever, Roscoe Dunjee Story," KOCO, Oklahoma City, 28 August 1981.
15. "The Negro Going Northward," *Black Dispatch*, 21 September 1917, 4.
16. "Senseless Negroes," *Black Dispatch*, 9 July 1920, 4.
17. Stewart interview.

18. Teall, *Black History*, 196.

19. Arthur L. Tolson, *Black Oklahomans: A History, 1541–1972* (New Orleans: Edwards, 1974), 176.

20. Ibid.

21. "If That Be Treason, Make the Most of It," *Black Dispatch*, 15 February 1941, 6.

22. "Open Letter About Jim Crow Injustice, Not Equal in Point of Safety," *Black Dispatch*, 5 October 1917, 1.

23. "Our Schools Badly Need a Truant Officer," *Black Dispatch*, 21 September 1917, 1.

24. "To the Governor—Copy of Letter Sent Chief Executive Who Failed in Manuscript to Mention Black Soldiers of Oklahoma," *Black Dispatch*, 30 November 1917, 1.

25. "NEW BATTLE NOW IN PROGRESS," *Tulsa World*, 1 June 1921, 1.

26. Teall, *Black History*, 204.

27. "Negroes Attempt to Protect Negro Boy Charged With Crime, Whites Try to Disarm Blacks," *Black Dispatch*, 3 June 1921, 1.

28. Ibid.

29. *Black Dispatch*, 3 June 1921, 1.

30. "Whites and Negroes Die in Tulsa Riots As 3,000 Armed Men Battle in Streets; 30 Blocks Burned, Military Rule in City," *New York Times*, 2 June 1921, 1.

31. Teall, *Black History*, 205.

32. "DEAD! Stop Spreading False Rumors," *Black Dispatch*, 3 June 1921, 1.

33. "LOOT, ARSON, MURDER! Four Million Dollars Lost—Sarah Page Not to Be Found," *Black Dispatch*, 10 June 1921, 1; and "Dick Rowland in South Omaha, No Trace of Girl," *Black Dispatch*, 17 June 1921, 1.

34. "$650.00 Had Been Raised," *Black Dispatch* 3 June 1921, 1; *Black Dispatch*, 10 June 1921, 1; "Dick Rowland in South Omaha, No Trace of Girl," *Black Dispatch*, 17 June 1921, 1.

35. "Negroes Fleeing from City; List of Dead Mounts," *Tulsa World*, 1 Jun. 1921, 1.

36. *Black Dispatch*, 10 June 1921, 1.

37. *Black Dispatch*, 17 June 1921, 1.

38. *Black Dispatch*, 10 June 1921, 1.

39. "Armed White Parties Are to Be Disbanded," *Tulsa World*, 1 June 1921, morning ed., third extra, 1.

40. *Black Dispatch*, 10 June 1921, 1.

41. Ibid.

42. "Freedom for All Forever, Roscoe Dunjee Story," KOCO, Oklahoma City, 28 August 1981.

Chapter 5

1. Julius Eric Thompson, "Mississippi," in *The Black Press in the South, 1865–1979*, ed. Henry Lewis Suggs (Westport, Conn.: Greenwood, 1983), 182.

2. Ibid.
3. Ibid., 179–180.
4. Ibid., 199.
5. George Alexander Sewell, *Mississippi Black History Makers* (Jackson: University Press of Mississippi, 1977), 265.
6. Ibid.
7. Ibid., 263–264.
8. Frederick G. Detweiler, *The Negro Press in the United States* (1922; reprint, College Park: University of Chicago Press and McGrath, 1968), 15.
9. Thompson, "Mississippi," 198.
10. Lee Finkle, *Forum for Protest: The Black Press During World War II* (Cranbury, N.J.: Associated University Presses, 1975), 19.
11. Ibid.
12. Detweiler, *Negro Press*, 15.
13. Henry Lewis Suggs, ed., *The Black Press in the South, 1865–1979* (Westport, Conn.: Greenwood, 1983), vii.
14. Detweiler, *Negro Press*, 75.
15. Augustus Low and Virgil A. Clift, eds., *Encyclopedia of Black America* (New York: McGraw, 1981), 640.
16. Thompson, "Mississippi," 182.

Chapter 6

1. Lee Finkle, *Forum for Protest: The Black Press During World War II* (Cranbury, N.J.: Associated University Presses, 1975), 48. The festering problem was the decision during World War I by W.E.B. DuBois, who had been a leader in launching racial attacks, but abruptly halted those attacks and called for the black press to "forget our special grievances and close our ranks ... with our own white fellow citizens...."
2. Ibid., 59.
3. Ibid., 54.
4. Ibid., 157.
5. Henry Lewis Suggs, ed., *The Black Press in the South: 1865–1979* (Westport, Conn.: Greenwood, 1983), 203.
6. Mabel E. Smythe, ed., *The Black American Reference Book* (Englewood Cliffs, N.J., Prentice Hall, 1976), 859.
7. Patrick S. Washburn, *A Question of Sedition: The Federal Government's Investigation of the Black Press During World War II* (New York: Oxford University Press, 1986), 39.
8. Franklin Frazier, *The Negro in the United States* (New York: Macmillan, 1949), 515.
9. Ibid.
10. George Alexander Sewell, *Mississippi Black History Makers* (Jackson: University Press of Mississippi, 1977), 265.

11. Washburn, *A Question of Sedition*, 84.

12. Ibid., 34.

13. Ibid.

14. "Used Men As Seagoing Chambermaids, Bell Hops, Dishwashers," *Pittsburgh Courier*, 5 October 1940, national ed., 1.

15. Washburn, *A Question of Sedition*, 35.

16. P. L. Prattis, "13 Messmen on U.S.S. Philadelphia Made 'Mistake' by Writing Their Side of Story and Signing Names," *Pittsburgh Courier*, 7 December 1940, national ed., 1.

17. "Used Men As Seagoing Chambermaids, Bell Hops, Dishwashers," *Pittsburgh Courier*, 5 October 1940, national ed., 1.

18. "Navy Messmen, in Prison, Cry Out for Help from Readers," *Pittsburgh Courier*, 9 November 1940, national ed., 1.

19. Finkle, *Forum for Protest*, 159.

20. Washburn, *A Question of Sedition*, 53–54.

21. Ibid.

22. Ibid., 11.

23. Ibid., 82.

24. Ibid., 32.

25. Ibid., 33.

26. Ibid., 62.

27. Ibid., 84.

28. Ibid., 32–33.

29. The newspapers under this chain were located in Baltimore, Philadelphia, Richmond, Va., Newark, N.J., and Washington, D.C.

30. Washburn, *A Question of Sedition*, 63–64.

31. Ibid., 59.

32. Ibid., 84.

33. *Pittsburgh Courier*, 20 December 1941, 6.

34. Washburn, *A Question of Sedition*, 64.

35. "Stand Together," *Black Dispatch*, 20 December 1941, editorial page.

36. "Japan and United States at War," *Jackson Advocate*, 13 December 1941, 8.

37. "News From the World at War," *Jackson Advocate*, 27 December 1941, 8.

38. Washburn, *A Question of Sedition*, 99.

39. Ibid.

40. "Race Support of War Effort Is Lukewarm, Say Conferees," *Pittsburgh Courier*, 17 January 1942, national ed., 1

41. "No Closed Ranks Now, Says *Crisis*," *Pittsburgh Courier*, 17 January 1942, national ed., 2.

42. James G. Thompson, "Should I Sacrifice to Live 'Half-American?'" *Pittsburgh Courier*, 31 January 1942, national ed., 3.

43. "Democracy, At Home, Abroad," *Pittsburgh Courier*, 7 February 1942, national ed., 7.

44. Washburn, *A Question of Sedition*, 54.

45. "The Courier's Double 'V' For A Double Victory Campaign Gets

Country-Wide Support," *Pittsburgh Courier*, 14 February 1942, national ed., 1.

46. Washburn, *A Question of Sedition*, 100.

47. Ibid., 82.

48. Finkle, *Forum for Protest*, 114.

49. Frazier, *Negro in the United States*, 514.

50. Washburn, *A Question of Sedition*, 100–101.

51. Ibid., 82.

52. Ibid., 103.

53. Ibid., 101–103.

54. Ibid., 102.

55. Ibid.

56. Ibid.

57. Ibid., 146–148.

58. Ibid., 145.

59. Ibid., 144.

60. Ibid., 144–146.

61. Ibid., 8.

62. *Jackson Advocate*, 13 December 1941, 1, 8.

63. "Peace on Earth, Goodwill Toward Men," *Jackson Advocate*, 20 December 1941, 8.

64. "Tid-Bits of Negro History," *Jackson Advocate*, 14 February 1942, 1.

65. "The Sikeston Lynching and Negro Morale," *Jackson Advocate*, 7 February 1942, 8.

66. "The Mississippi Power And Light Company Contributes To Negro Morale," *Jackson Advocate*, 21 February 1942, 8.

67. "The Mississippi Negro Their Civil Rights and the Twentieth Century Carpetbaggers," *Jackson Advocate*, 2 February 1963, 4.

68. "The Mississippi Negro and His Schools," *Jackson Advocate*, 13 March 1965, 4.

69. Washburn, *A Question of Sedition*, 180.

70. Ibid., 175.

71. "Writer Lauds Russia's Treatment of Negroes," *Jackson Advocate*, 6 December 1941, 8.

72. Washburn, *A Question of Sedition*, 176.

73. Ibid., 170.

74. Ibid., 183.

75. "Identifying the Communists," *Black Dispatch*, 10 October 1942, 6.

76. Washburn, *A Question of Sedition*, 183.

77. Ibid., 192.

78. Ibid., 166.

79. Ibid., 105.

80. Ibid., 174.

81. Ibid., 8–9.

82. Ibid., 5.

83. Edward Carter, *The Story of Oklahoma Newspapers, 1844–1984* (Muskogee: Western Heritage Books, 1984), 191.

84. Jimmy Stewart, personal interview, May 10, 1982.
85. Ibid.
86. Note the difference in the spelling of the last names: Roscoe Dunjee and John Dungee.
87. Stewart interview.
88. Ibid.
89. Ibid.

Chapter 7

1. John Hope Franklin, *From Slavery to Freedom: A History of Negro Americans*, 3d ed. (New York: Alfred A. Knopf, 1967), 623–38.
2. Benjamin Muse, *The American Negro Revolution* (Bloomington: Indiana University Press, 1968), 54.
3. Neil R. McMillen, "Development of Civil Rights, 1956–1970," in *A History of Mississippi*, vol. II, ed. Richard A. McLemore (Hattiesburg: University and College Press of Mississippi, 1973), 155–156.
4. Ibid., 155–156.
5. Mildred Pitts Walter, *Mississippi Challenge* (New York: Bradbury, 1992), 53–54.
6. "Education in the United States," *Prodigy Interactive Personal Service* (Grolier Electronic Publishing, 1994).
7. McMillen, "Development of Civil Rights," 155.
8. Ibid., 160.
9. The State Sovereignty Commission's files were so secretive, in fact, that the state legislators have sealed those public records for the next 50 years.
10. Mississippi, Record Group 42, Sovereignty Commission, Report on State Sovereignty Commission, vol. 15: 1964–1967.
11. "A&T Students Stage Sit-Down at Woolworths," *Pittsburgh Courier*, 13 February 1960, 4.
12. Franklin, *From Slavery to Freedom*, 623.
13. James Farmer, *Lay Bare the Heart: An Autobiography of the Civil Rights Movement* (New York: Penguin, 1985), 192.
14. "A&T Students Stage Sit-Down at Woolworths," *Pittsburgh Courier*, 13 February 1960, 4.
15. Sanford Wexler, *The Civil Rights Movement: An Eyewitness History* (New York: Facts on File, 1993), 125.
16. Herbert Aptheker, comp. and ed., *A Documentary History of the Negro People in the United States, 1960–1968*, vol. 7 (New York: Carol, 1994), 31; and David R. Goldfield, *Black, White, and Southern: Race Relations and Southern Culture* (Baton Rouge: Louisiana State University Press, 1990), 118–119.
17. Mortimer J. Adler, Charles Van Doren, and George Ducas, eds., *The Negro in American History* (n.p.: Encyclopaedia Britannica Educational Corporation, 1969), 282.

18. Aptheker, *Documentary History*, 30.

19. Walter, *Mississippi Challenge*, 7.

20. Peter B. Levy, ed., *Documentary History of the Modern Civil Rights Movement* (New York: Greenwood, 1992), 74.

21. "A&T Students Stage Sit-Down at Woolworths," *Pittsburgh Courier* 13 Feb. 1960: 4.

22. "Student Protest Spreads to S.C.," *Pittsburgh Courier*, 20 February 1960, 3.

23. *Pittsburgh Courier*, 5 March 1960, 1–3.

24. *Pittsburgh Courier*, 12 March 1960, 2–9.

25. "The '11' Commandments—For Southern Students, White and Colored, Fighting Segregation," *Pittsburgh Courier* 12 March 1960, 3.

26. "Must Abide by Local Customs," *Pittsburgh Courier*, 12 March 1960, 8.

27. "Students 'Sitdown' Protest Spreads to Virginia, Tenn.," *Daily Defender*, 16 February 1960, 3.

28. *Daily Defender*, 16 February 1960, 3.

29. "Sit-Down Background—4 Students Spark Spreading Drive," *Daily Defender*, 3 March 1960, 9.

30. "Lunch Counter Protest Spreads All Over Nation," *Black Dispatch*, 26 February 1960, 1.

31. "He Can't Live with Them, He Can't Live without Them," *Black Dispatch*, 26 February 1960, 5.

32. "City-By-City Round-up On Sit-Down Strikes," *Black Dispatch*, 25 March 1960, 3.

33. "NAACP Officials Call off Planned Demonstration," *Black Dispatch*, 1 April 1960, 1.

34. "State Group Eyes Lunch Counter Jim Crow Fight," *Black Dispatch*, 15 Apr. 1960, 1.

35. "Sitdown Protest Darkens U.S. Race Picture," *Jackson Advocate*, 5 March 1960, 1.

36. "The Sitdown Protests and the Future of American Negroes," *Jackson Advocate*, 5 March 1960, 4.

37. Ibid.

38. Peter M. Bergman, *The Chronological History of the Negro in America* (New York: Harper & Row, 1969), 568.

39. "Harlem Pickets Woolworth in Support Southern Students," *Jackson Advocate*, 5 March 1960, 1.

40. "Ohio Students Win; Cafe Drops Race Bar," *Pittsburgh Courier*, 9 March 1960, 3.

41. "Sit-Ins Win Victories in Eight Dixie Cities," *Daily Defender*, 8 June 1960, 5.

42. "Score Sit-In Results in Tallahassee," *Daily Defender*, 6 June 1960, 2.

43. "Sit-Ins Win Victories in Eight Dixie Cities," *Daily Defender*, 8 June 1960, 5.

44. Aptheker, *Documentary History*, 32–33.

45. Julius Eric Thompson, "Mississippi," in *The Black Press in the South, 1865–1979*, ed. Henry Lewis Suggs (Westport, Conn.: Greenwood, 1983), 192.

46. Ibid., 192.

47. George Alexander Sewell, *Mississippi Black History Makers* (Jackson's University Press of Mississippi, 1977), 263–264.

48. "Friendly Relations with White People Still the Mississippi Negro's Greatest Asset," *Jackson Advocate*, 21 November 1959, 4.

49. "Hooray For Georgia," *Jackson Advocate*, 27 May 1961, 4.

50. "'Reds Exploit Sit-Ins,' Truman Says on TV," *Daily Defender*, 13 June 1960, 2.

51. "HST Tells Viewers, 'Niggers Must Grow Up,'" *Daily Defender*, 14 June 1960, 3.

52. "ABC-TV Officials Deny Harry Truman Slur," *Daily Defender*, 15 June 1960, 3.

53. "Mrs. Roosevelt Denies Reds Back Sit-Ins," *Daily Defender*, 20 June 1960, 2.

54. "Irrepressible Mr. Truman," *Daily Defender*, 21 June 1960, 10.

55. "FBI Director Says Communist Influence in Negro Movement," *Jackson Advocate*, 25 April 1964, 1.

56. "Wake-Up Mississippi Negro Wake-Up," *Jackson Advocate*, 25 April 1964, 4.

57. "Percy Greene Tells Why He Switched," *Pittsburgh Courier*, 21 January 1961, 2.

58. "Friendly Relations with White People Still the Mississippi Negro's Greatest Asset," *Jackson Advocate*, 21 November 1959, 4.

59. "No Role for Martin Luther King," *Jackson Advocate*, 13 January 1962, 4.

60. Alton Hornsby, Jr., *The Black Almanac*, rev. ed. (New York: Barron's Educational Series, 1973), 80. Although the *Courier*'s report showed a date of May 17, 1945, the actual date was May 17, 1954, for the *Brown vs Board of Education* of Topeka decision.

61. "Percy Greene Tells Why He Switched," *Pittsburgh Courier*, 21 January 1961, 2.

62. "The Medgar Evers Story," *Jackson Advocate*, 8 November 1958, 4.

63. "Wanted—Another Booker T. Washington," *Jackson Advocate*, 29 November 1958, 4.

64. *Jackson Advocate*, 29 November 1958, 5.

65. Erle Johnston, *Mississippi's Defiant Years* (Forest, Miss.: Lake Harbor, 1990), 231.

66. Wexler, *Civil Rights Movement*, 111.

67. "Atlanta Mayor Raps 'Rabble Rousers,'" *Pittsburgh Courier*, 15 April 1961, sec. 2, 2.

68. Bergman, *Chronological History*, 573.

69. Anthony Lewis and the *New York Times*, *Portrait of a Decade: The Second American Revolution* (New York: Random House, 1964), 87.

70. Howard Zinn, *A People's History of the United States* (New York: Harper Perennial, 1980), 444.

71. Farmer, *Lay Bare the Heart*, 195–196.

72. Patricia and Frederick McKissack, *The Civil Rights Movement in America from 1865 to the Present* (Chicago: Children's Press, 1987), 211.

73. Farmer, *Lay Bare the Heart*, 199.

74. Ibid., 197.

75. Henry Hampton and Steve Fayer with Sarah Flynn, *Voices Freedom: An Oral History of the Civil Rights Movement from the 1950s through the 1980s* (New York: Bantam Books, 1990), 77.

76. Farmer, *Lay Bare the Heart*, 196–204.

77. Hampton, *Voices of Freedom*, 77–78.

78. Farmer, *Lay Bare the Heart*, 202.

79. Ibid.

80. Hampton, *Voices of Freedom*, 78.

81. "Alabama Leaders Blame Bus-Riding Travelers for Trouble," *Black Dispatch*, 26 May 1961, 1.

82. *Black Dispatch*, 26 May 1961, 1.

83. "Patterson's Words a 'Mockery' to Victims of Alabama Racists," *Pittsburgh Courier*, 3 June 1961, sec. 2, 1.

84. "Alabama Leaders Blame Bus-Riding Travelers for Trouble," *Black Dispatch*, 26 May 1961, 1.

85. Hampton, *Voices of Freedom*, 79.

86. Ibid.

87. Farmer, *Lay Bare the Heart*, 203.

88. *Daily Defender*, 16 May 1961, 3.

89. "Alabama Hoodlums," *Daily Defender*, 17 May 1961, 11.

90. Wexler, *Civil Rights Movement*, 122.

91. "'We're Ready to Die,' Vow Beaten 'Freedom Riders' After Riots," *Pittsburgh Courier*, 3 June 1961, sec. 2, 2.

92. Zinn, *People's History*, 441.

93. David R. Goldfield, *Black, White, and Southern: Race Relations and Southern Culture, 1940 to the Present* (Baton Rouge: Louisiana State University Press, 1990), 127.

94. Hampton, *Voices of Freedom*, 89.

95. Ibid., 88–90.

96. "Was Beating of Whites Racists' Big Mistake?" *Pittsburgh Courier*, 3 June 1961, sec. 2, 2.

97. Wexler, *Civil Rights Movement*, 118.

98. Hampton, *Voices of Freedom*, 90.

99. "Send 200 More Marshals to Ala.," *Daily Defender*, 23 May 1961, 3.

100. "Says Klans Gird for Race Fight," *Daily Defender*, 23 May 1961, 3.

101. Ibid.

102. "On the Alabama Riots," *Black Dispatch*, 2 June 1961, 6.

103. Ibid.

104. Ibid.

105. "Cool Off? ... For What? 'The Mob Must Not Win,'" *Pittsburgh Courier*, 3 June 1961, sec. 1, 2.

106. "UL Raps Bob Kennedy For 'Cool Off' Plea," *Pittsburgh Courier*, 10 June 1961, 2.
107. Aptheker, *Documentary History*, 96–97.
108. Ibid., 98.
109. Edgar A. Toppin, *A Biographical History of Blacks in America Since 1528* (New York: David McKay, 1971), 168.
110. Aptheker, 98.
111. Ibid.
112. Hampton, *Voices of Freedom*, 92.
113. "We'll Fill Their Jails," *Pittsburgh Courier*, 10 June 1961, 3.
114. Hampton, *Voices of Freedom*, 94.
115. "Jail 25 Freedom Riders In Miss.," *Daily Defender*, 25 May 1961, sec. 1, 3.
116. "'Freedom Riders' Hijacked, Lawyer Says of Convicted 27," *Daily Defender*, 29 May 1961, sec. 1, 2.
117. "Ride On, Freedom Riders," *Daily Defender*, 29 May 1961, sec. 1, 11.
118. "Vandiver Vows to Keep Order for 'Mixing,' *Pittsburgh Courier*, 17 July 1961, sec. 1, 2.
119. "Truman Blasts, 'Rocky' Boost 'Freedom Riders,'" *Pittsburgh Courier* 17 Jul. 1961, sec. 1: 2.
120. Wexler, *Civil Rights Movement*, 132–133.
121. Ibid., 133.
122. "Jail 25 Freedom Riders in Miss.," *Daily Defender*, 25 May 1961, sec. 1, 3.
123. Lewis and the *New York Times*, 214.
124. "Court Orders Meredith Enrolled at University of Mississippi," *Jackson Advocate*, 30 June 1962, 1.
125. "The Decision in the University of Mississippi Case," *Jackson Advocate*, 30 June 1962, 4.
126. "Meredith Loses His Bid for Immediate Entry at Ole Miss," *Jackson Advocate*, 14 July 1962, 1.
127. Hampton, *Voices of Freedom*, 116.
128. Ibid.
129. Ibid., 118.
130. Ibid., 116.
131. Ibid., 119–120.
132. Ibid., 120.
133. "The Ole Miss Crisis and History's Challenge to Mississippi Negroes," *Jackson Advocate*, 13 October 1962, 4.
134. Farmer, *Lay Bare the Heart*, 202.
135. Hampton, *Voices of Freedom*, 124.
136. Ibid., 128.
137. Ibid., 125.
138. Ibid.
139. Muse, *American Negro Revolution*, 5.
140. Hampton, *Voices of Freedom*, 124.
141. Ibid., 125–126.

142. Ibid., 127.
143. C. S. Hammond, *Year's Pictorial History of the American Negro* (New York: Year Inc., 1965), 100.
144. Goldfield, *Black, White, and Southern*, 135.
145. Hampton, *Voices of Freedom*, 129.
146. Goldfield, *Black, White, and Southern*, 135.
147. Ibid.
148. "Negro Leaders Rejects Call of U.S. Attorney Gen. Kennedy," *Jackson Advocate*, 13 April 1963, 1.
149. Hammond, *Pictorial History*, 101.
150. Hampton, *Voices of Freedom*, 133.
151. Goldfield, *Black, White, and Southern*, 140.
152. Hampton, *Voices of Freedom*, 134.
153. "Rev. Shuttlesworth Alive, 'Bull' Sorry," *Pittsburgh Courier*, 18 May 1963, sec. 1, 1; "Bull Conner Says He's Sorry Blast Did Not Kill Pastor," *Black Dispatch*, 24 May 1963, 10.
154. "Alabama's Like a 'Foreign' Land, Asserts Atty.-Gen. Bob Kennedy," *Pittsburgh Courier*, 4 May 1963, sec. 1, 1.
155. "Editorial Comment," *Black Dispatch*, 19 April 1963, 6.
156. Ibid.
157. Ibid.
158. Ibid.
159. "More Negroes Leave Miss. Than from Any Other State," *Pittsburgh Courier*, 1 April 1961, sec. 2, 5.
160. "Civil Rights Groups Invade Leflore County," *Jackson Advocate*, 9 March 1963, 1.
161. Ibid. It is not certain if Wiley A. Branton, Negro lawyer and director of the Voter Education Project, is the same person as Wiley Brandon of Pine Bluff, Arkansas (see page 120).
162. Ibid.
163. "Protection for Voting Rights," *Jackson Advocate*, 9 March 1963, 4.
164. "Second Shooting in Greenwood Is Reported Within a Week," *Jackson Advocate*, 16 March 1963, 1.
165. "Incidents Mounting In Leflore County As Fire Is Set to SNCC Office Shotgun Blast Home of Dewey Green's Parents," *Jackson Advocate*, 30 March 1963, 1.
166. "Miss. Cop, Dog Scatter 100 in Voting March," *Daily Defender*, 28 March 1963, 3.
167. "Russians Flay Travel Curb to Mississippi," *Daily Defender*, 10 April 1963, 4.
168. "Soviet Journalist Say Mississippi Negroes Afraid," *Jackson Advocate* 21 Mar. 1964: 1.
169. "Dick Gregory In Greenwood," *Jackson Advocate*, 6 April 1963, 1.
170. "Miss. Cops Manhandle Gregory in Vote March," *Daily Defender*, 3 April 1996, 2.
171. "Greene Blasts Gregory for 'Butting In,'" *Black Dispatch* 19 April 1963, 1.

172. "2 Negro Editors Make 'Uncle Tom' Appeals to Negroes to Reject Civil Rights Drive," *Black Dispatch*, 31 May 1993, 10.

173. "Mayor Pleased with Greenwood Negro Citizens," *Jackson Advocate*, 13 April 1963, 1.

174. "Say Jackson Least Civilized Spot in State," *Jackson Advocate*, 27 April 1963, 1.

175. "Violence Flares As NAACP Backed Sit-Ins Start Here," *Jackson Advocate*, 1 June 1963, 1.

176. "Sit-ins Now Have 'Green' Light—Jack," *Pittsburgh Courier*, 1 June 1963, 1.

177. "NAACP's Roy Wilkins Jailed in Jackson; Calls Mississippi 'Nazi State,'" *Pittsburgh Courier*, 8 June 1963, 1.

178. Walter, *Mississippi Challenge*, 107.

179. Goldfield, *Black, White, and Southern*, 156.

180. Peter B. Levy, ed., *Documentary History of the Modern Civil Rights Movement* (New York: Greenwood, 1992), 139; Walter, *Mississippi Challenge* 109–110.

181. Hampton, *Voices of Freedom*, 142.

182. Ibid., 141.

183. Ibid., 150.

184. Levy, *Documentary History*, 167.

185. Hampton, *Voices of Freedom*, 152.

186. Ibid., 155.

187. Ibid., 154–155.

188. "Kennedy Shocked by 'Barbaric' Murder of Evers," *Daily Defender*, 13 June 1963, 3; "NAACP Chief's 3 Tots Beg Dad Not to Die," *Daily Defender*, 13 June 1963, 3.

189. "Medgar Evers Slain by Bullet from Sniper's Rifle," *Jackson Advocate*, 15 June 1963, 1.

190. "Evers' Killer Was Expert Shot," *Black Dispatch*, 21 June 1963, 1.

191. "Bury 'Tall Quiet Man' from Decatur, Miss.," *Pittsburgh Courier*, 22 June 1963, 1; "Jackson's Police Holding 'Suspect,'" *Pittsburgh Courier*, 22 June 1963, 1.

192. "Medgar Evers Laid to Rest Among Nation's Heroes," *Jackson Advocate*, 22 June 1963, 1; "Evers Brother New State NAACP Secy.," *Jackson Advocate*, 22 June 1963, 1.

193. "Mississippi Negro Editor Blasts Northern 'Niggers,' *Black Dispatch*, 28 June 1963, 3.

194. "Accused Slayer of Medgar Evers Awaits Action Hinds Grand Jury," *Jackson Advocate*, 29 June 1963, 1.

195. "Beckwith Must Face Second Trial as Jurors Disagree," *Pittsburgh Courier*, 15 February 1964, 1.

196. "La Beckwith Free on Bond," *Pittsburgh Courier*, 25 April 1964, 1.

197. *Jackson Advocate*, 17 August 1963, 1.

198. Editorial, *Black Dispatch*, 13 September 1963, 6.

199. Ibid.

200. Ibid.

201. Ibid.
202. "Many Washington Marchers Beaten, Arrested When They Return to Southern Homes," *Black Dispatch*, 20 September 1963, 11.
203. McKissack, *Civil Rights Movement*, 225; Levy, *Documentary History*, 125.
204. "A Look at the Recent Birmingham Church Bombing," *Jackson Advocate*, 28 September 1963, editorial page.
205. "John F. Kennedy an American Immortal," *Jackson Advocate*, 30 November 1963, 4.
206. "Hatred Bears Bitter Fruit," *Pittsburgh Courier*, 30 November 1963, 10.
207. Wexler, *Civil Rights Movement*, 196–197.
208. Ibid., 289.
209. McMiller, "Development of Civil Rights," 166–670.
210. Walter, *Mississippi Challenge*, 136.
211. Dorothy Sterling, *Tear Down the Walls! A History of the American Civil Rights Movement* (Garden City, N.Y.: Doubleday, 1968), 212.
212. Walter, *Mississippi Challenge*, 135.
213. Sterling, *Tear Down the Walls!* 212.
214. Wexler, *Civil Rights Movement*, 199–200.
215. "Was Trio Killed? Miss. Invasion Set," *Daily Defender*, 25 June 1964, 3.
216. "Mutilated Bodies of Negroes Spurs Call for Federal Action," *Black Dispatch*, 31 July 1964, 8.
217. "Find Bodies of Summer Project Workers," *Jackson Advocate*, 8 August 1964, 1.
218. "World Watches Outcome of Miss. Lynching," *Black Dispatch*, 14 August 1964, 3.
219. Levy, *Documentary History*, 135.
220. "Senseless Negroes," *Black Dispatch*, 19 July 1920, 4.
221. Aptheker, *Documentary History*, 463.
222. McMillen, "Development of Civil Rights," 166–167.
223. Ibid., 167.
224. "Civil Rights Groups Invade Leflore County," *Jackson Advocate*, 9 March 1963, 1.
225. "Protection for Voting Rights," *Jackson Advocate*, 9 March 1963, 4.
226. Anne Moody, *Coming of Age in Mississippi* (New York: Dial, 1968), 290.
227. "The Mississippi Negro Their Civil Rights and the Twentieth Century Carpetbaggers," *Jackson Advocate*, 2 February 1963, 4.
228. Ibid.
229. Ibid.
230. Thompson, "Mississippi," 193.
231. Ibid., 192, 197.
232. Ibid., 193.
233. Ibid.
234. "This Is How It Happens," *Jackson Advocate*, 2 February 1963, 4.

235. Robert Hooker, "Race and the Mississippi Press," *New South* (Winter 1971): 56.
236. "A Call for New Negro Leaders," *Jackson Advocate*, 13 April 1963, 4.
237. "Charles Evers Our Right to Freedom of Speech and the Right of Freedom of the Press," *Jackson Advocate*, 20 April 1968, 4.

Conclusions

1. "Lynching Must Be Stopped by Shotgun," *Chicago Defender*, 7 March 1914, 1.
2. A service yet to be identified.
3. According to the ACLU in Jackson, Mississippi, although the state had no public records law, their position was that "there should be a presumption that these [the Mississippi State Sovereignty Commission records] are public records." Also there was no state legislation which could be used to legally seal these records. Nevertheless, the state legislature sealed these records in 1977 using a Mississippi Code (1972) 31-9-61, 31-9-63, and 31-9-65, which was never passed by the legislature.

A SELECTED
BIBLIOGRAPHY

Newspapers

Black Dispatch (Oklahoma City)
Chicago Defender
Daily Defender (Chicago)
Jackson Advocate (Jackson, Mississippi)
New York Times
Pittsburgh Courier
Tulsa World

Selected Works

Aptheker, Herbert, comp. and ed. *A Documentary History of the Negro People in the United States, 1960-1968*. Vol 7. New York: Citadel, 1994.

Barger, Harold M. *Political Content of Black Newspapers: Chicago and Nation, 1969-1970*. Evanston, Ill.: Northwestern University, 1971.

Belles, A. Gilbert. "The Black Press in Illinois." *Journal of the Illinois State Historical Society* (1975): 344-52.

Bergman, Peter M. *The Chronological History of the Negro in America*. New York: Harper & Row, 1969.

Bittner, John R. *Mass Communication: An Introduction*. 5th ed. Englewood Cliffs, N.J.: Prentice Hall, 1989.

Black Press Handbook, 1977. Washington: National Newspaper Publishers Association, 1977.

Boris, Joseph J., ed. *Who's Who in Colored America—1927: A Biographical Dictionary of Notable Living Persons of Negro Descent in America*. Vol 1. New York: Who's Who in Colored America Corp., 1927.

Broderick, Francis L. *W.E.B. DuBois: Negro Leader in a Time of Crisis*. Stanford: Stanford University Press, 1959.

Buni, Andrew. *Robert L. Vann of "The Pittsburgh Courier."* Pittsburgh: University of Pittsburgh Press, 1974.

Carter, Edward L. *The Story of Oklahoma Newspapers, 1844 to 1984*. Muskogee: Western Heritage Books, 1984.

Chicago Commission of Race Relations. *The Negro in Chicago: A Study of Race Relations and a Race Riot.* 1922. Reprint. New York: Arno and the *New York Times*, 1968.

Davis, John P., ed. *The American Negro Reference Book.* Englewood Cliffs, N.J.: Prentice-Hall, 1966.

Davis, Thomas J. "Louisiana." In *The Black Press in the South, 1865-1979*, edited by Henry Lewis Suggs, 151-76. Westport, Conn.: Greenwood, 1983.

Detweiler, Frederick G. *The Negro Press in the United States.* 1922. Reprint. College Park: University of Chicago and McGrath, 1968.

Drake, St. Clair, and Horace R. Cayton. *Black Metropolis.* 1922. Reprint. New York: Harcourt, Brace, 1945.

Duster, Alfreda M., ed. *The Autobiography of Ida B. Wells.* Chicago: University of Chicago Press, 1970.

Editors of *Ebony*, comp. *The Negro Handbook.* Chicago: Johnson Publishing, 1966.

Editors of *Ebony. The Negro Handbook.* Chicago: Johnson Publishing, 1974.

Farmer, James. *Lay Bare the Heart: An Autobiography of the Civil Rights Movement.* New York: Penguin, 1986.

Finkle, Lee. *Forum for Protest: The Black Press During World War II.* Cranbury, N.J.: Associated University Presses, 1975.

Finley, Gravelly E. Personal interview, May 12, 1982.

Franklin, John Hope. *From Slavery to Freedom: A History of Negro Americans.* 3d ed. New York: Alfred A. Knopf, 1967.

Frazier, E. Franklin. *The Negro in the United States.* New York: Macmillan, 1949.

"Freedom for All Forever: Roscoe Dunjee Story." KOCO, Oklahoma City. August 28, 1981.

Garrett, Romeo B. *Famous First Facts About Negroes.* New York: Arno, 1972.

Goldfield, David R. *Black, White, and Southern: Race Relations and Southern Culture, 1940 to the Present.* Baton Rouge: Louisiana State University Press, 1990.

Goldston, Robert. *The Negro Revolution.* Toronto: Macmillan, Collier-Macmillan Canada, Ltd., 1968.

Gordon, Eugene F. "Outstanding Negro Newspapers." *Opportunity* (December 1924): 365–67.

_____, "Outstanding Negro Newspapers—Reiteration and Detail." *Opportunity* (February 1925): 51–54.

_____, "Outstanding Negro Newspapers, 1927." *Opportunity* (December 1927): 358–63.

Gorham, Thelma Thurston. *The Negro Press: Past, Present & Future.* New York: U.S. Negro World, 1967.

Grose, Charles William. *Black Newspapers in Texas, 1868–1970.* University of Texas at Austin, 1972.

Gross, Bella. "Freedom's Journal and The Rights of All." *Journal of Negro History* 15 (July 1932): 241–86.

Guzman, Jessie Parkhurst, ed. *Negro Year Book: 1941-1946.* Tuskegee Institute: Department of Records and Research, 1947.

_____, *Negro Year Book: 1952.* New York: William H. Wise, 1952.

Hammond, C. S. *Year's Pictorial History of the American Negro.* New York: Year Inc., 1965.

Hampton, Henry, and Steve Fayer with Sarah Flynn. *Voices of Freedom: An Oral History of the Civil Rights Movement from the 1950s Through the 1980s.* New York: Bantam Books, 1990.

Henri, Florette. *Black Migration: Movement North, 1900–1920.* Garden City, N.Y.: Anchor Press/Doubleday, 1975.

Hogan, Lawrence D. *A Black National News Service: The Associated Negro Press and Claude Barnett, 1919–1945.* Rutherford, N.J.: Fairleigh Dickinson University Press, 1984.

Hooker, Robert. "Race and the Mississippi Press." *New South* (Winter 1971): 55–62.

Hornsby, Alton, Jr. *The Black Almanac.* Rev. ed. New York: Barron's Educational Series, 1973.

Hughes, Langston, Milton Meltzer, and C. Eric Lincoln. *A Pictorial History of Black Americans.* New York: Crown, 1983.

Hynds, Ernest C. *American Newspapers in the 1970s.* New York: Hastings House, 1975.

Johnston, Erle. *Mississippi's Defiant Years, 1953-1973.* Forest: Lake Harbor, 1990.

Jones, Lester M. "The Editorial Policy of the Negro Newspapers of 1917–1918 as Compared with That of 1941–1942." *Journal of Negro History* 29 (January 1944): 24–31.

Kerlin, Robert T. *The Voice of the Negro—1919.* 1920. Reprint. New York: Arno and the *New York Times,* 1968.

Koontz, E. C. "Pittsburgh Courier Leads Fight for American Negro Equality." *Quill* 54, 10 (October 1966): 44.

Levy, Peter B., ed. *Documentary History of the Modern Civil Rights Movement.* New York: Greenwood, 1992.

Lewis, Anthony, and the *New York Times. Portrait of a Decade: The Second American Revolution.* New York: Random House, 1964.

Lochard, Metz T. P. "Robert S. Abbott—'Race Leader.'" *Phylon* 8 (Second Quarter 1947): 124–132.

Low, W. Augustus, and Virgin A. Clift, eds. *Encyclopedia of Black America.* New York: McGraw-Hill, 1981.

McAdam, Doug. *Freedom Summer.* New York: Oxford University Press, 1988.

McKissack, Patricia and Frederick. *The Civil Rights Movement in America from 1865 to the Present.* Chicago: Children's Press, 1987.

McMillen, Neil R. "Development of Civil Rights, 1956–1970." In *A History of Mississippi,* vol. 2, edited by Richard A. McLemore. Hattiesburg: University and College Press of Mississippi, 1973.

Meier, August. "Booker T. Washington and the Negro Press: With Special Reference to the *Colored American Magazine." Journal of Negro History* 38 (January 1953): 67–90.

_____, *Negro Thought in America, 1880–1915.* Ann Arbor: University of Michigan Press, 1969.

Mississippi. Record Group 42 Sovereignty Commission. Report on State Sovereignty Commission. Vol. 15, 1964–1967.

"Mississippi—Thought Control." *Time*. 28 April 1961: 16–17.

"Mississippi to Hire Secret Race Police." *Christian Century*, 30 May 1956, 659–60.

Moody, Anne. *Coming of Age in Mississippi*. New York: Dial, 1968.

Muse, Benjamin. *The American Negro Revolution*. Bloomington: Indiana University Press, 1968.

Myrdal, Gunnar. *An American Dilemma*. New York: Harper & Row, 1962.

Nash, Richard Keaton. Personal interview, February 17, 1982.

National Association for the Advancement of Colored People. *Thirty Years of Lynching in the United States, 1889–1918*. 1919. Reprint. New York: Arno Press and the *New York Times*, 1969.

Oklahoma Historical Society. Roscoe Dunjee family papers.

Ottley, Roi. *The Life and Times of Robert S. Abbott*. Chicago: Henry Regnery, 1955.

Penn, I. Garland. *The Afro-American Press and Its Editors*. 1891. Reprint. New York: Arno and the *New York Times*, 1969.

Perry, Russell M. Personal interview, April 1982.

Ploski, Harry A., and Ernest Kaiser, eds. and comps. *The Negro Almanac: A Reference Work on the African American*. Detroit: Gale Research, 1989.

Powell, George P. *American Newspaper Directory*. Boston: n.p., 1868–1908.

Prattis, P. L. "The Role of the Negro Press in Race Relations." *Phylon* 7 (Third Quarter 1946): 273–83.

Pride, Armistead S. "A Register and History of Negro Newspapers in the United States: 1827–1950." Ph.D. diss., Northwestern University, 1950.

Rathbun, Lou K. *The Rise of the Modern American Negro Press: 1880–1914*. Ann Arbor: University Microfilm International, 1979.

Reddick, Dewitt C. *The Mass Media and the School Newspaper*. 2d ed. Belmont: Wadsworth, 1985.

Sandman, Peter M. and David M., and David B. Sachsman, *Media: An Introductory Analysis to American Mass Communications*. 3d ed. Englewood Cliffs, N.J.: Prentice-Hall, 1982.

Sanford, Johnson W. Personal interview, May 19, 1982.

Senna, Carl. *The Black Press and the Struggle for Civil Rights*. New York: African-American Experience, 1993.

Sewell, George Alexander. *Mississippi Black History Makers*. Jackson: University Press of Mississippi, 1977.

Shannon, Samuel. "Tennessee." In *The Black Press in the South, 1865–1979*, edited by Henry Lewis Suggs. Westport, Conn.: Greenwood, 1983.

Smythe, Mabel M., ed. *The Black American Reference Book*. Englewood Cliffs, N.J.: Prentice-Hall, 1976.

Snorgrass, J. William, and Gloria T. Woody. *Blacks and Media: A Selected, Annotated Bibliography, 1962–1982*. Tallahassee: Florida A&M University Press, 1985.

Spear, Allan H. *Black Chicago: The Making of a Negro Ghetto, 1890–1920*. Chicago: University of Chicago Press, 1967.

Sterling, Dorothy. *Tear Down the Walls! A History of the American Civil Rights Movement*. Garden City, N.Y.: Doubleday, 1968.

Stewart, Jimmy. Personal interview, May 10, 1982.

Suggs, Henry Lewis, ed. *The Black Press in the South: 1865–1979*. Westport, Conn.: Greenwood, 1983.

Syrjamaki, John. "The Negro Press in 1938." *Sociology and Social Research* (September-October 1939): 43–52.

Teall, Kaye M., ed. *Black History in Oklahoma: A Resource Book*. Oklahoma City: Oklahoma City Public Schools, 1971.

Thompson, Julius Eric. "Mississippi." In *The Black Press in the South, 1865–1979*, edited by Henry Lewis Suggs, 177–210. Westport, Conn.: Greenwood, 1983.

Thornbrough, Emma L. "American Negro Newspapers, 1880–1914." *Business History Review* 40, no. 4 (Winter 1966): 467–490.

Tolson, Arthur L. *The Black Oklahomans: A History, 1541–1972*. New Orleans: Edwards, 1974.

Toppin, Edgar A. *A Biographical History of Blacks in America Since 1528*. New York: David McKay, 1971.

U.S. Department of Commerce, Bureau of the Census. *Negroes in the United States, 1920–1932*, 1935. Reprint. New York: Arno and the *New York Times*, 1969.

A Walk Through the 20th Century with Bill Moyers—The Second American Revolution, Part II. Videocassette. Prod. Corporation for Entertainment and Learning. PBS VIDEO, 1988. 58 min.

Walter, Mildred Pitts. *Mississippi Challenge*. New York: Bradbury, 1992.

Washburn, Patrick S. *A Question of Sedition: The Federal Government's Investigation of the Black Press During World War II*. New York: Oxford University Press, 1986.

Washington, Booker T. *Up from Slavery*. New York: Dodd, Mead, 1965.

Wexler, Sanford. *The Civil Rights Movement: An Eyewitness History*. New York: Facts on File, 1993.

Wolseley, Roland E. *The Black Press, U.S.A.* Ames: Iowa State University Press, 1971.

Zinn, Howard. *A People's History of the United States*. New York: Harper Perennial, 1980.

INDEX

Abbott, Robert S. 7, 27–41, 43–45, 51–52, 59, 61, 64–66, 70–73, 82, 156, 159–160, 164–165
ACMHR *see* Alabama Christian Movement for Human Right
Advertiser (Lexington, Miss.) 157
African Sentinel (Albany, N.Y.) 11
Afro-American (Baltimore) 53, 85, 122
Afro-American (Washington, D.C.) 81
Afro-American chain 75
Afro-American Press and Its Editors 2
Alabama Christian Movement for Human Rights (ACMHR) 128
Albany Argus 11
Amsterdam Star-News (New York) 81
Anderson, Trezzvant 108–109
Arkansas Freeman (Little Rock, Ark.) 15
Atlanta Constitution 109, 116, 133
Atlanta Daily World 75, 102, 117–119, 144

Baker, Ella 97
Baptist Leader (Birmingham, Ala.) 66–67
Barclay, Frank F. 14
Barnett, Ross 109, 125–126, 142, 144
Barry, Marion 97, 106
Beckwith, Byron De La 144–145
Bee (Washington, D.C.) 23, 39

Benevolent Banner (Edwards, Miss.) 63
Bennett, James Gordon 29–30
Bennett College, Greensboro, N.C. 96
Bethune, Mary McLeod 86
Bethune-Cookman College, Daytona Beach, Fla. 86
Biddle, Francis 87–88
Bigelow, Albert 111
Birmingham News (Alabama) 132
Birmingham World (Alabama) 75, 118
Black Dispatch (Fort Worth, Tex.) 52
Black Dispatch (Oklahoma City) 4, 7, 51–53, 55–56, 58, 60, 63, 65, 70, 72, 76, 78, 83, 85–87, 89–90, 99–100, 103, 111, 116, 122, 132, 138, 142, 146–150, 153, 158, 161, 163
Black Republican (New Orleans) 52
Black Republican and Office Holder's Journal (New York) 52
Blair, Ezell, Jr. 96
Boise Valley Herald (Middletown, Idaho) 83
Bolden, Frank 75
Bookertee Searchlight (Oklahoma) 52
Boutwell, Albert C. 128, 130, 133
Boynton v. Virginia (1960) 111
Brandon, Wiley 120
Branton, Wiley A. 135

California Eagle (Los Angeles) 45
Carter, Hodding 138
Central Intelligence Agency (CIA) 152
Chaney, James 152–153, 155
Chase, William Calvin 39
Chicago Commission on Race Relations 40
Chicago Conservator 16, 23
Chicago Defender 6–8, 25, 27–30, 32–40, 43–47, 49, 51, 53–54, 63, 65–67, 70–72, 77–78, 81–83, 85–86, 90, 156, 160, 164; see also *Daily Defender*
Chicago Tribune 40
Chicago Whip 30
Christian Recorder (Philadelphia) 29, 32, 37
Christian Science Monitor (Boston) 136
Churchill, Winston 80
CIA *see* Central Intelligence Agency
Civil War 1, 13, 15–16, 20, 117
Clark College, Atlanta, Ga. 109
Cleveland Gazette 23
Close Ranks Proposal 39, 79, 82, 88
COFO *see* Council of Federated Organizations
Collins, Addie Mae 148
Colonization Society 9, 11, 66, 163
Colorado Statesman (Denver) 85
Colored Agricultural and Normal University, Langston, Okla. 52
Colored American (Augusta, Ga.) 10, 15
Colored American (New York) 10
Colored American (Philadelphia) 10
Colored Citizen (Vicksburg, Miss.) 15
Colored Tennessean (Nashville) 15
Community Citizen (New Albany, Miss.) 103
Congress of Racial Equality (CORE) 97, 101, 110, 113, 117–118, 121, 138–140, 152–153

Connor, Eugene (Bull) 112, 128, 130–133
Conservator (Chicago) 16, 23
CORE *see* Congress of Racial Equality
Cornish, Samuel 10–11, 66, 72, 159
Council of Federated Organizations (COFO) 140–141, 151–154 158
Courier (Hazlehurst, Miss.) 38
Courier Journal (Louisville, Ky.) 116
Craig, C.F. 116
Crisis magazine (New York) 22, 39, 47, 79, 85

Daily Defender (Chicago) 99, 103–105, 113, 116, 120, 122, 137, 142, 144, 146, 148–150; see also *Chicago Defender*
Daily News (Chicago) 38
Dallas Express 32
Dann, Martin E. 1
Dees, Henry 153
Dennis, Dave 140
Denver Star (Denver) 85
Detweiler, Frederick G. 67
Dies, Martin 86–87
Diggs, Charles C. 142
Doar, John 114, 126
Double V Campaign 80–81, 85
Douglass, Frederick 12–13, 27–28, 165
DuBois, W.E.B. 6, 22–23
Dulles, Allen W. 152
Dungee, John 90, 99–100, 156
Dunjee, Roscoe 4, 7, 51–57, 59–61, 64–65, 72, 76–77, 84, 86–87, 89–90, 100, 154, 156, 158, 161, 163, 165
Dutuit, Louis 14

Eagle Eye (Jackson, Miss.) 63
Eastland, James O. 95, 120–121, 154

Editorial philosophies 5–6, 14–16, 18, 25–26, 49, 51, 53, 63, 65, 70, 78, 87–89, 92, 106, 108, 118, 136, 160–163
Edmondson, J. Howard 100
Elevator (Albany, N.Y.) 11
Emancipation Proclamation 13, 37, 54, 165
Emancipator and Free American (Boston) 11
Enquirer Sun (Columbus, Ga.) 38
Evers, Charles 142, 153, 157–158
Evers, Medger 91, 107–108, 140–145, 148–150, 157–158, 165
Evers, Merlie 141

Fair Play (Meridian, Miss.) 63
Farmer, James 97, 110, 135–136, 153
Federal Bureau of Investigation (FBI) 74–77, 84–88, 106, 112, 152–153
Finkle, Lee 66
Finley, Gravelly 90
First Negro newspapers—Confederate States: Alabama (Mobile) *Nationalist* 15; Arkansas (Little Rock) *Arkansas Freeman* 15; Florida (Gainesville) *New Era* 15; Georgia (Augusta) *Colored American* 15; Louisiana (New Orleans) *L'Union* 13–15; Mississippi (Vicksburg) *Colored Citizen* 15; North Carolina (Raleigh) *Journal of Freedom* 15; South Carolina (Charleston) *Leader* 15; Tennessee (Nashville) *Colored Tennessean* 15; Texas (Austin) *Freeman's Press* 15; Virginia (Norfolk) *True Southerner* 15
Fleming, J.L. 19
Forman, James 135
Fortune, T. Thomas 19
40 Acres and a Mule (Jackson, Miss.) 63

Frazier, E. Franklin 86
Free Press (Chattanooga, Tenn.) 146
Free Speech and Headlight (Memphis) 16, 19, 21, 26, 40, 49, 72, 163
Freedom Riders 91, 103, 110–123, 127, 130, 132, 135, 137
Freedom Summer Projects 91, 151, 153, 155, 165
Freedom's Journal (New York) 5, 9–10, 12, 20, 66, 72
Freeman's Press (Austin, TX) 15

Garvey, Marcus M. 48–49
Gillespie, Jessie 103
The Golden Rule (Quitman, Miss.) 63
Goodman, Andrew 152, 155
Gordon, Eugene 50
Greeley, Horace 14
Greenberg, Jack 139
Greene, Percy 8, 63–65, 67, 72, 77–78, 84–86, 90, 101, 103–104, 106–110, 122–125, 127, 131, 134–140, 142–144, 147–150, 154–158 161–163
Gregory, Dick 137–138, 147, 156
Guardian (Boston) 22–23, 118

Hall, R.N. 66
Hamer, Fannie Lou 140, 154
Hampton, Henry 125
Hampton Institute, Hampton, Va. 28
Hance, William N. 44
Harleston, Edwin Nathaniel 43–44
Harpers Ferry Messenger (W. Va.) 47
Harriman, Averell 106
Hartsfield, William B. 109, 127,
Hayes, Rutherford B. 16
Hearst, William Randolph 27–28, 30, 40

Hendrick, Leon 145
Henri, Florette 34
Henry, Aaron 140, 153
Herald (Biloxi, Miss.) 38
Hodges, Willis T. 12, 27, 159
Hoover, J. Edgar 75, 77, 87–88, 106
Hop-Toad Whistle (Assbray, Miss.) 63
Human Relations Committee 100

Inquirer (Philadelphia) 147

Jackson Advocate (Miss.) 8, 11, 13, 63–64, 67, 72, 77–78, 84–86, 90, 103–104, 108–109, 117–118, 122–124, 127, 134–139, 142–145, 147–148, 150, 153–154, 156, 158, 161–163
Jackson Index (Miss.) 15
Jackson State College, Jackson, Miss. 64, 123
Johnson, Lyndon B. 150–151
Johnston, Earle 109
Jones, J.W. 103
Journal of Freedom (Raleigh, N.C.) 15

Kansas Blackman (Coffeyville) 52
Kansas Blackman (Topeka) 52
Kansas City Call (Mo.) 53
Kennedy, John F. 91, 110, 115, 123, 126, 130, 134, 136, 142–143, 146, 149–151, 165
Kennedy, Robert F. 114–117, 120, 131–132, 142, 146, 153
Kent College of Law, Chicago, Ill. 28
King, Martin Luther, Jr. 92, 97–99, 108, 128, 130–131, 134–135, 142–144, 148, 157
Ku Klux Klan 36, 66, 111, 116, 129, 152

Lawson, James 120
Leader (Charleston) 15
Legal Educational Advisory Committee 94
Lewis, Ira 45
Lewis, John 111
Lexington Adviser (Miss.) 157
Liberian Herald (Liberia, Africa) 11
Little Rock Gazette (Ark.) 133
Los Angeles Sentinel 85
Lynching Era 21

McCain, Franklin 96
McKay, Cliff 75
McNair, Denese 148
McNeil, Joseph 96
Macon Telegraph (Ga.) 37
March on Washington 145–148
Marshall, Burk 125
Marshall, Thurgood 97, 105
Memphis Commercial 19
Memphis Scimitar 19, 147
Meredith, James 123–127, 156
Messenger magazine (New York) 47
Michigan Chronicle (Detroit) 85
Mid-South Informer (Walls, Miss.) 103
Militant (New York) 83
Miller, Dorie 74
Miller, Willie J. 138
Mississippi Constitutional Convention of 1890 18, 64
Mississippi Enterprise (Jackson) 138
Mississippi Free Press (Jackson) 155–157
Mississippi Plan 64
Mississippi's Defiant Years, 1953–1973, University of Mississippi, Oxford, Miss. 91, 123–125
Montgomery, Isaiah 18, 64, 95
Montgomery Bus Boycott 2, 108, 92, 96
Moody, Anne 155
Moore, Jamie 133

Morehouse College, Atlanta, Ga. 109
Morris Brown College, Atlanta, Ga. 109
Moses, Bob 140
Myrdal, Gunnar 21
Mystery (Pittsburgh, Pa.) 11

NAACP *see* National Association for the Advancement of Colored People
Nashville Tennessean 116, 133
National Association for the Advancement of Colored People (NAACP) 21, 48, 82–83, 96, 100, 105–106, 108, 123, 136, 138–143, 145, 153, 157–158
National Negro Publishing Association (NNPA) 70
National Red Cross 57, 79
National Watchman (Troy, N.Y.) 11
Nationalist (Mobile, Ala.) 15
Negro World (New York) 48, 83
New Era (Gainesville, Fla.) 15
New Orleans Tribune 14–15
New York Age 16, 19, 32
New York Enquirer 9
New York Herald 30
New York News 32
New York Sun 11–12, 19
New York Times 58, 147
Nightingale, Taylor 16, 159
NNPA *see* National Negro Publishing Association
Noah, Mordecai M. 9
Norfolk Journal and Guide (Va.) 53, 74, 81
North Carolina A&T College, Greensboro, N.C. 96
North Carolina Women's College, Greensboro, N.C. 96
North Star (Rochester, N.Y.) 12–13

OFF *see* Office of Facts and Figures

Office of Censorship 84
Office of Facts and Figures (OFF) 81–83
Office of War Information 84, 87
Oklahoma Federation for Constitutional Rights 56
Opportunity (New York) 85
Our Brother in Black (Muskogee, Okla.) 52

Page, Sarah 58–59
Page, William N. 44
Palladium of Liberty (Columbus, Ohio) 11
Palmer, Will 148
Parrish, Mary E. Jones 58
Pathfinder (Greenville, Miss.) 63
Patterson, John 112, 116
Peck, James A. 111, 113, 121
Penman, Edward 43–44
Penn, I. Garland 2, 10, 12, 23
People's Relief (Jackson, Miss.) 63
People's Voice (New York) 81, 85
Phillips, Leon C. 55–56
Pickens, William 86
Pittsburgh Courier 7–8, 43–47, 49–50, 54, 61, 63, 65, 67, 70, 72–76, 78–83, 85–87, 90, 97–98, 101, 103, 106, 108–109, 112, 115, 117, 121–122, 132, 134, 139, 142, 145, 147–148, 150, 153, 156, 160, 164
Pittsburgh, University of, Pittsburgh, Pa. 44
Policies, separate but equal 94
Posey, Cumberland, Sr. 44
Prattis, Percival L. 73–76, 79–80, 82, 90, 108, 156, 160–161, 164–165
Press Scimitar (Memphis) 147
Pride, Armistead S. 2, 14, 53
Princeton University, Princeton, N.J. 100
Public Ledger (Memphis) 17
Pulitzer, Joseph 28
Purdy, C.M. 99

Queens College, Flushing, N.Y.
152

Race Pride (Okolona, Miss.) 63
Racial Digest (Detroit) 85
Ram's Horn (New York) 12, 27, 159
Randolph, A. Phillip 47
Record (Columbia, S.C.) 146
Rensselaer, Thomas Van 12, 159
Richmond, David 96
Richmond Planet 23
Rights of All (New York) 11
Robertson, Carole 148
Rockefeller, Nelson 121
Rogers, Leslie 39
Roosevelt, Eleanor 105
Roosevelt, Franklin D. 80, 82, 84
Rosemound, Samuel 44
Roudanez, L.C. 15
Rowe, Billy 86
Rowland, Dick 58–59
Rusk, Dean 143
Russia see Union of Soviet Social-
ist Republics
Russwurm, Samuel 10–11, 72, 159,
163

Sampson, Charles E. 136, 138
Sanders, Carl 144
Savannah Tribune 29
Schuyler, George 47–49
Schwerner, Mickey 152, 155
SCLC see Southern Christian
Leadership Conference
Scottsboro, Alabama 49
Seawell, Malcolm 99
Seigenthaler, John 114–115
Sengstacke, John 77, 83, 90, 149,
156, 165
Shaw University, Raleigh, N.C. 97
Shelton, Bobby 116
Shuttlesworth, Fred 117, 128–132
Sillers, Walter 95
Simkins, George 96
Simmons, William 126

Sit-in demonstrations 2, 91, 96–99,
101–102, 104–106, 109–110, 117,
127, 129–130, 137–139, 143
Sixteenth Street Baptist Church
129, 131, 148
Smiley, J. Hockley 28, 30, 37
Smythe, Mable 37
SNCC see Student Non-violent
Coordinating Committee
South Carolina Leader (Charleston)
15
Southern Christian Leadership
Conference (SCLC) 97, 108,
113, 119, 128–132, 134, 139
Spear, Allan 35
Spelman College, Atlanta, Ga.
109
Spirit of the Times (New York) 11
Star of Zion (Charlotte, N.C.) 37
State Sovereignty Commission
(Mississippi) 95, 109, 154,
156–157, 162–163
Staton, Dakota 143
Steeger, Henry 117
Stern, Laurence 143
Stewart, Jimmy 52, 55
Student Non-violent Coordinating
Committee (SNCC) 97, 106,
113, 136, 139–141

Tanner, Harvey 43–44
Tennessean (Nashville) 116, 133
Tennessee Bible Institute,
Nashville, Tenn. 111
Terry, Wallace 143
Thompson, Allen C. 141–143
Thompson, James G. 79
Thompson, Julius Eric 66–67
Times-Picayune (New Orleans)
32
A Toiler's Life (Pittsburgh, Pa.)
43
Travis, James 135
Trevigne, Paul 14
La Tribune de la Nouvelle-Orléans
(New Orleans) 15

Trotter, William Monroe 22–23, 118
True Southerner (Norfolk, Va.) 15
Truman, Harry S 104–106, 121
Tucker, C. Ewbank 149
Tulsa World (Okla.) 57, 59
Tuskegee Institute, Tuskegee, Ala. 21–22, 48
Tutwiler Whirlwind (Clarksdale, Miss.) 63

Underground Railroad 13
Understanding Clause 18, 94
UNIA *see* Universal Negro Improvement Association
Union (New Orleans, La.) 14–16
L'Union (New Orleans) 13–15
Union of Soviet Socialist Republics (U.S.S.R.) 86, 137
Universal Negro Improvement Association (UNIA) 48
Urban League 117, 146
U.S. Army 70, 73, 75, 77–79, 84
U.S. Coast Guard 70, 79
U.S. Department of Labor 38
U.S. Justice Department 46, 83, 88, 112, 114, 116, 121, 126
U.S. Marine Corps 70
U.S. Navy 70, 73–74, 77, 79; Naval Academy 70
U.S. Post Office 83–84, 88
U.S. State Department 137, 143
U.S.S. *Philadelphia* 73

Vandiver, S. Ernest 121
Vann, Robert S. 43–47, 49, 51, 55, 61, 64–65, 72–73, 88, 156, 160, 165
Vardaman, James 38

Virginia Union University, Richmond, Va. 44
Voter Education Project 135

Walker, Wyatt Tee 119, 129
Wallace, George C. 128, 132–133
Waller, Bill 144
War Department 73, 76
War Production Board 84
Washburn, Patrick 81
Washington, Booker T. 1, 6, 18, 21–24, 30, 48, 108, 138, 158, 162, 165
Washington Post (Washington, D.C.) 143
Waters Normal Institute, Winton, N.C. 44
Weekly Advocate (New York) 11
Weekly Avalanche (Memphis) 17
Wells, Ida B. 16–20, 23,28, 40–41, 49, 72, 159–160, 164–165
Wesley, Cynthia 148
White, Hugh Lawson 95
White, Walter 82–83
White Citizen's Council 95, 125–126, 128, 144, 156–157
The White House 73, 84, 88, 105
Wilkins, Roy 135, 139, 142
William, Robert L. 57
W.P.A. Writers Project of the Oklahoma Historical Society 58
Wood, Scott 43
World War I 1, 7, 25, 29, 38–39, 72, 74, 79, 81–82, 88, 159–160, 164
World War II 1, 7, 8, 66, 69–70, 72–74, 81, 88–89, 81, 106–107, 111, 160–161, 164

Young, P.B., Sr. 74